CONTENTS AT A GLANCE

INTRODUCTION xix

CHAPTER 1   Introduction 1

CHAPTER 2   Tuning Techniques for Cost Optimization. 29

CHAPTER 3   Inference Techniques for Cost Optimization 49

CHAPTER 4   Model Selection and Alternatives. 89

CHAPTER 5   Infrastructure and Deployment Tuning Strategies 123

CONCLUSION 163

INDEX 181

Large Language Model–Based Solutions

Large Language Model–Based Solutions

HOW TO DELIVER VALUE WITH COST-EFFECTIVE GENERATIVE AI APPLICATIONS

Shreyas Subramanian

WILEY

To my wife, Divya Prabhakar, for her infinite patience, love, and support. For being the spark, the melody, and the joy in every chapter, and for always making me the hero of our story.

ABOUT THE AUTHOR

Dr. Shreyas Subramanian has been at the forefront of driving revolutionary advancements in machine learning (ML) and artificial intelligence that resonate with businesses and researchers alike. With a PhD in aerospace engineering from Purdue University, Dr. Subramanian currently serves as a principal data scientist at Amazon, a position held by few people worldwide. His prolific research record includes 26 academic papers and six patents, with significant citations to date. His two previous books in the field of AI have sold thousands of copies, with his latest book, *Applied Machine Learning and High-Performance Computing*, being one of the top 50 books covering AI sold on Amazon and one of the only books bridging the gap between HPC and AI. His earlier AWS AI certification guide was ranked the top 9th bestseller in the AI category worldwide.

With a rich and extensive career, Dr. Subramanian has championed the development and application of AI/ML models while carving a distinct leadership path within Amazon. His achievements range from implementing AI/ML solutions for use cases in core verticals, including manufacturing, aerospace, automotive, financial services, and healthcare, to fundamental Artificial Intelligence research. Particularly noteworthy is his role as the creator of the open-source ML package *ezsmdeploy*, which simplifies the deployment of models on the cloud to a single-line API call and has garnered more than 50,000 downloads so far. Most recently, Dr. Subramanian has been involved in helping train generative large language models like ChatGPT for customers of Amazon Web Services in a cost-efficient way. This speaks volumes about his influence in democratizing ML and fostering a community of practitioners.

Dr. Subramanian's PhD dissertation focused on developing algorithms for complex aerospace systems design problems. Since then, he has published several seminal papers on topics such as evolutionary algorithms, surrogate modeling, distributed optimization, deep learning, and language modeling. Dr. Subramanian's comprehensive expertise extends to academia and industry, where he has served as a reviewer for prominent journals and conferences, contributing to the academic community. Recently, Dr. Subramanian won the Best Presentation Award at the Pattern Recognition and Machine Learning 2023 conference for his work on a novel scheduler for faster language model training. He has also been an invited judge and session chair for major conferences such as IEEE, INFORMS, and AIAA.

Dr. Subramanian's research has attracted significant interest from government funding agencies. He was invited to serve on five NSF review panels on artificial intelligence to evaluate proposals worth up to $2 million in Small Business Innovation Research grants for startups and small businesses. One of Dr. Subramanian's significant contributions lies in his ability to secure funding for pioneering projects in topics related to applied machine learning. His skill in proposal writing secured more than $4.6 million in funding from NASA while he was the director of research at a NASA subcontractor, where he helped identify and solve problems related to aviation safety using AI/ML tools on the cloud. Dr. Subramanian exemplifies leadership in the AI research community with elite academic credentials and impactful real-world contributions. He was recently nominated and selected to be an IEEE senior member, a distinction held by only 8% of IEEE's 400,000+ members worldwide.

In his current role as a principal data scientist at Amazon, Dr. Subramanian's contributions have led to substantial cost savings for numerous businesses. His efforts in architecting, building, and scaling large ML models have resulted in remarkable annual savings of hundreds of thousands of dollars for clients. Moreover, his guidance has led to the success of end-to-end advanced driver assistance systems (ADASs) and self-driving car projects, underpinning the vital intersection of ML and automotive technology, which is currently considered a key milestone in the field of AI. At Amazon, Dr. Subramanian leads a team of machine learning solutions architects and researchers across several projects. Internally at Amazon, several of his ideas have been incorporated into new product features for Amazon's machine learning services. By identifying areas of cost optimization within machine learning operations, Dr. Subramanian has collectively saved millions of dollars for clients. For example, he reduced production costs by 8% per quarter for one of the world's largest contract manufacturers, saving millions of dollars. In another instance, Dr. Subramanian reduced the cost of tuning a large number of models for a customer by more than 99%, from hundreds of thousands of dollars per year to just dozens.

This extreme interest in applying cost optimization principles to "do more with less" has led to this book on optimizing performance with cost in the era of large language models.

Dr. Subramanian continues publishing cutting-edge papers in the field of AI, filing high-value patents, writing books with a unique viewpoint, and speaking at major AI conferences.

ABOUT THE TECHNICAL EDITOR

Rabi Jay is a renowned expert in digital transformation and enterprise AI, boasting more than 15 years of rich experience in guiding businesses through the complexities of technology-driven change. His expertise encompasses a wide range of areas, including AI-driven martech innovation, platform modernization, enterprise asset consolidation, and efficiency enhancement through automated workflows. Jay's proficiency is further reinforced by an impressive array of certifications spanning AWS, Azure, SAP, ITIL, TOGAF, and SAFe Agile, demonstrating his comprehensive understanding of both the technical and strategic aspects of digital transformation.

Beyond his technical acumen, Jay has demonstrated exceptional leadership and global strategic insight as a global alliance manager with Deloitte. He skillfully leads large-scale, multinational projects across diverse sectors such as retail, food, consumer products, aerospace, and software technology. As a VP of digital transformation, he championed an integrated practice using human-centered design, AI platforms, and change management built upon the principles of design thinking and process reengineering. An accomplished author and speaker, Jay has contributed significantly to the thought leadership on AI and cloud technologies, with notable books including *SAP NetWeaver Portal Technology: The Complete Reference* (McGraw-Hill, 2008) and *Enterprise AI in the Cloud: A Practical Guide to Deploying End-to-End Machine Learning and ChatGPT Solutions* (Wiley, 2024). His LinkedIn newsletter, "Enterprise AI Transformation: Playbook for Professionals and Businesses to Implement AI," is a testament to his passion for sharing knowledge and best practices in generative AI, cloud adoption, and AI implementation. Outside his professional pursuits, Jay is an avid traveler, golfer, ping-pong enthusiast, and dedicated self-development coach with a keen interest in yoga and meditation.

CONTENTS

INTRODUCTION   *xix*

CHAPTER 1: INTRODUCTION   1

  Overview of GenAI Applications and Large Language Models   1
    The Rise of Large Language Models   1
    Neural Networks, Transformers, and Beyond   2
    GenAI vs. LLMs: What's the Difference?   5
    The Three-Layer GenAI Application Stack   6
      The Infrastructure Layer   6
      The Model Layer   7
      The Application Layer   8
  Paths to Productionizing GenAI Applications   9
      Sample LLM-Powered Chat Application   11
  The Importance of Cost Optimization   12
    Cost Assessment of the Model Inference Component   12
    Cost Assessment of the Vector Database Component   19
      Benchmarking Setup and Results   20
      Other Factors to Consider   23
    Cost Assessment of the Large Language Model Component   24
  Summary   27

CHAPTER 2: TUNING TECHNIQUES FOR COST OPTIMIZATION   29

  Fine-Tuning and Customizability   29
    Basic Scaling Laws You Should Know   30
  Parameter-Efficient Fine-Tuning Methods   32
    Adapters Under the Hood   33
      Prompt Tuning   34
      Prefix Tuning   36
      P-tuning   39
      IA3   40
    Low-Rank Adaptation   44
  Cost and Performance Implications of PEFT Methods   46
  Summary   48

CHAPTER 3: INFERENCE TECHNIQUES FOR COST OPTIMIZATION 49

Introduction to Inference Techniques 49
Prompt Engineering 50
  Impact of Prompt Engineering on Cost 50
    Estimating Costs for Other Models 52
  Clear and Direct Prompts 53
    Adding Qualifying Words for Brief Responses 53
    Breaking Down the Request 54
    Example of Using Claude for PII Removal 55
    Conclusion 59
  Providing Context 59
    Examples of Providing Context 60
    RAG and Long Context Models 60
    Recent Work Comparing RAG with Long Content Models 61
    Conclusion 62
    Context and Model Limitations 62
  Indicating a Desired Format 63
    Example of Formatted Extraction with Claude 63
    Trade-Off Between Verbosity and Clarity 66
Caching with Vector Stores 66
    What Is a Vector Store? 66
    How to Implement Caching Using Vector Stores 66
    Conclusion 69
Chains for Long Documents 69
    What Is Chaining? 69
  Implementing Chains 69
    Example Use Case 70
    Common Components 70
    Tools That Implement Chains 72
    Comparing Results 76
    Conclusion 76
Summarization 77
  Summarization in the Context of Cost and Performance 77
    Efficiency in Data Processing 77
    Cost-Effective Storage 77
    Enhanced Downstream Applications 77
    Improved Cache Utilization 77
    Summarization as a Preprocessing Step 77
    Enhanced User Experience 77
    Conclusion 77

Batch Prompting for Efficient Inference   78
  Batch Inference   78
    Experimental Results   80
    Using the accelerate Library   81
    Using the DeepSpeed Library   81
  Batch Prompting   82
    Example of Using Batch Prompting   83
Model Optimization Methods   83
  Quantization   83
  Code Example   84
  Recent Advancements: GPTQ   85
Parameter-Efficient Fine-Tuning Methods   85
  Recap of PEFT Methods   85
  Code Example   86
Cost and Performance Implications   87
Summary   88
References   88

CHAPTER 4: MODEL SELECTION AND ALTERNATIVES   89

Introduction to Model Selection   89
Motivating Example: The Tale of Two Models   89
The Role of Compact and Nimble Models   90
Examples of Successful Smaller Models   91
  Quantization for Powerful but Smaller Models   91
  Text Generation with Mistral 7B   93
  Zephyr 7B and Aligned Smaller Models   94
  CogVLM for Language-Vision Multimodality   95
  Prometheus for Fine-Grained Text Evaluation   96
  Orca 2 and Teaching Smaller Models to Reason   98
  Breaking Traditional Scaling Laws with Gemini and Phi   99
  Phi 1, 1.5, and 2 B Models   100
  Gemini Models   102
Domain-Specific Models   104
  Step 1 - Training Your Own Tokenizer   105
  Step 2 - Training Your Own Domain-Specific Model   107
    More References for Fine-Tuning   114
    Evaluating Domain-Specific Models vs. Generic Models   115
The Power of Prompting with General-Purpose Models   120
Summary   122

CHAPTER 5: INFRASTRUCTURE AND DEPLOYMENT TUNING STRATEGIES   **123**

Introduction to Tuning Strategies   123
Hardware Utilization and Batch Tuning   124
   Memory Occupancy   126
   Strategies to Fit Larger Models in Memory   128
   KV Caching   130
   PagedAttention   131
     How Does PagedAttention Work?   131
     Comparisons, Limitations, and Cost Considerations   131
   AlphaServe   133
     How Does AlphaServe Work?   133
     Impact of Batching   134
     Cost and Performance Considerations   134
   S3: Scheduling Sequences with Speculation   134
     How Does S3 Work?   135
     Performance and Cost   135
   Streaming LLMs with Attention Sinks   136
     Fixed to Sliding Window Attention   137
     Extending the Context Length   137
     Working with Infinite Length Context   137
     How Does StreamingLLM Work?   138
     Performance and Results   139
     Cost Considerations   139
   Batch Size Tuning   140
     Frameworks for Deployment Configuration Testing   141
     Cloud-Native Inference Frameworks   142
     Deep Dive into Serving Stack Choices   142
     Batching Options   143
     Options in DJL Serving   144
     High-Level Guidance for Selecting Serving Parameters   146
   Automatically Finding Good Inference Configurations   146
     Creating a Generic Template   148
     Defining a HPO Space   149
     Searching the Space for Optimal Configurations   151
     Results of Inference HPO   153
Inference Acceleration Tools   155
   TensorRT and GPU Acceleration Tools   156
   CPU Acceleration Tools   156
Monitoring and Observability   157

LLMOps and Monitoring   157
    Why Is Monitoring Important for LLMs?   159
    Monitoring and Updating Guardrails   160
Summary   161

CONCLUSION   *163*
INDEX   *181*

Introduction

WHAT'S IN THIS CHAPTER?

➤ GenAI Applications and Large Language Models

➤ Importance of Cost Optimization

➤ Micro Case Studies

➤ Who Is This Book For?

GenAI APPLICATIONS AND LARGE LANGUAGE MODELS

Large language models (LLMs) have evolved to become a cornerstone in the domain of text-based content generation. They can produce coherent and contextually relevant text for a variety of applications, making them invaluable assets in today's digital landscape. One notable example is OpenAI's GPT-4, which reportedly ranked in the 90th percentile of human test takers on the Uniform BAR Examination, showcasing its advanced language understanding and generation capabilities. Generative AI tools (like ChatGPT, for example) may use LLMs, but also other kinds of large models (e.g., foundational vision models). These models serve as the backbone for many modern applications, facilitating a multitude of tasks that would otherwise require substantial human effort for building bespoke, application-specific models. The capabilities of these models to understand, interpret, and generate human-like text are not only pushing the boundaries of what's achievable with AI but also unlocking new avenues for innovation across different sectors. To reemphasize what's already obvious, Figure 1 shows Google Trends interest over time for the term *Generative AI* worldwide.

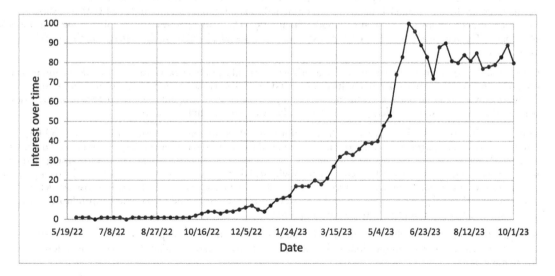

FIGURE 1: Google Trends chart of interest over time for the term *Generative AI* worldwide

Generative AI (GenAI) and LLMs represent two interlinked domains within artificial intelligence, both focusing on content generation but from slightly different angles. GenAI encompasses a broader category of AI technologies aimed at creating original content. While LLMs excel at text processing and production, GenAI places a broader emphasis on creativity and content generation across different mediums. Understanding the distinctions and potential synergies between these two areas is crucial to fully harness the benefits of AI in various applications, ranging from automated customer service and content creation to more complex tasks such as code generation and debugging. This field has seen rapid advancements, enabling enterprises to automate intelligence across multiple domains and significantly accelerate innovation in AI development. On the other hand, LLMs, being a subset of GenAI, are specialized in processing and generating text. They have demonstrated remarkable capabilities, notably in natural language processing tasks and beyond, with a substantial influx of research contributions propelling their success.

The proliferation of LLMs and GenAI applications has been fueled by both competitive advancements and collaborative efforts within the AI community, with various stakeholders including tech giants, academic institutions, and individual researchers contributing to the rapid progress witnessed in recent years. In the following sections, we will talk about the importance of cost optimization in this era of LLMs, explore a few case studies of successful companies in this area, and describe the scope of the rest of the book.

IMPORTANCE OF COST OPTIMIZATION

The importance of cost optimization in the development and operation of GenAI applications and LLMs cannot be understated. Cost can ultimately make or break the progress toward a company's adoption of GenAI. This necessity stems from various aspects of these technologically advanced models. GenAI and LLMs are resource-intensive by nature, necessitating substantial computational resources to perform complex tasks. Training state-of-the-art LLMs such as OpenAI's GPT-3 can involve weeks or even months of high-performance computing. This extensive computational demand translates into increased costs for organizations leveraging cloud infrastructure and operating models.

The financial burden of developing GenAI models is considerable. For instance, McKinsey estimates that developing a single generative AI model costs up to $200 million, with up to $10 million required to customize an existing model with internal data and up to $2 million needed for deployment. Moreover, the cost per token generated during inference for newer models like GPT-4 is estimated to be 30 times more than that of GPT-3.5, showing a trend of rising costs with advancements in model capabilities. The daily operational cost for running large models like ChatGPT is significant as well, with OpenAI reported to spend $700,000 daily to maintain the model's operations.

GenAI models require high utilization of specialized hardware like graphics processing units (GPUs) and tensor processing units (TPUs) to accelerate model training and inference. These specialized hardware units come at a premium cost in cloud infrastructure, further driving up the expenses. Companies trying to do this on-premises, without the help of cloud providers, may need a significant, up-front capital investment.

Beyond compute requirements, large-scale, high-performance **data storage** is imperative for training and fine-tuning GenAI models, with the storage and management of extensive datasets incurring additional cloud storage costs. As AI models evolve and adapt to ever-increasing stores of data (like the Internet), ongoing storage requirements further contribute to overall expenses. This is why scalability poses a significant challenge in cost optimization. Rapid scaling to accommodate the resource demands of GenAI applications can lead to cost inefficiencies if not managed effectively. Overscaling can result in underutilized resources and unnecessary expenditure, whereas underscaling may hinder model performance and productivity.

Strategies to optimize costs while scaling GenAI in large organizations include prioritizing **education** across all teams, creating spaces for **innovation**, and reviewing **internal processes** to adapt for faster innovation where possible.

Pre-training a large language model to perform fundamental tasks serves as a foundation for an AI system, which can then be fine-tuned at a lower cost to perform a wide range of specific tasks. This approach aids in cost optimization while retaining model effectiveness for specific tasks.

Conducting a thorough **cost-value assessment** to rank and prioritize GenAI implementations based on potential impact, cost, and complexity can lead to better financial management and realization of ROI in GenAI initiatives. Lastly, the most common pattern seen today is for "model providers" to spend and try to recoup their costs by providing an API and for "model consumers" to heavily optimize their costs by using GenAI model APIs without the need for any up-front investment or even data.

Challenges and Opportunities

The pathway to cost optimization in GenAI applications with large language models is laden with both challenges and opportunities. These arise from the inherent complexities of the models and the evolving landscape of AI technologies. The following are the principal challenges and the accompanying opportunities in this domain:

Computational demands: LLMs like GPT-3 or BERT require substantial computational resources for training and inference. The high computational demands translate to increased operational costs and energy consumption, which may create barriers, especially for small to medium-sized enterprises (SMEs) with limited resources.

Opportunity: The challenge of computational demands opens the door for innovation in developing more efficient algorithms, hardware accelerators, and cloud-based solutions that can reduce the cost and energy footprint of operating LLMs.

Model complexity: The complexity of LLMs, both in terms of architecture and the amount of training data required, presents challenges in achieving cost optimization. The model's size often correlates with its performance, with larger models generally delivering better results at the expense of increased costs.

Opportunity: This challenge catalyzes the exploration and adoption of techniques such as model pruning, quantization, and knowledge distillation that aim to reduce model size while retaining or even enhancing performance.

Data privacy and security: Handling sensitive data securely is a paramount concern, especially in sectors such as healthcare and finance. The cost of ensuring data privacy and security while training and deploying LLMs can be significant.

Opportunity: The necessity for robust data privacy and security solutions fosters innovation in privacy-preserving techniques, such as federated learning, differential privacy, and encrypted computation.

Scalability: Scaling GenAI applications to accommodate growing data and user demands without a proportional increase in costs is a formidable challenge.

Opportunity: This challenge drives the advancement of scalable architectures and technologies that allow for efficient scaling, such as microservices, container orchestration, and serverless computing.

Model generalizability and domain adaptation: Achieving high performance on domain-specific tasks often requires fine-tuning LLMs with additional data, which can be cost-intensive.

Opportunity: This creates a niche for developing techniques and frameworks that facilitate efficient domain adaptation and transfer learning, enabling cost-effective customization of LLMs for various domain-specific applications.

Evolving regulatory landscape: The regulatory landscape surrounding AI and data usage is continually evolving, potentially incurring compliance costs.

Opportunity: The dynamic regulatory environment stimulates the development of adaptable AI systems and compliance monitoring tools that can mitigate the risks and costs associated with regulatory compliance.

Each of these challenges, while posing hurdles, concurrently lays the groundwork for innovation and advancements that can significantly contribute to cost optimization in GenAI applications with large foundational models. The confluence of these challenges is an important factor in propelling the field of GenAI forward, fostering the development of cost-effective, efficient, and robust GenAI packages, software, and solutions. The myriad of factors contributing to the high costs in the development, deployment, and operation of GenAI and LLMs necessitates a structured approach toward cost optimization to ensure the sustainable adoption and scalability of these transformative technologies. This book dives into the details of what makes GenAI applications powerful but costly and highlights several aspects of balancing performance with cost to ensure the success of organizations that make use of large foundational models. Next, we will look at a few case studies as motivation for the rest of the book.

MICRO CASE STUDIES

This section focuses on three different companies that have "walked the walk" in terms of putting large models in production. What "in production" means is different for different companies, as you will see in the following studies. The case studies should provide a glimpse into the kind of effort and investment required to be involved in the deployment and production usage of foundational models like LLMs in the form of GenAI applications.

OpenAI: Leading the Way

Founded in 2015, OpenAI embarked on a mission to ensure that artificial general intelligence (AGI) benefits all of humanity. Initially operating as a nonprofit, it pledged to collaborate freely with other institutions and researchers, making its patents and research public. The early years saw the launch of OpenAI Gym and Universe, platforms dedicated to reinforcing learning research and measuring AI's general intelligence across a spectrum of tasks.

As AI technology advanced, OpenAI rolled out GPT-1 in 2018, marking its venture into robust language models. GPT-1, with 117 million parameters, showcased the potential of generating coherent language from prompts, although it had its limitations such as generating repetitive text. Addressing these challenges, OpenAI unveiled GPT-2 in 2019 with 1.5 billion parameters, offering improved text generation capabilities. In 2020, the release of GPT-3, a behemoth with 175 billion parameters, set a new standard in the NLP realm. GPT-3's ability to generate sophisticated responses across a variety of tasks and create novel content such as computer code and art showcased a significant leap in AI capabilities.

By late 2022, OpenAI transitioned ChatGPT to GPT-3.5 and eventually introduced GPT-4 in March 2023, further enhancing the system's multimodal capabilities and user engagement with a subscription model, ChatGPT Plus. OpenAI's trajectory has been significantly bolstered by robust financial backing, amassing a total of $11.3 billion in funding over 10 rounds until August 2023. Noteworthy is the $13 billion investment from Microsoft, which has provided not only a substantial financial runway but also strategic partnerships in various ventures.

OpenAI operates on a pricing model hinging on cost per request and monthly quotas, providing a straightforward and flexible pricing structure for its users. The pricing varies with the type of model, with distinct models like OpenAI Ada and OpenAI Babbage priced differently for different use cases. The revenue landscape of OpenAI is on an upswing, with projections indicating a surge from $10 million in 2022 to $200 million in 2023, and a staggering $1 billion by 2024.

OpenAI's CEO, Sam Altman, revealed a revenue pace crossing a $1.3 billion annualized rate, demonstrating a significant revenue potential with the growing user base and subscription services. The launch of ChatGPT saw a rapid user base expansion, reaching 100 million monthly active users within just two months post-launch. Moreover, the introduction of a paid subscription service, ChatGPT Plus, didn't deter the growth, indicating a strong user willingness to pay for enhanced services. The substantial user engagement, especially from large revenue companies, correlates directly with the rising revenue trajectory.

OpenAI's journey elucidates a nuanced navigation through technological advancements, financial fortification, and a user-centric operational model. The continual investment in cutting-edge AI models, coupled with a growing user base and strategic financial backing, underscores OpenAI's substantial impact in the AI domain and its potential for further revenue generation and technological innovation.

Hugging Face: Open-Source Community Building

Founded in 2016, Hugging Face pioneered an open ecosystem for natural language processing (NLP) based on sharing pre-trained models. By 2022, its website hosted more than 100,000 daily active users accessing a broad range of AI capabilities. However, the emergence of LLMs—AI systems with billions of parameters—threatened Hugging Face's ability to support user growth economically. This case examines how Hugging Face adapted its platform architecture and operations to scale out and serve massive user demand while keeping costs contained even as model sizes exploded.

In recent years, AI models have grown exponentially larger. For example, OpenAI's GPT-3 contained 175 billion parameters in 2020. The trend accelerated in 2021 and 2022, with models reaching trillions of parameters. Practically, we see that this vertical scaling to larger and larger models may not be sustainable, so several companies are considering hosting a collection of large (as opposed to one very large) model. These LLMs demonstrated new NLP capabilities but required massive compute resources for training and inference. For Hugging Face, LLMs presented a dilemma. Users expected access to cutting-edge models like GPT-3, but running them required costly cloud computing resources. As a small startup, Hugging Face had limited ability to absorb these costs, especially as user counts approached six figures. Providing LLMs through their existing infrastructure would force Hugging Face to either restrict access, pass costs to users, or operate at a loss. A new approach was needed to economically scale out AI: optimizing model hosting. Hugging Face's first initiative focused on optimizing their model hosting architecture. In their original setup, models were stored together with code in a monolithic GitHub repository. This might have worked initially but did not allow computational separation of storage and inference. Engineers redesigned the architecture as microservices, splitting storage and compute. Models were moved to scalable cloud object storage like S3, while compute happened in isolated containers on demand. This allowed independently scaling storage and compute to match user demand. Large models could be affordably stored while compute scaled elastically with usage.

Next, Hugging Face optimized inference itself. Out-of-the-box PyTorch and TensorFlow were flexible but slow. So, engineers created optimized model servers that reduced overhead. For example, request batching allowed amortizing costs over multiple inferences. Execution was also streamlined by eliminating excess framework code. Together, these optimizations reduced compute requirements by up to 3x. Additional savings came from aggressively right-sizing instances. Usage patterns and models were analyzed to select ideal CPU/GPU configurations. The result was inference costs cut by nearly 80% compared to off-the-shelf solutions.

Democratizing access with caching despite optimizations, LLMs still carried high compute costs. To further reduce expenses, Hugging Face deployed aggressive caching: once a model produced an output for a given input, the result was cached. Subsequent identical requests reused the cached output rather than rerunning inference. Popular models saw cache hit rates above 90%, greatly reducing compute needs. This worked thanks to Hugging Face's scale; similar inputs recurred frequently across the large user base. Caching allowed democratizing access to expensive LLMs that would otherwise be available to only few users. The cache layer also added monitoring capabilities for usage insights.

As usage grew, Hugging Face needed further scalability. Its final strategy was pooling community resources via a federated compute network. Users could volunteer spare computing power in return for platform credit. Requests were dynamically routed to volunteer resources based on load, geographic proximity, and costs. This federated architecture achieved almost unlimited scale at low costs by tapping underutilized capacity. Volunteers benefited by earning credits for their own platform usage. The network was unified through a blockchain-based coordination layer for secure decentralized orchestration. Hugging Face's architectural optimizations and federated model enabled scaling to serve more than 100,000 daily users at just $0.001 inference cost per request. Despite exponential LLM growth, costs remained contained through efficiency gains. Platform contributions also increased as volunteers shared resources in exchange for credits.

This scalable, open-source oriented approach unlocked AI for the entire community. By innovatively pooling collective capacity, Hugging Face democratized access to capabilities once available only to tech giants. This story provides lessons for sustainably scaling out AI alongside the relentless growth in model size and complexity.

Bloomberg GPT: LLMs in Large Commercial Institutions

Bloomberg, known worldwide for its financial data and analytics, took a big step by developing its large language model called Bloomberg GPT. This was driven by the growing need for better NLP capabilities in finance to help with decision-making and customer interactions.

Bloomberg's venture into the realm of LLMs represents a forward-thinking endeavor to harness the potential of AI in financial analytics and services. With an ambitious goal, Bloomberg aimed to develop a model capable of understanding and generating human-like text, tailored to the financial sector's nuanced needs. The project was not only a technological endeavor but also a strategic move to stay ahead in the highly competitive financial information services arena.

The model, boasting 50 billion parameters, is a testament to Bloomberg's commitment to cutting-edge innovation. This extensive model size necessitated a significant investment in computational resources. The training phase consumed a staggering 1.3 million hours of GPU time, showcasing the intensive computational demand that large language models entail. Yet, it was a necessary venture to develop a model with a deep understanding of financial lexicon and concepts.

Bloomberg's approach was unique. The company engaged in reinforcement learning from human feedback (RLHF), a method that utilized human feedback to fine-tune the model iteratively. This approach enabled the model to better understand and generate financial text, improving its performance significantly over several iterations. The in-house development allowed for a tailored approach, ensuring the model's alignment with Bloomberg's specific requirements in financial analytics and reporting.

The financial commitment to this project was substantial, reflecting Bloomberg's strategic investment in AI as a long-term asset. While the exact figures remain undisclosed, industry estimates place the development of such models in the range of tens to hundreds of millions of dollars. The investment extends beyond the model itself to a robust infrastructure capable of supporting the model's computational demands and the talent required to develop and maintain such a sophisticated AI system.

The ability to provide insightful financial analytics and generate human-like text proved to be a valuable asset, offering a competitive advantage in the fast-paced financial services sector. Several months after the publication of the model, no other organization of the same scale has publicly announced a competitive foundational model for finance. The model's success also demonstrates the significant potential and value that large language models hold in specialized domains.

As of this writing, Bloomberg plans to commercialize this technology by integrating it into its existing suite of financial analytics tools. The model will power new features, providing more in-depth insights and analytics to Bloomberg's clientele. Additionally, the model serves as a foundation for future internal and external-facing AI projects, showcasing the company's capability and commitment to leveraging AI for better financial analysis and decision-making.

The Bloomberg GPT project underscores the substantial financial and computational investments required to develop specialized large language models. It also illustrates the strategic importance of AI in the financial sector, not only as a tool for better analytics but as a competitive differentiator in a market where timely and accurate information is crucial.

WHO IS THIS BOOK FOR?

This book was crafted with a broad spectrum of readers in mind, encompassing a range of individuals who are either enthralled by the promise of GenAI or actively engaged in its exploration and application. Whether you are a budding enthusiast, a citizen data scientist, a seasoned researcher, a rockstar engineer, or a visionary decision-maker, this book has insights that can help you along the pathway to cost-effective GenAI applications.

AI practitioners: For those immersed in the day-to-day endeavor of building, tuning, and deploying AI models, this book offers a collection of strategies and techniques for cost optimization, helping to maximize the value and impact of your work while minimizing expenditure.

Researchers: Academics and researchers delving into the frontiers of GenAI and large language models will find a structured discourse on the economic aspects that underpin the practical deployment of research findings. This book aims to bridge the chasm between academic exploration and real-world application, shedding light on cost-effectiveness as a critical vector.

Engineers: Engineers standing at the confluence of software, hardware, and AI will discover a wealth of knowledge on how to architect, implement, and optimize systems for cost efficiency while harnessing the potential of large language models.

Educators and students: Educators aiming to equip students with a holistic understanding of GenAI will find this book a valuable resource. Similarly, students aspiring to delve into this exciting domain will garner a pragmatic understanding of the cost dynamics involved.

Tech enthusiasts: If you are captivated by the unfolding narrative of AI and its potential to shape the future, this book offers a lens through which you can appreciate the economic dimensions that are integral to making this promise a reality.

Policy makers: Those engaged in shaping the policy framework around AI and data utilization will find insightful discussions on the cost considerations that are imperative for fostering a sustainable and inclusive AI ecosystem.

Decision-makers: For decision-makers steering the strategic direction of organizations, this book provides a lucid understanding of the economic landscape of GenAI applications. It elucidates the cost implications, risks, and opportunities that accompany the journey toward leveraging GenAI for business advantage.

In essence, this book caters to a large and diverse readership, aiming to engender a nuanced understanding of cost optimization in the realm of GenAI and large language models. Through a blend of technical exposition, real-world case studies, and strategic insights, it seeks to foster an informed dialogue and pragmatic action toward cost-effective and responsible AI deployment.

SUMMARY

This chapter introduced the world of GenAI and LLMs and highlighted the importance of cost optimization. It presented three micro case studies to help you further understand what it takes for even large, well-funded organizations to achieve scale while controlling costs.

Large Language Model–Based Solutions

1

Introduction

WHAT'S IN THIS CHAPTER?

➤ Overview of GenAI Applications and Large Language Models

➤ Paths to Productionizing GenAI Applications

➤ The Importance of Cost Optimization

OVERVIEW OF GenAI APPLICATIONS AND LARGE LANGUAGE MODELS

In this section, we introduce GenAI applications and large language models.

The Rise of Large Language Models

Large language models (LLMs) have become a cornerstone of artificial intelligence (AI) research and applications, transforming the way we interact with technology and enabling breakthroughs in natural language processing (NLP). These models have evolved rapidly, with their origins dating back to the 1950s and 1960s, when researchers at IBM and Georgetown University developed a system to automatically translate a collection of phrases from Russian to English. The early pioneers were optimistic that human-level intelligence would soon be within reach. However, building thinking machines akin to the human mind proved more challenging than anticipated. In the initial decades, research in AI was focused on symbolic reasoning and logic-based systems. But these early AI systems were quite brittle and limited in their capabilities. They struggled with commonsense knowledge and making inferences in the real world.

By the 1980s, AI researchers realized that rule-based programming alone could not replicate the versatility and robustness of human intelligence. This led to the emergence of machine learning techniques, where algorithms are trained on large amounts of data to pick up statistical patterns. Instead of hard-coding complex rules, the key idea was to have systems automatically learn from experience and improve their performance. Machine learning enabled progress in specialized domains such as computer vision and speech recognition. But the overarching goal of achieving artificial general intelligence remained distant.

The limitations of earlier approaches led scientists to look at AI through a new lens. Rather than explicit programming, perhaps deep learning neural networks could be the answer. Neural networks are computing systems inspired by the biological neural networks in the human brain. They consist of layers of interconnected nodes that transmit signals between input and output. By training on huge amounts of data, these multilayered networks could potentially learn representations and patterns too complex for humans to hard-code using rules.

> **NOTE** *Language is a complex and intricate system of human expressions governed by grammatical rules. It therefore poses a significant challenge to develop capable AI algorithms for comprehending and grasping a language. Language modeling is one of the major approaches to advancing machine language intelligence. In general, language modeling aims to model the generative likelihood of word sequences, so as to predict the probabilities of future (or missing) tokens. Language modeling research has received extensive attention in the literature, which can be divided into four major development stages: statistical language models (SLMs), neural language models (NLMs), pre-trained language models (PLMs), and large language models.*

In the 2010s, deep learning finally enabled a breakthrough in AI capabilities. With sufficient data and computing power, deep neural networks achieved remarkable accuracy in perception tasks such as image classification and speech recognition. However, these systems were narrow in scope, focused on pattern recognition in specific domains. Another challenge was that they required massive labeled datasets for supervised training. Obtaining such rich annotation at scale for complex cognitive tasks proved infeasible.

This is where self-supervised generative modeling opened new possibilities. By training massive neural network models to generate representations from unlabeled data itself, systems could learn powerful feature representations. Self-supervised learning could scale more easily by utilizing the abundant digital data available on the Internet and elsewhere. Language modeling emerged as a promising approach, where neural networks are trained to predict the next word in a sequence of text.

Neural Networks, Transformers, and Beyond

Language modeling has been studied for decades using statistical methods like n-gram models. But neural network architectures were found to be much more effective, leading to the field of neural language modeling. Word vectors trained with language modeling formed useful representations that could be leveraged for various natural language processing tasks.

Around 2013, an unsupervised learning approach called **word2vec** became popular. It allowed efficiently training shallow neural networks to generate word embeddings from unlabeled text data. The word2vec embeddings were useful for downstream NLP tasks when used as input features. This demonstrated the power of pre-training word representations on large textual data.

The next major development was the proposal of **ELMo** by Allen Institute researchers in 2018. ELMo introduced deep contextualized word representations using pre-trained bidirectional long short-term memory (LSTM). The internal states of the bidirectional LSTM (BiLSTM) over a sentence were used as powerful context-based word embeddings. ELMo embeddings led to big performance gains in question answering and other language understanding tasks.

Later in 2018, Google AI proposed the revolutionary Bidirectional Encoders from Transformers (**BERT**) model. BERT is a novel self-attention neural architecture. BERT introduced a new pre-training approach called *masked language modeling* on unlabeled text. The pre-trained BERT model achieved huge performance gains across diverse NLP tasks by merely fine-tuning on task datasets.

The immense success of BERT established the "pre-train and fine-tune" paradigm in NLP. Many more transformer-based pre-trained language models were proposed after BERT, such as XLNet, RoBERTa, T5, etc. Scaling model size as well as unsupervised pre-training strategies yielded better transfer learning performance on downstream tasks.

However, model sizes were still limited to hundreds of millions of parameters in most cases. In 2020, OpenAI proposed **GPT-3**, which scaled up model parameters to an unprecedented 175 billion! GPT-3 demonstrated zero-shot, few-shot learning capabilities never observed before, stunning the AI community. Without any gradient updates or fine-tuning, GPT-3 could perform NLP tasks from just task descriptions and a few examples. As such, GPT-3 highlighted the power of scale in language models. Its surprising effectiveness motivated intense research interest in training even larger models. This led to the exploration of LLMs with model parameters in the trillion+ range. Startups such as Anthropic and public efforts such as PaLM, Gopher, and LLaMA pushed model scale drastically with significant investments in the space. Several tech companies and startups are now using (and training their own) LLMs with hundreds of billions or even a trillion plus parameters. Models like PaLM, Flan, LaMDA, and LLaMA have demonstrated the scalability of language modeling objectives using the transformer architecture. At the time of this writing, Anthropic has developed Claude, the first LLM to be openly released with conversational abilities rivaling GPT-3.

You can see that all the models mentioned are related, much like the Tree of Life. In other words, anatomical similarities and differences in a phylogenetic tree are similar to the architectural similarities found in language models. For example, Figure 1.1 shows the evolutionary tree of LLMs and highlights some of the most popular models used in production so far. The models that belong to the same branch are more closely related, and the vertical position of each model on the timeline indicates when it was released. The transformer models are represented by colors other than gray: decoder-only models like **GPT, OPT** and their derivatives, encoder-only models like **BERT**, and the encoder-decoder models T5 and **Switch** are shown in separate main branches. As mentioned earlier, models have successively "grown" larger. Interestingly, this is visually and objectively similar to the evolution of intelligent species, as shown in Figure 1.2. A deeper comparison is out of the scope of this book, but for more information on either of these evolutionary trees, refer to the links in the captions.

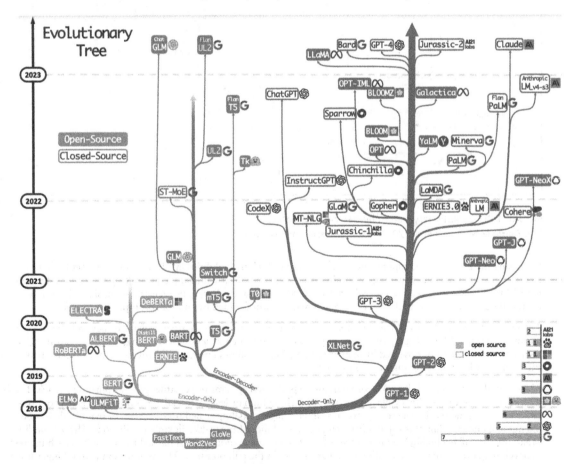

FIGURE 1.1: Evolutionary tree of language models
(see Rice University / `https://arxiv.org/pdf/2304.13712.pdf` / last accessed December 12, 2023.)

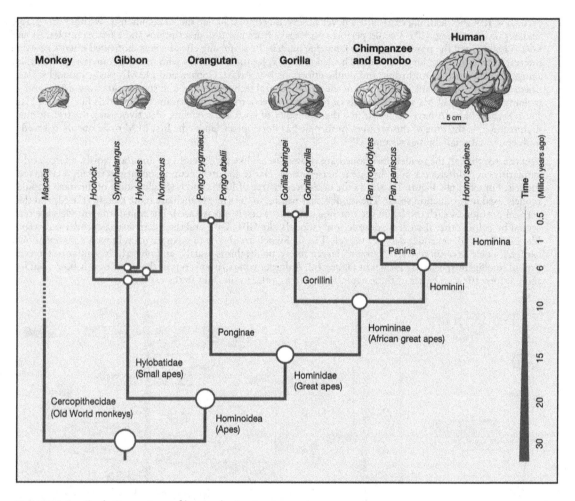

FIGURE 1.2: Evolutionary tree of human brain structure
(see André M.M. Sousa et al., 2017/ with permission of Elsevier.)

Increasing the model size, compute, and data seems to unlock new abilities in LLMs, which exhibit impressive performance on question answering, reasoning, and text generation with simple prompting techniques. By training LLMs to generate code, models such as AlphaCode and Codex display proficient coding skills. LLMs can chat, translate, summarize, and even write mathematical proofs aided by suitable prompting strategies.

The key shift from PLMs to LLMs is that scale seems to bring about qualitative transitions beyond just incremental improvements. LLMs display certain emergent capabilities such as few-shot learning, chain of reasoning, and instruction following not observed in smaller models. These abilities emerge suddenly once model scale crosses a sufficient threshold, defying smooth scaling trends.

LLMs entail a paradigm shift in AI from narrowly specialized systems to versatile, general-purpose models. Leading experts feel recent LLMs display signs of approaching human-level artificial general intelligence. From statistical to neural networks, the steady progress in language modeling scaled up by orders of magnitude has been the missing link enabling this rapid advancement toward more human-like flexible intelligence. The astounding capabilities of GPT-3 highlighted the power of scale in language models. This has led to intense research interest in developing even larger LLMs with model parameters in the trillion range. The assumption is that bigger is better when it comes to language AI. Scaling model size along with compute and data seems to unlock new abilities and performance improvements.

The largest LLMs have shown the ability to perform human-level question answering and reasoning in many domains without any fine-tuning. With proper prompting techniques like chain of thought, they can solve complex arithmetic, logical, and symbolic reasoning problems. LLMs can intelligently manipulate symbols, numbers, concepts, and perform multistep inferences when presented with the right examples.

But of course, language generation is the main area where LLMs' capabilities have taken a huge leap. LLMs can generate fluent, coherent, and human-like text spanning news articles, poetry, dialogue, code, mathematical proofs, and more. The creativity and versatility displayed in conditional and unconditioned text generation are remarkable. Few-shot prompting allows controlling attributes such as length, style, content, etc. Text-to-image generation has also made rapid progress leveraging LLMs. The exponential growth in model parameters has been matched by the computing power and datasets availability. Modern GPU clusters, the emergence of model parallelism techniques, and optimized software libraries have enabled training LLMs with trillions of parameters. Massive text corpora for pre-training are sourced from the Internet and digitization initiatives.

All this has fueled tremendous excitement and optimism about the future of AI. LLMs display a form of algorithmic and statistical intelligence to solve many problems automatically given the right data. Leading AI experts believe rapid recent progress is bringing us closer to artificial general intelligence than before. Large language models may be the missing piece that enables machines to learn concepts, infer chains of reasoning, and solve problems by formulating algorithms like humans.

LLMs still have major limitations. They are expensive and difficult to put into production, prone to hallucination, lack common sense, and struggle with complex symbolic reasoning. Model capabilities are also severely constrained by the training data distribution. LLMs can propagate harmful biases, generate toxic outputs, and be manipulated in dangerous ways. There are rising concerns around AI ethics, governance, and risks that merit careful consideration. Responsible development of AI aligned with human values is necessary. However, we already see several generative AI (GenAI) applications with these LLMs at their core! GenAI heralds a paradigm shift from narrow analytical intelligence toward creative and versatile systems. GenAI applications powered by models such as GPT-3, PaLM, and Claude are displaying remarkable abilities previously thought impossible for machines.

GenAI vs. LLMs: What's the Difference?

While both GenAI and LLMs deal with generating content, their scopes and applications differ. GenAI is a broader term that encompasses AI systems capable of creating various types of content, such as text, images, videos, and other media. LLMs, on the other hand, are a specific class of deep learning models designed to process and understand natural language data. LLMs are used as a core component in GenAI applications to generate human-like text. GenAI applications, on the other hand, use LLMs to create more comprehensive and interactive experiences for users. While LLMs are responsible for understanding and generating human-like text, GenAI applications utilize these capabilities to create more comprehensive and interactive experiences for users.

GenAI applications are full end-to-end applications that could involve LLMs as their core. For example, ChatGPT is a GenAI application with GPT-3.5 and GPT-4 at its core. This means that while LLMs are responsible for understanding and generating human-like text, GenAI applications utilize these capabilities to create more comprehensive and interactive experiences for users. Putting LLMs into production as GenAI applications requires overcoming several challenges, including aligning LLMs with human values and preferences, training LLMs due to their huge model size, adapting LLMs for specific downstream tasks, and evaluating the abilities of LLMs. Despite these challenges, LLMs have the potential to revolutionize the way we develop and use AI algorithms, and they are poised to have a significant impact on the AI community, and society in general.

LLMs have enabled remarkable advances in GenAI applications in recent years. By learning from vast amounts of text data, LLMs like GPT-3 and PaLM can generate highly fluent and coherent language. This capability has been harnessed to power a diverse range of GenAI applications that were previously infeasible. Let's discuss some popular GenAI applications here:

Conversational agents and chatbots: One of the most popular applications of LLMs is conversational agents and chatbots. Systems like Anthropic's Claude and Google's LaMDA leverage the language generation skills of LLMs to conduct natural conversations. They can answer questions, offer advice, and discuss open-ended topics through multiturn dialogue. The conversational abilities of these agents derive from the pre-training of LLMs on massive dialogue corpora. Fine-tuning further adapts them for smooth and consistent conversations.

Code completion and programming assistants: LLMs have proven adept at code generation and completion. Tools such as GitHub Copilot and TabNine auto-complete code based on natural language comments and existing context. This assists programmers by reducing boilerplate and speeding up development. LLMs can also generate entire code snippets or functions given high-level descriptions. Their training on large code corpora enables robust translation of natural language to programming languages. Beyond autocompletion, LLMs could serve as AI pair programmers that suggest improvements to code.

Language translation machine translation: This has benefited enormously from LLMs. Models such as Google's Translation LM achieve state-of-the-art results by learning representations from massive text corpora. They can translate between languages with higher accuracy and more contextual fidelity than previous phrase-based translation systems. LLMs retain knowledge about linguistics, grammar, and semantics that improves translation quality. Their training methodology also facilitates zero-shot translation between multiple languages.

Text summarization and generation LLMs: These are unmatched at summarizing lengthy text into concise overviews. They distill key points while preserving semantic consistency. Applications built using LLMs can summarize emails, articles, legal documents, and other sources as a text companion. Conditional generation allows summarization to be tailored for different lengths, styles, or perspectives. Text generation applications powered by LLMs can produce original long-form content such as stories, poems, and articles.

Even with this broad and deep set of capabilities and active research, companies around the world today may be concerned about the following aspects around productionizing GenAI-based applications:

➤ Access to high-performing LLMs is limited, costly, and not straightforward; commercial models are black boxes behind a paywall, and open-source models are mostly licensed for academic and research use, not for commercial applications.

➤ Building advanced applications that seamlessly integrate with existing databases and analytical applications is not trivial.

➤ There is no transparent architecture that ensures privacy and confidentiality of internal customer data while fine-tuning or using foundational models through an API. Questions around copyrights, trust, and safety are important and far from fully solved today.

In the next section, we begin to dive deeper into these concepts, starting with a framework to think of how a typical GenAI application is built today.

The Three-Layer GenAI Application Stack

The rapid advancements in large language models like GPT-3, Claude, and PaLM have enabled new generative AI applications that can produce high-quality text, code, images, and more. However, developing and deploying these GenAI applications requires bringing together diverse components into an integrated technology stack. We will discuss the three main layers of a GenAI application stack—the infrastructure layer, the model layer, and the application layer—and delve into the details of each.

The Infrastructure Layer

The infrastructure layer provides the foundational data, compute, and tooling resources needed to develop, train, and serve LLMs.

Data storage and management: LLMs require massive, labeled datasets, often petabytes in size, to train the models. Many public datasets like Common Crawl and Wikipedia provide broad coverage for pre-training foundation models. Custom datasets tailored to specific domains or applications are also curated for fine-tuning. This training data needs to be stored, managed, and accessed efficiently. Distributed object storage systems like Amazon S3, Azure Blob Storage, and Google Cloud Storage allow storing the vast datasets affordably. Data lakes built on cloud storage act as centralized repositories to gather, clean, and process heterogeneous data from diverse sources.

Metadata catalogs like AWS Glue, Azure Purview, and Google Data Catalog maintain schemas, trace data lineage, and enable discovery. Versioning capabilities track data changes over time. Data quality tools monitor and profile datasets. Overall, a robust data management platform is essential for LLMs to benefit from high-quality, well-organized training data.

Vector databases: LLMs rely on representing words and documents as dense numeric vectors that encode semantic meaning. Vector databases like Anthropic's Constitutional AI, Pinecone, Weaviate, and Milvus specialize in storing and indexing billions of vectors to enable efficient similarity search and retrieval.

They allow embedding large text corpora into vector spaces where semantic relationships are captured through distance metrics such as cosine similarity. This powers capabilities such as semantic search that go beyond keyword matching. Using vector databases decouples storing embeddings from model training and serving, enabling shared knowledge representation across applications.

Compute infrastructure: Training and running LLMs places intense computational demands, requiring access to extensive GPU/TPU resources. For example, training GPT-3 took 3,640 petaflop/s-days on more than 10,000 GPUs.

Cloud infrastructure providers such as AWS, Azure, and GCP offer GPU/TPU-optimized virtual machine instances. For example, AWS provides P4d instances with up to eight GPUs for machine learning workloads. GCP's Cloud TPU VMs give direct access to TPU chips tailored for ML.

Autoscaling groups dynamically match resources like GPUs to fluctuating training and inference demands. Orchestrators like Kubernetes facilitate deploying distributed LLMs at scale. The compute fabric should provide high-throughput, low-latency networking to support parallel model training across GPU clusters.

The Model Layer

The model layer is the heart of a GenAI application stack, where the choice and adaptation of a large language model are crucial. This layer plays a pivotal role in determining the capabilities, efficiency, and effectiveness of the generative AI application.

Choosing the right LLM: When selecting an LLM as the foundation for your application, several key factors must be considered.

> **Model capability:** The first consideration is the model's inherent capability. Different LLMs may excel in various tasks. For instance, models like Google's BERT are renowned for their understanding of contextual information, while autoregressive models like OpenAI's GPT series are exceptional at generating coherent text.

> **Computational efficiency:** The computational resources required to train and deploy the chosen LLM are essential. Some models may be more resource-intensive than others, which can impact the scalability and cost of your application.

> **Commercial availability:** The availability of the model can be crucial. Many tech companies have open-sourced LLMs, allowing developers to use them freely. Alternatively, cloud providers offer LLMs via APIs, making them accessible but often with associated costs.

> **Problem domain suitability:** Consider the specific problem domain your application targets. Certain LLMs may be better suited for tasks such as text summarization (e.g., T5), while others shine in creative text generation (e.g., GPT).

Fine-tuning the LLM: Once you've selected an LLM as your foundation, fine-tuning becomes essential to adapt it to your application's unique requirements. Fine-tuning techniques, often based on transfer learning, are employed to achieve this adaptation. Take targeted datasets, for example.

> **Targeted datasets:** Fine-tuning typically involves training the LLM on smaller, domain-specific datasets. This helps the model become more proficient in specialized tasks while preserving its general intelligence.

Enhancing capabilities: By fine-tuning, you can improve the LLM's performance in specific areas, such as dialogue systems, reasoning, or knowledge retrieval. Anthropic's Claude, for instance, undergoes fine-tuning to enhance its dialogue capabilities without compromising its overall intelligence.

Avoiding catastrophic forgetting: Care must be taken during fine-tuning to avoid "catastrophic forgetting," where the model loses previously learned knowledge. Techniques such as gradient clipping and selective fine-tuning of specific layers are used to mitigate this risk.

Integrating the LLM: The integration of the selected and fine-tuned LLM into the application is a critical step.

Data transformation: Application code needs to convert input data, such as text or other types of data, into formats suitable for the LLM, typically token embeddings. This transformation is essential to ensure that the model can process the data effectively.

Model architecture: The architecture of the LLM plays a significant role in how it processes input data. Factors like how self-attention is applied across input tokens determine the model's ability to capture long-range dependencies in the data.

Scaling innovations: Recent advancements enable the efficient scaling of LLMs. Techniques such as sparsely gated mixture-of-experts partition model layers into multiple expert groups, enhancing scalability. This technique uses a trainable portion of the neural network to conditionally pass through some inputs, based on the actual contents of the input itself. For more information about this interesting advancement, refer to https://arxiv.org/pdf/1701.06538.pdf.

Additionally, efficient attention mechanisms like BigBird and Reformer reduce self-attention complexity for handling long sequences efficiently.

> **NOTE** *The mixture of experts (MoE) layer consists of a number of neural network experts, each typically a simple feedforward network, along with a trainable gating network. The gating network selects a sparse combination of a small number of experts to process each input example. This allows the overall layer to contain a large number of parameters while activating only a small portion of them per example, drastically reducing computational costs. Specifically, noisy top-k gating adds Gaussian noise and then selects only the top k experts by gate value. The experts become specialized based on different input semantics and syntax. With up to thousands of experts and sparsity levels exceeding 99.99%, the MoE enables models with more than 100 billion parameters while maintaining reasonable computational efficiency. The convolutional application of MoE between recurrent neural network (RNN) layers enables different expert selections per timestep. Overall, the MoE layer enables massive increases in model capacity, leading to significantly improved results in language modeling and translation compared to prior state-of-the-art models. The extreme model parallelism allows continued benefits from increased model scale and data.*

The Application Layer

The application layer focuses on streamlining GenAI application development and deployment leveraging integrated LLMs.

Application development frameworks: GenAI development frameworks are built around LLM APIs, such as Claude, Cohere, GPT-3, Genie, and LangChain, which simplify building applications using LLMs. They provide developer-friendly APIs and SDKs to access model inferencing without dealing with deployment details. These services encapsulate infrastructure provisioning, autoscaling, availability, networking, and other complexities. Developers just integrate the framework's APIs to invoke the LLM capabilities from application code. The frameworks scale seamlessly as request volumes grow rather than requiring changes to application logic.

Some frameworks also offer additional capabilities. For instance, Genie focuses on personalization, version management, and result caching to optimize LLM usage. Claude provides data versioning, monitoring, and safety tools in addition to streamlined model deployment.

Building the application: Developers incorporate LLM capabilities into the application using the framework's interfaces. The business logic sends user inputs to the framework API and processes the inferencing results. The application manages functionality such as identity, security, privacy, personalization, and monitoring on top of the LLM integration.

For conversational applications, the dialogue flow manages directing user utterances to the LLM API and rendering responses. Monitoring tools track metrics such as latency, errors, and resource consumption to maintain performance. User interactions are transformed into suitable LLM inputs, and outputs are post-processed if needed before returning responses.

The layered stack discussed in this section allows assembling the diverse components needed for impactful GenAI applications in a modular, scalable, and extensible architecture. As LLMs continue advancing at a rapid pace, the ability to iterate on and refine each layer independently will become increasingly critical. Companies that embrace and invest in optimized GenAI stacks will gain valuable advantages in deploying and harnessing LLMs to solve real-world problems.

PATHS TO PRODUCTIONIZING GenAI APPLICATIONS

Despite fast-growing fundamental research and awareness around LLMs, GenAI applications are not widespread. They are large and costly to run and are difficult to put into production. However, we are seeing several startups and large enterprises building applications and interfaces to LLMs. Although a full architecture of GenAI applications is similar to any other enterprise architecture on the cloud, we would like to focus more on key components that make GenAI applications special. Throughout the book, we will discover more about LLMs, LLM APIs, and important components such as vector databases.

But first, let's dive deeper into the main ways used to develop these applications. The previous section presented some example GenAI applications. What do you see under the hood of the actual LLM or LLM API components of these architectures? How exactly do you use these APIs? Are there standard names for these methods used for interacting with LLMs? While there are several resources to answer these questions, let's dive right in and look at the key ways you can choose to interact with LLMs or LLM APIs.

Zero-shot LLM prediction: Pre-trained LLMs are used behind an API layer for prediction tasks; this includes simple classification tasks (such as sentiment analysis or topic modeling) and zero-shot chain of thought (CoT) reasoning. For example, an Amazon.com review such as "This is an excellent phone case, good value" along with candidate labels (positive, negative) can be passed into an LLM that can provide a prediction, even if it was not previously trained specifically for sentiment analysis tasks. Interestingly, the same model can be used to extract multiple dimensions or tags from raw data, which can augment and add value to the unstructured data owned by customers today.

Few-shot in-context learning: With a few examples as part of the input, LLMs can perform even better at multiple tasks. As an example, you can provide pairs of natural language statements and corresponding SQL queries to a model as context and provide a new natural language sentence for prediction and expect the right SQL query as an output. Here, the input distribution, output distribution, correctness, and input-output mapping have significant impact (more details explained below).

Prompt engineering and prompt templates: Developers of GenAI applications use prompts to interact with, improve the safety of, and augment LLMs with domain-specific knowledge. Prompt templates provide structure and a format to help LLMs return responses that are usable in downstream applications. Specifically designed prompts allow the LLM to provide better, structured results. Prompt templates are useful for zero-shot, few-shot, chain-of-thought, Reason+Act, and instruction synthesis frameworks.

For example, a zero-shot prompt template may look like this:

```
Answer the question based on the context below. Keep the answer short and concise.
Respond "Unsure about answer" if not sure about the answer.
Context: < ... >
Question: < ... >
Answer:
```

Multiturn chat agents: One-and-done style predictions are not suitable for complex tasks. When we need a more complex dive into a topic that is conversational, an LLM-based chatbot works very well. Examples of applications in production with this architecture include ChatGPT, BingChat, Bard from Google, OpenAssistant from LAION, Claude from Anthropic, Ernie Bot from Baidu, etc. The basic steps to create a chatbot style application (in the training phase) were outlined in the InstructGPT paper by OpenAI (https://browse.arxiv.org/pdf/2203.02155.pdf).

➤ Collect high-quality examples of instruction-fulfillment from human labelers and fine-tune an LLM.

➤ A new dataset is created based on multiple outputs from a single prompt, which is then used to train a supervised *reward model* based on ranks provided from a human labeler.

➤ Use reinforcement learning based on human feedback (RLHF) to produce a policy that uses the previous two items.

All these steps can be built and managed as modules using tools such as SageMaker Groundtruth and SageMaker's training and reinforcement learning capabilities. Existing open implementations of LLM-based chatbots also provide a monolithic Docker implementation to deploy the application as a full stack.

Langchain: Langchain is both a concept and a specific tool/framework to develop applications powered by LLMs. Langchain links several useful components, including LLMs to achieve an output that is more useful to end users. Langchain components include standard prompt templates, indexes, memory, connectors, and an SDK that provides access to not only these components for creating custom chains but also some tailored, use-case-specific chains that are useful out of the box. The simplest chain can include three steps: use a prompt template to parse the input, pass this processed input to an LLM, and parse and process the output before displaying. More complex chains can involve components that have access to tools (such as the Google Search API or a calculator or database access). Learn more about Langchain at www.langchain.com.

LLM-based autonomous agents: Langchain and related concepts allow users to construct a chain of steps that solves a use case. However, in some cases, it is impossible to predetermine the different combination of steps and components involved to complete the task posed by a user. Agents use a toolkit full of different tools to interact with the outside world; popular tools may include calculator, file system tools, the Python terminal, Google Search, WolframAlpha, Wikipedia API, etc. Autonomous agents such as AutoGPT, babyAGI, AgentGPT, etc., are agents that automatically combine components and reason steps and try to find solutions to your tasks. To achieve the final goal, the autonomous agent needs to add intermediate tasks and complete them in order to step closer toward the goal. Goals can be simple or very abstract and stated in natural language. As a result, autonomous agents will research the Internet, create tasks, execute these tasks, self-improve if needed, and create more tasks until the final goal is met. For example, try AgentGPT at https://agentgpt.reworkd.ai.

Foundational model training/fine-tuning: Foundational model training involves training a large model from scratch using a diverse dataset that makes use of significant compute resources. This produces a generalized model that can be adapted to multiple tasks. While few organizations have the resources to train an LLM from scratch and then deploy it for providing access at scale, most organizations will be able to fine-tune or use one of the previous methods to achieve success in their use cases. Fine-tuning involves taking a pre-trained foundational model and training it on a specific, smaller dataset. This takes less computational resources and time compared to foundational model training. The performance of a fine-tuned model can be significantly better than a large foundational model that is good at multiple tasks.

Now that you have an overview of the types of applications that can be built within the three-layer GenAI application stack, we will use a hypothetical use case of constructing a GenAI-based enterprise chat application by assembling components of the three-layer GenAI stack and techniques discussed.

Sample LLM-Powered Chat Application

As mentioned, chat applications such as ChatGPT are examples of popular GenAI applications. As with any GenAI stack, the infrastructure layer provides the data, compute, and tooling to support large-scale LLMs. Vector databases enable embedding knowledge into vector spaces for efficient retrieval. Distributed GPU/TPU resources provide the computing muscle for LLM training and inference, and this is sometimes abstracted behind a managed API provided by LLM API providers so that end users do not need to worry about hosting and maintaining these models in production. The model layer focuses on choosing, fine-tuning, and optimally integrating the most appropriate LLMs into the application. Finally, the application layer leverages frameworks to simplify access to the deployed models. Figure 1.3 shows an example flow diagram with components that could be used to create a powerful LLM-based chat application.

Figure 1.3 illustrates the request flow in the LLM-powered chatbot application. The diagram provides a comprehensive overview of the request flow in the GenAI application, highlighting the interactions between the different components involved. The user sends a request to the chatbot, which then forwards the request to the application API. The API performs preprocessing on the request, followed by model inference and postprocessing. The processed response is returned to the API, which then sends it back to the chatbot. Finally, the chatbot delivers the response to the user.

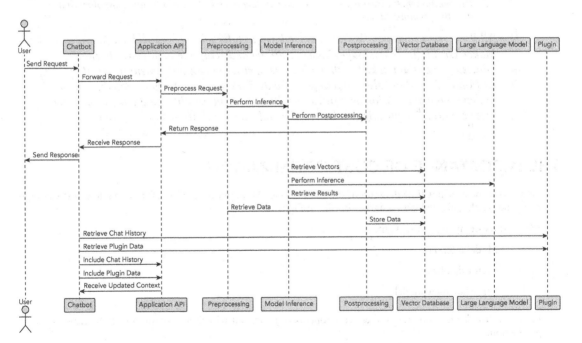

FIGURE 1.3: Sequence diagram of the request flow through a GenAI chatbot application

During the model inference stage, the inference component interacts with the vector database to retrieve vectors and with the LLM to perform the actual inference. Additionally, the preprocessing and postprocessing stages may interact with the vector database to retrieve and store data.

The chatbot component also interacts with the plugin component to retrieve chat history and plugin data. The chatbot includes this information in the request sent to the API, and the API incorporates it into the processing. The API then sends the updated context back to the chatbot.

Next, we will discuss how each of the components in the sample chatbot architecture needs to be tested for performance and how to generate and interpret pricing estimates for GenAI applications.

> **NOTE** *In this chapter, we leave out the fact that training a "chat-ready" LLM is itself a costly endeavor. One-and-done predictions without storing a session history are not suitable for complex tasks. When we need a more complex dive into a conversational topic, an LLM-based chatbot works well. Examples of applications in production with this architecture include ChatGPT, BingChat, Bard from Google, OpenAssistant from LAION, Claude from Anthropic, Ernie Bot from Baidu, etc. The basic steps to create a chatbot-style application (in the training phase) were outlined in the InstructGPT paper by OpenAI available at* `https://arxiv.org/pdf/2203.02155.pdf.`
>
> 1. *Collect high-quality examples of instruction fulfillment from human labelers and fine-tune an LLM.*
>
> 2. *A new dataset is created based on multiple outputs from a single prompt, which is then used to train a supervised reward model based on ranks provided from a human labeler.*
>
> 3. *Use reinforcement learning based on human feedback (RLHF) to produce a policy that uses the previous two steps.*
>
> *All these steps can be built and managed as modules using tools such as Sage-Maker Groundtruth and SageMaker's training and reinforcement learning capabilities on the cloud, which will incur costs. Existing open implementations of LLM-based chatbots also sometimes provide a monolithic Docker implementation to deploy the application as a full stack. But the responsibility (and cost) of hosting these container applications are with the end user (or chatbot service provider).*

THE IMPORTANCE OF COST OPTIMIZATION

Let's revisit the previous flow diagram of the chatbot (GenAI) application with a focus on a few costly components that are highlighted with a darker border in Figure 1.4.

We see three components highlighted.

➤ Model inference

➤ Vector database

➤ Large language model

Let's first dive deeper into each of these components to figure out why they may turn out to be expensive in production.

Cost Assessment of the Model Inference Component

The model inference component is a core component at the center of all GenAI chat applications. It is a component that does the following things:

1. Receives a request to perform inference on.

2. Analyzes the request and allows/disallows the inference to continue. This can be for parameter validation, for safety, and to prevent malicious use.

3. Retrieves vectors from the vector database, or in cases where the vector database provides a similarity search API, directly receives similar items from the database.

4. Constructs the prompt for prediction with the LLM.

5. Receives response from the LLM.

6. Performs any post-processing of the response received from the LLM.

7. Returns the response to the client application if successful and returns an appropriate error code otherwise.

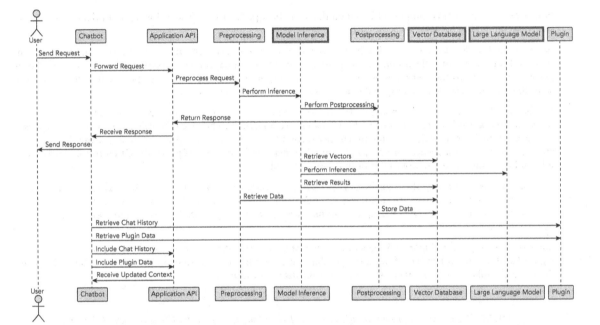

FIGURE 1.4: Sequence diagram of the request flow through a GenAI chatbot application, with a focus on three costly components

> **NOTE** *In many cases, the model inference component may include preprocessing and post-processing. In some cases, the model inference container also hosts the entire LLM. In practice, several LLM-as-an-API providers, such as OpenAI, Anthropic, and Amazon Web Services (AWS) offer competitive pricing and extremely easy-to-use APIs that obviate the need to build and host an LLM on your own in the model inference component.*

Why could this component be costly? Depending on how you choose to create this component, there could be costs associated with hosting your model inference code. In AWS, for example, there are services that can help host this component. For example, you can use one of the following services, in increasing order of complexity:

➤ AWS Lambda, which lets you run your code without having to manage servers (see https://aws.amazon.com/pm/lambda)

> ➤ AWS Fargate, which is a serverless compute engine to orchestrate container-based applications (see `https://aws.amazon.com/fargate`)

> ➤ Amazon SageMaker, which is an end-to-end managed service for machine learning including hosting LLMs (`https://aws.amazon.com/sagemaker`)

> ➤ Amazon EC2, which is a secure and resizable compute for any workload including hosting LLMs (`https://aws.amazon.com/ec2`).

Similar serverless and server based options exist on other cloud providers such as Microsoft Azure or Google Cloud Platform (GCP).

Now let's try to price this component based on the available options today. The following is a pricing exercise that you can modify for your own use case.

As mentioned earlier, it is anticipated to have about 100 concurrent users chatting with the assistant at any given time, and each user will make about 100 requests per hour through natural conversation with the assistant. For a given user, this means the user takes 60/100 ~= 0.6 minutes, or 36 seconds, on average per request; this is realistic since the user needs some time to type the next question in the chat session.

We then need to benchmark the model itself, since the architecture of the model inference component changes based on how fast the hosted LLM or LLM API can make inferences. The metric to calculate for this purpose is tokens generated per second, or simply tokens per second (TPS). If you aren't already familiar with tokens, they are commonly found sequences or groups of characters that can be used to form words. Often entire words are tokens. For example, for an input prompt that looks like this:

```
As a customer support executive, you are assisting a customer who claims that their
previous bill is still showing as due despite making the payment last week.
Write a reply by reviewing the cusstomer's bill payment history and resolving
the issue.
```

the tokens correspond to Figure 1.5 (generated using `https://platform.openai.com/tokenizer`). Figure 1.6 shows the token IDs of the corresponding tokens in the previous sentence, which are index pointers to these specific tokens in the sentence found in the tokenizer's vocabulary.

> **NOTE** *If you want a programmatic interface to the tokenizer used by ChatGPT and GPT models, check out* `https://github.com/openai/tiktoken`.

To benchmark TPS for a hosted LLM or LLM API, first choose a benchmark prompt or set of prompts. It is important to control the number of tokens generated, either using an appropriate max token count parameter in an API call or using a smart prompt. Let's use a long sentence from *Don Quixote*, written in 1605, and considered a classic, foundational literary work in Western literature. Here is the sentence:

About this time, when some rain began to fall, Sancho proposed that they should shelter themselves in the fulling-mill, but Don Quixote had conceived such abhorrence for it, on account of what was past, that he would no means set foot within its wall; wherefore, turning to the right-hand, they chanced to fall in with a road different from that in which they had traveled the day before; they had not gone far, when the knight discovered a man riding with something on his head, that glittered like polished gold, and scarce had he descried this phenomenon, when turning to Sancho, 'I find,' said he, 'that every proverb is strictly true; indeed, all of them are apophthegms dictated by experience herself; more especially, that which says, 'shut one door, and another will soon open': this I mention, because, if last night, fortune shut against us the door we fought to enter, by deceiving us with the fulling-hammers; today another stands wide open, in proffering to use us, another greater and more certain adventure, by which, if I fail to enter, it shall be my own fault, and not imputed to my ignorance of fulling-mills, or the darkness of the night.

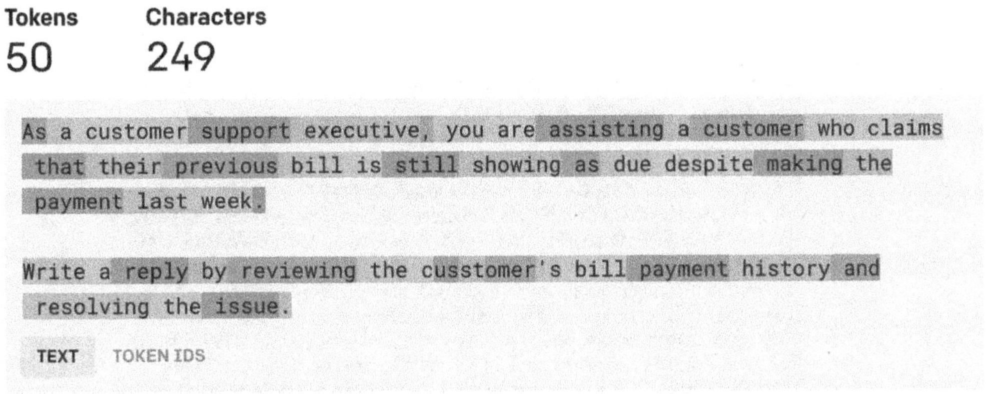

Tokens   Characters

50   249

As a customer support executive, you are assisting a customer who claims
that their previous bill is still showing as due despite making the
payment last week.

Write a reply by reviewing the cusstomer's bill payment history and
resolving the issue.

TEXT   TOKEN IDS

FIGURE 1.5: Tokens generated for the text prompt. Notice how the misspelled word "cusstomer" and its apostrophe get split into their own different tokens.

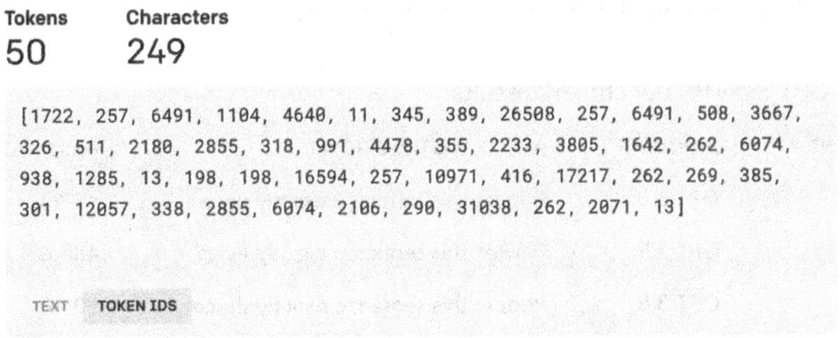

Tokens   Characters

50   249

```
[1722, 257, 6491, 1104, 4640, 11, 345, 389, 26508, 257, 6491, 508, 3667,
326, 511, 2180, 2855, 318, 991, 4478, 355, 2233, 3805, 1642, 262, 6074,
938, 1285, 13, 198, 198, 16594, 257, 10971, 416, 17217, 262, 269, 385,
301, 12057, 338, 2855, 6074, 2106, 290, 31038, 262, 2071, 13]
```

TEXT   **TOKEN IDS**

FIGURE 1.6: Token IDs of the tokens generated from the original text prompt and shown in Figure 1.5

This long, single sentence paragraph from *Don Quixote* has 1,158 characters and 269 tokens, as shown Figure 1.7. It is not necessary to use a long sentence, and when repeating the benchmark, you can use a set of examples relevant to your business.

Through the API, or from the console, we can calculate the total time for repeating this sentence. Add an instruction to the previous like "repeat the following sentence exactly once." Since most models faithfully repeat the fixed, known number of tokens, asking the same question to multiple models may result in varying answers with a different number of tokens. Also, we can modify the instruction by saying "repeat the following sentence exactly twice," or thrice, four times, etc. The process that generates these tokens is not linear, so testing the number of tokens across these cases is important. It is also a good idea to repeat each experiment at least five times and report the best and worst TPS for each experiment.

Table 1.1 is a sample result table using the previous sentence with GPT 3.5. Note that the model prediction is timed using the free research preview of the ChatGPT application and is not representative of a real benchmark; it is shown here to explain the ways to read results, even if the actual experiment is done from the model inference component being designed, and via an API call.

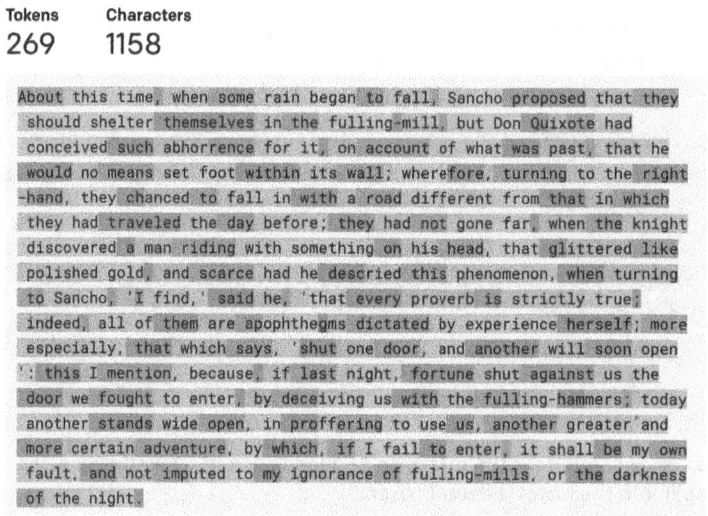

Tokens   **Characters**
269   1158

About this time, when some rain began to fall, Sancho proposed that they should shelter themselves in the fulling-mill, but Don Quixote had conceived such abhorrence for it, on account of what was past, that he would no means set foot within its wall; wherefore, turning to the right-hand, they chanced to fall in with a road different from that in which they had traveled the day before; they had not gone far, when the knight discovered a man riding with something on his head, that glittered like polished gold, and scarce had he descried this phenomenon, when turning to Sancho, 'I find,' said he, 'that every proverb is strictly true; indeed, all of them are apophthegms dictated by experience herself; more especially, that which says, 'shut one door, and another will soon open'; this I mention, because, if last night, fortune shut against us the door we fought to enter, by deceiving us with the fulling-hammers; today another stands wide open, in proffering to use us, another greater and more certain adventure, by which, if I fail to enter, it shall be my own fault, and not imputed to my ignorance of fulling-mills, or the darkness of the night.

FIGURE 1.7:   Tokens generated for the long example sentence

TABLE 1.1:   GPT 3.5 TPS benchmark results

EXPERIMENT #	MODEL	PREFIX INSTRUCTIONS	BEST/WORST TPS
1	GPT 3.5	Repeat this sentence exactly once	45/13
2	GPT 3.5	Repeat this sentence exactly twice	48/26
3	GPT 3.5	Repeat this sentence exactly thrice	50/10
4	GPT 3.5	Repeat this sentence exactly four times	46/40

Here are a few observations about Table 1.1:

➤ The best-case scenarios across experiments seem to be consistent, at around 48 TPS.

➤ The worst-case numbers for TPS have a huge range, from as low as 10 TPS to 40 TPS.

➤ Across all experiments conducted, the average TPS was around 35 TPS. Most teams will design their application for the expected demand based on the average TPS.

➤ More experiments with other models may inform your choices, especially if you are left with little control over the hosting infrastructure and you are mainly interfacing with managed APIs. While managed LLM APIs provide limits and strive to provide consistently high performance, the onus of performing benchmarks still lies with the application building team.

Now that we have a number for the average TPS (35), we also need to make some assumptions on the average token size per text prompt. In the previous test, about 250 tokens were returned as a response, and this is a good, representative response size. The response per turn will then take 250/35, which is around 7 seconds. The worst-case response time is 250/10, or 25 seconds. The worst-case response is better than the requirement of about 36 seconds per response. This will work for a single user, with requests being queued up and sent back to back, sequentially. We also have an orthogonal requirement of 100 concurrent users doing 100 requests each per hour. Additionally, LLM API providers will enforce rate limits on the requests you make over three dimensions: TPS, requests per second (RPS), and concurrency. Requests are throttled if any of these limits are exceeded.

> **NOTE** *Rate limits in LLM APIs play a crucial role by setting rules on how frequently users can request information within a specific timeframe. These limits serve multiple purposes. First, they safeguard the API from misuse or abuse, preventing malicious actors from overloading the system. Second, rate limits ensure equitable access for all users, preventing any single user from monopolizing resources and slowing down the API for others. Last, they help maintain the API's performance and prevent server strain during periods of high usage, ensuring a smooth experience for all users using the API. This is especially important with LLM APIs, since all users hit the same logical base model, but behind the scenes, the LLM API providers have to massively scale out their inference workload to support tens of thousands of concurrent users.*

Based on the benchmark, only about 10 users will receive their response within the minute with one request going out per second (1 RPS); with 10 RPS, we should be able to service 100 sessions. However, this may not be completely true.

Assume that we have the following limits from the LLM API provider: a TPS limit of 600, an RPS of 10, and a concurrency of 1. These look like very stringent limits for our discussion but are realistic since they are around the same limits offered today by leading LLM API providers. From our previous benchmark, we expect the model to produce tokens at about 35 TPS when tested from a client application. Since we expect 100 users to do 100 requests per hour, the total throughput of RPS required is $100*100/(60*60)$, which is 2.7 RPS on average. These two to three requests may not consistently happen at every second; we expect this to be the average RPS over a long period of time. However, from our benchmark, we see that we can only do about 10 requests per minute, which is less than 1 RPS. With 100 user sessions running and a RPS limit of 10 from the LLM API provider, combined with the concurrency limit of 1, the model inference application may be quickly throttled, even though the API calls are below the TPS limit.

Practically, the model inference component can implement its own queue, use an external service as a queue, or, even simpler, use exponential backoff implemented by a library. In Python, it would look like this:

```python
import backoff
import LLMapi

@backoff.on_exception(backoff.expo, LLMapi.ThrottleError)
def predict_with_backoff(**kwargs):
    return LLMapi.predict(**kwargs)

predict_with_backoff(prompt="...")
```

Note that in the previous example, since we are still not hitting the TPS limit, we can batch multiple requests from the model inference component. Typically, the LLM API backend will send back a batched response much quicker than sequentially running it. This API call may look like the following:

```python
predict_with_backoff(prompt=["...","...","...","...","...","..."] )
```

This effectively multiplies the achieved RPS to help service more users in parallel, once again subject to the multiple limits mentioned earlier. The model inference component then has to stay alive for the time it takes to complete that particular request, batched or otherwise. This tells us which of the various options (serverless, managed server) to use. For a complex model inference server that is serving multiple users, it may be worthwhile considering an always-on system such as a long-running container or a VM. Serverless options usually will suffer from a cold start but can be cost effective. A one-second cold start means your inference does not actually begin for 1 second. Container-based serverless solutions can be slower to come up. Nevertheless, there are great use cases for model inference components to be on services like AWS Lambda. Let's look at how to calculate price when using AWS Lambda (adapted from https://aws.amazon.com/lambda/pricing for our example).

In our scenario with 100 concurrent users making 100 requests per hour, on the average case, we receive 35 TPS from the LLM API.

```
Monthly compute charges:
Total compute duration per request (seconds) = 269 tokens / 35 tokens/second =
7.6857 seconds (rounded to 7.69 seconds)
Total compute duration per user per hour (seconds) = 100 requests/hour * 7.69
seconds/request = 769 seconds
Total compute duration per user per month (seconds) = 769 seconds * 30 days/month =
23,070 seconds
Total compute duration for all users per month (seconds) = 100 users * 23,070
seconds = 2,307,000 seconds
Total compute (GB-s) = 2,307,000 seconds * 4096 MB / 1024 MB = 9,228,000 GB-s
Total compute - AWS Free Tier compute = Monthly billable compute GB-s
9,228,000 GB-s - 400,000 free tier GB-s = 8,828,000 GB-s
Monthly compute charges = 8,828,000 * $0.0000166667 = $147.13
Monthly request charges:
Total requests per user per hour = 100 requests/hour
Total requests per user per month = 100 requests/hour * 24 hours/day * 30 days/
month = 72,000 requests
Total requests for all users per month = 100 users * 72,000 requests = 7,200,000
requests
Total request charges = 7,200,000 / 1,000,000 * $0.20 = $1.44
Total monthly charges:
Total charges = Compute charges + Request charges = $147.13 + $1.44 =
$148.57 per month
```

In this updated scenario with 100 concurrent users making 100 requests per hour, where each request involves generating about 269 tokens, and on average, you get 35 tokens per second generated from the back end, your total monthly charges would be approximately $148.57.

In our end-to-end application, however, the cold start of having these AWS Lambda functions is non-negligible. With complex model inference components that do pre- and post-processing of requests, the additional startup latency could be significant. Additionally, without provisioned capacity on AWS Lambda, the time it takes to serve requests increases as the number of requests increases. For example, let us start off with our case where each request takes around 7.69 seconds. We can perform a benchmark using a load testing tool like ab (https://httpd.apache.org/docs/2.4/programs/ab.html) or locust (https://locust.io), where we first have no provisioned capacity set up and send 100s of requests to this endpoint. Now, since we don't want to pay the LLM provider for these benchmarks, it is a good idea to simply emulate these requests and sleep for 7.69 seconds on average for every request coming in from these benchmarking tools. With provisioned concurrency disabled, we get the results shown in Table 1.2 for completed predictions.

TABLE 1.2:   Percentage of requests served within a certain time period in seconds

PERCENTAGE OF REQUESTS	MAX SECONDS ALLOWED
50%	7.69 s
66%	7.85 s
75%	8.35 s
80%	8.62 s
90%	9.46 s
95%	29.85 s
98%	35.61 s
99%	36.69 s
100%	42.29 s

As we can see from Table 1.2, with hundreds of requests coming in and with no provisioned capacity, it could take several times the originally assumed 7.69 seconds to serve all requests. Provisioned capacity on AWS Lambda is a feature where your serverless functions can be kept warm or initialized, waiting for requests so that there is minimal startup latency. With this, functions can be made ready to respond within double-digit milliseconds. However, going back to the theme of cost to performance, this obviously means it will cost more. But how much more? Let's perform the same costing exercise with provisioned capacity. Let's assume your functions receive requests from 100 users 100 times per hour. Each request takes about 7.69 seconds. Provisioned concurrency is enabled throughout the month, 16 hours a day. You configure your function with 4,096 MB of memory on an x86-based processor and set Provisioned Concurrency at 100.

```
Monthly Provisioned Concurrency charges:
The Provisioned Concurrency price is $0.0000041667 per GB-s.
Total period of time for which Provisioned Concurrency is enabled (seconds) = 30
days * 16 hours * 3,600 seconds = 1,728,000 seconds.
Total concurrency configured (GB): 100 * 4096 MB / 1024 MB = 400 GB.
Total Provisioned Concurrency amount (GB-s) = 400 GB * 1,728,000 seconds =
691,200,000 GB-s.
Provisioned Concurrency charges = 691,200,000 GB-s * $0.0000041667 = $2,880.00.
Monthly Compute charges while Provisioned Concurrency is enabled:
The compute price is $0.0000097222 per GB-s.
Total compute duration (seconds) = 100 users * 100 requests * 7.69 seconds per
request = 76,900 seconds per hour.
Total compute duration for the month = 76,900 seconds per hour * 16 hours per day *
30 days = 36,993,600 seconds per month.
Total compute (GB-s) = 36,993,600 seconds * 4096 MB / 1024 MB = 147,974,400 GB-s.
Total compute charges = 147,974,400 GB-s * $0.0000097222 = $1,440.88.
Monthly request charges:
The monthly request price is $0.20 per 1 million requests.
Monthly request charges = (100 users * 100 requests per hour * 16 hours per day *
30 days) / 1,000,000 * $0.20 = $768.00.
Total monthly charges:
Total charges = Provisioned Concurrency charges + Compute charges while Provisioned
Concurrency is enabled + Request charges = $2,880.00 + $1,440.88 + $768.00 =
$4,088.88.
```

We see a huge increase in cost, from close to $150 to now $4,000 a month. I hope you now see why evaluating the cost of each component in your architecture, getting representative benchmark numbers, and balancing cost to performance are important. Let's continue this discussion with another important component of the architecture, vector databases.

Cost Assessment of the Vector Database Component

Vector databases have emerged as a critical technology for solving complex problems in areas such as recommendation systems, natural language processing, computer vision, and now retrieval augmented generation (RAG) applications with LLMs. The ability of vector databases to perform ultra-fast similarity search on large datasets of high-dimensional vectors enables transformative applications. However, with a plethora of vector database solutions available, from open-source systems to cloud services, selecting the right one for your use case can be challenging. This highlights the importance of benchmarking to evaluate different options on crucial performance factors, which includes cost. As you will notice throughout the book, cost-based benchmarking is not useful without considering performance.

This section covers the key components to test, benchmark design considerations, test cases to include, metrics to track, guidelines for fair evaluation, and best practices when choosing a vector database for your application. The goal is to equip you with the knowledge to thoroughly assess vector databases and select the optimal one for your needs. Benchmarking the performance of a vector database is critical to understanding how it will operate under real-world production workloads.

Several key components determine the performance of a vector database. A rigorous benchmark must evaluate the following aspects thoroughly:

Index building time: This measures the time taken to build search indexes on a vector dataset, which enables fast retrieval. Index building involves steps such as data loading, normalization, graph structure creation, etc. Not all indexes are built using all these components; most indexes are just vector databases with additional metadata. Faster index building allows quick start of production workloads.

Insertion throughput: Insertion throughput indicates how fast the database can ingest new vectors. This matters both for initial bulk loading and for incremental inserts during production. Key metrics to track here are the number of vectors inserted per second and the total time for bulk loading.

Search latency: Search latency measures the time taken to execute search queries after indexes are built. Lower latency allows real-time response for time-sensitive applications. Testing latency under different workloads reveals responsiveness. The key metrics to track are average, median, 95th and 99th percentile latencies.

Search throughput: While latency focuses on a single query, throughput measures how many search queries can be processed per second concurrently. Higher throughput supports heavy production workloads with many users. The key metric to track here is queries per second (QPS).

Scalability: Testing these metrics on varied data and workload sizes reveals how well performance scales. Benchmarking should cover small to huge datasets and moderate to high concurrency.

Accuracy: Search accuracy depends on the matching logic. Benchmarking must test relevant accuracy metrics such as precision, recall, etc., under different conditions. Key metrics are recall and F1 score for search results.

Resource efficiency and cost: Given similar hardware, a database that achieves better performance per CPU core, RAM utilization, etc., is more resource efficient. When the compute chosen is more efficient, operational costs are lowered. This also includes the benchmarking of filtering search results by predicates without scanning all vectors, which is crucial for efficiency in production. Benchmarking must test filtering throughput and latency for diverse filtering ratios. Key metrics to track are end-to-end query latencies, cost, recovery time after failures, and carbon footprint. Finally, looking at the end-to-end cost to performance ratio is important, including factors such as hardware, software, operating, and maintenance expenses. This helps in determining the overall value of the database for specific use cases.

As you can see from the various dimensions of benchmarks to test, results could be very case specific. Several benchmarking tools are available for evaluating the performance of vector databases. Some of these tools include the following:

VectorDBBench: An open-source vector database benchmark tool that provides unbiased vector database benchmark results for mainstream vector databases and cloud services; see `https://zilliz.com/vector-database-benchmark-tool`

Qdrant: An open-source vector search engine that provides a comparative benchmark and benchmarking framework for vector search engines and vector databases; see `https://qdrant.tech/benchmarks`

ANN Benchmark: A popular benchmark that evaluates both scientific libraries and vector databases, providing a starting point for performance comparison; see `https://ann-benchmarks.com`

Benchmarking Setup and Results

Now, similar to the previous section on creating your own benchmarking table for the model inference component, we can create our own benchmarking numbers for the vector database component. It is likely that this benchmarking exercise is a large undertaking for a team of any size, so the only caution is to use as many open benchmarks as possible before deciding and set up your own benchmarking architecture only if required.

Let's assume you have a need to run your own benchmarking; cloud providers offer several services that can be stitched up to do this. There is no "standard" architecture and no widely accepted set of tools either. The following is a discussion of one of the various ways to set this up.

First, we discuss some principles of setting up a benchmark for the vector database component.

Benchmark vector embedding components in isolation: Since we want to test metrics associated with ingest and latency of queries for just this component, we need to isolate other components in our architecture and eliminate latency from these other sources. For example, one of the most important aspects of building a vector database is embedding vectors. LLM API providers offer APIs to return high-quality vectors for each input sequence. However, these APIs are highly throttled and may add time to our total measurement. So, in this case, it is a good idea to host your own embedding model that generates similar sized vectors as the final intended embedding model.

Use a representative input dataset: This should contain the same order of magnitude of text documents that you need to test for. Even if you plan to use a smaller portion of the full dataset, size your resources for the full dataset to make sure you have the right performance and cost estimates.

Plan to do an end-to-end benchmark: This is in addition to vector embedding benchmarks alone. An end-to-end benchmark could be measuring search quality or accuracy, with vector embeddings being part of a larger system.

Figure 1.8 shows a general architecture to measure two very important KPIs related to vector databases: ingestion time and query latency.

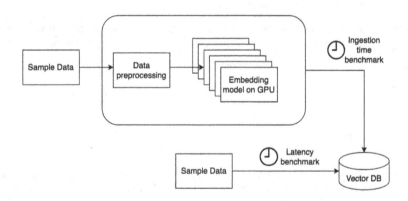

FIGURE 1.8: Vector DB benchmarking architecture

Let's walk through the components of this benchmark architecture. The sample architecture diagram in Figure 1.8 displays the core components involved in a typical vector database benchmarking pipeline. Raw text data first goes through several preprocessing steps before getting converted into embedding vectors. Preprocessing includes cleaning, such as removing HTML tags, fixing encoding issues, and handling malformed data. The text is tokenized by splitting it into individual words, phrases, or sentences. All text is converted to lowercase for consistency and common stop words like *a*, *and*, and *the* are removed as they add little semantic meaning. Words are stemmed or lemmatized to their root form to reduce vocabulary size. For example, *running* is converted to *run*. Finally, documents are broken into smaller chunks to allow parallel embedding. This preprocessed text is fed as input to the embedding model, hosted on GPU servers to leverage massive parallelism for efficient computation. The model converts each text chunk into a dense high-dimensional vector representation encoding its semantic meaning. These embeddings are floating-point vectors that are typically 1,000 dimensions for each chunk of text but can vary based on the embedding model used.

The generated vectors are loaded into the vector database, which stores them optimized for low-latency similarity search and retrieval. The database provides APIs to ingest vectors and enables querying using algorithms such as cosine similarity and locality sensitive hashing (LSH). The vectorized dataset powers downstream applications such as search, classification, and recommendations, and in the case of our GenAI chatbot solution, it can be used to augment LLM results by providing useful context from real data.

Two key performance metrics highlighted are total data ingestion time and query latency. Ingestion time measures the complete end-to-end duration to process raw data through embedding and storing vectors in the database.

Query latency indicates how rapidly the database can retrieve similar vectors for a given input. A specific instantiation of this architecture may involve the following setup:

➤ Using a sample benchmark dataset for indexing such as OSCAR (`https://huggingface.co/datasets/oscar-corpus/OSCAR-2301`)

➤ Using a library like ray.io (`https://github.com/ray-project/ray`) to both process the data and locally host embedding models in a GPU cluster

➤ Using an embedding model like `https://huggingface.co/sentence-transformers/all-mpnet-base-v2`

Once again, remember that we can use different data sources, different ways to distribute the ingestion workload and host models, and various embedding models. When running a benchmark using the previous sample architecture and a variety of vector databases, we get the results in Table 1.3:

TABLE 1.3: Benchmark results for vector DB

DATABASE	AVERAGE INGESTION TIME (MS)	P99 INGESTION TIME (MS)	AVERAGE QUERY LATENCY (MS)	P99 QUERY LATENCY (MS)
OpenSearch	2.13	35.0	11	16
Amazon RDS	1.60	7.7	83	210
Pinecone	3.80	5.1	81	113

Table 1.3 compares the performance of three vector databases: OpenSearch (`https://aws.amazon.com/opensearch-service`), RDS with PG Vector (`https://aws.amazon.com/about-aws/whats-new/2023/05/amazon-rds-postgresql-pgvector-ml-model-integration`), and Pinecone (`https://docs.pinecone.io/docs/python-client`). The test performed uses a 1% sample of the dataset (the full dataset contains more than 600 million records). Metrics are provided for average and 99th percentile (P99) latency when ingesting a single record as well as querying for a single vector.

For ingestion latency, OpenSearch took an average of 2.1 ms to ingest a record. Its P99 latency was 35 ms, indicating 99% of ingests finished within 35 ms. RDS had a faster average ingestion latency of 1.6 ms per record. However, its P99 latency was higher at 7.7 ms. Pinecone had the highest ingestion latency, averaging 3.8 ms per record. Its P99 latency was the lowest at 5.1 ms.

For query latency, OpenSearch averaged 11 ms per query with a P99 of 16 ms. RDS had higher latency at an average of 83 ms per query and P99 of 210 ms. Pinecone also had a high query latency, averaging 81 ms per query and P99 of 113 ms.

As we can see from the results, there is no clear winner, and this is not surprising. While PG Vector on RDS provided the lowest average ingestion speed per record, query latencies are higher for this small benchmark. While OpenSearch had the lowest average query latency, it had the highest P99 ingest time per record (once again, for this particular benchmark). This shows how nuanced benchmarks can be and why we need to carefully look at performance numbers.

The main factor affecting total ingestion time is the database write throughput; in fact, if you isolated every other component, the only thing that affects total ingestion time is the write speed. Practically, unless you write the software for the actual vector database, it is not possible to isolate this component. Therefore, the total time to ingest data into the vector database is also affected by the complexity of the embedding model as discussed, GPU resources available (as running multiple copies of the model parallelized across more GPU cores reduces processing time), network transfer speed between embedding servers and the database, and vector dimensionality (as higher dimensions require more time to generate and ingest). Tuning these factors improves ingestion time. Choosing a simpler and lower-dimensional model, adding GPUs, improving network speed, and using a high write throughput database will reduce overall ingestion duration.

On the other hand, the vector database's query latency is impacted by what indexing algorithms are used. Algorithms like Locality Sensitive Hashing (LSH) can provide faster similarity search than brute-force cosine similarity. Using higher vector dimensions means that you have to process more data during the retrieval step. When setting up a system that uses queues, heavier concurrent loads will lead to longer queues and delays seen across users. Optimizing query latency involves efficient indexing like LSH, reducing vector dimensions, provisioning sufficient read throughput, and testing under peak load.

Other Factors to Consider

Two other factors are important when we look at the bigger picture: cost and accuracy.

As mentioned earlier, it is important to price out these options based on the full expected workload. Pricing options that are pay-as-you-go and look simple may end up being expensive for indexes with hundreds of millions of records. On the other hand, providers offering a licensing model with tiered pricing may have a nonlinear pricing structure that does not scale with the number of records. For example, the cost would be about $21,000 per month for holding the entire OSCAR dataset in OpenSearch, $17,000 per month for RDS, and $8,400 per month for Pinecone. While the vector database is only a component of a search system, sophisticated, managed services like Amazon Kendra that offer an end-to-end user experience with secure connectors and data parsers from various enterprise data sources may cost an order of magnitude higher for hundreds of millions of records.

The other aspect to look at is accuracy, with the backdrop of how one might trade off cost and performance. The optimal embedding model really depends on balancing accuracy, speed, compute resources, and cost. Simpler models embed efficiently on CPUs, while complex models require GPUs but achieve superior quality. For example, more complex models like BERT and GPT produce higher-quality embeddings but require more processing time versus simpler models such as word2vec. These larger models with more parameters generate better embeddings but are slower to execute, and you may be able to execute only these on GPUs, which increases the cost (unless they are distilled or quantized). Domain-specific models improve performance on related text compared to general-purpose embeddings, especially when these models are available and can be used for your specific use case. Lastly, a larger context window captures greater semantic nuances but needs increased compute power.

Several pre-trained embedding models are available out of the box through libraries such as Hugging Face Transformers. For example, Sentence Transformers (www.sbert.net/) provides optimized sentence embedding models like all-MiniLM-L6 (https://huggingface.co/sentence-transformers/all-MiniLM-L6-v2), which is compact and efficient. Multilingual models such as mLUKE (https://arxiv.org/abs/2110.08151) can handle diverse languages, if that is one of your requirements. Domain-specific models exist as well, like BioClinicalBERT (https://arxiv.org/abs/1904.03323) for biomedical texts. If resources are available, it is also a good idea to train or fine-tune your own embedding model for improved search quality. OpenAI's text-embedding-ada-002 uses a large 8,192-token context window for high accuracy. Rather than using ray.io as we showed in this example, you can also consider using Spark for distributed calculation of embeddings. The Spark NLP 5.0 library offers highly optimized models like INSTRUCTOR that can be run on a Spark cluster (www.johnsnowlabs.com/spark-nlp-5-0-its-all-about-that-search).

If you are building your own index using libraries like FAISS, you have much more flexibility in terms of indexing as well as search performance. The FAISS package by Meta provides excellent guidelines on when to use certain indexing algorithms (https://engineering.fb.com/2017/03/29/data-infrastructure/faiss-a-library-for-efficient-similarity-search).

To summarize this guidance, the optimal index for a vector database depends on the planned number of searches. For less than 10,000 searches, direct computation with a flat index is the most efficient as there is no amortization of build time. Exact search results require using the flat index, as it does not compress vectors or add overhead. When memory is a concern, if exact results are not needed, RAM becomes the constraint to optimize by picking an index that balances precision and speed. With ample memory or a small dataset, the HNSW index provides fast and highly accurate searches through its graph traversal algorithm but uses more RAM with its 4 to 64 links per vector.

Alternatively, an inverted file index with product quantization compresses vectors through OPQ dimension reduction and PQ quantization into codes using less memory, with two tuning parameters of reranking k and nprobe for the precision versus speed trade-off. As dataset size grows, clustering vectors first via k-means or HNSW graph partitioning into IVF buckets optimizes storage and lookup time, with nprobe buckets scanned per search. Training set size and number of clusters increase with data volume. Multilevel clustering further improves indexing of more than 100 million vectors. Finally, GPU support may be required, in which case flat, OPQ, and IVFK work on GPUs, while HNSW is CPU-only currently. Considering these factors holistically based on the use case leads to selecting the optimal indexing approach.

Thoroughly benchmarking ingestion and query performance under realistic workloads is key for an efficient vector database pipeline. The choice of embedding model and tasks, such as optimizing GPU resources, minimizing network transfers, leveraging fast ingest and retrieval algorithms, and provisioning adequate database throughput are important considerations. Benchmarks can predict production behavior and highlight areas for optimization; however, benchmarks like the ones discussed in this section can be nuanced and have to be used carefully in deciding what vector database to go with for production use cases. If you are interested in another view of the same discussion, take a look at this resource that compares some of the vector DBs mentioned here: https://benchmark.vectorview.ai/vectordbs.html.

Cost Assessment of the Large Language Model Component

Now let's look at another important component in the GenAI chatbot architecture; arguably this is the most important, central component. There are generally three ways to access LLMs today.

➤ Through a console application (e.g., ChatGPT, claude.ai)

➤ Through an API to a chat model, without the need to host the model itself

➤ Through a self-hosted API that includes the LLM and any serving stack

These three ways of accessing LLMs incur varying costs. When building a conversational AI application like a chatbot, virtual assistant, or content generation tool, a key component is selecting the right large language model to power the underlying AI. As AI continues to permeate our digital lives, more companies are launching LLMs with varying capabilities and pricing models.

How does one pick the most cost-effective LLM while meeting the performance needs of the application? We will be uncovering this question through several chapters that follow, focusing on ways to optimize cost. But first let's explore this question by revisiting the hypothetical scenario with a virtual assistant that is being built to handle multiple user sessions in parallel. Once again, it is anticipated to have 100 concurrent users chatting with the assistant at any given time. Based on user testing, it is estimated each user will make around 100 requests per hour through natural conversation with the assistant. If you have played around with applications like ChatGPT, this estimate may match what you experience in practice. You may use it to help you with work and may interact with it once a minute (and even that may be an overestimate).

Figures 1.9 and 1.10 explore this hypothetical scenario by changing a few variables that impact the price per hour for this application. Detailed pricing and usage comparison tables can provide critical insights when evaluating large language models. The tables compare leading LLMs like GPT-3, Claude, and Amazon SageMaker across metrics including cost per hour, requests per minute, usage limits, and optimizations like batching. By analyzing the variables in the tables for a projected workload, you can select an optimal LLM based on performance needs and cost constraints.

The tables shown in Figures 1.9 and 1.10 are snapshots of a cost calculator highlighting how factors such as scaling out instances and leveraging innovations such as continuous batching can transform an LLM from a cost-prohibitive to a cost-effective solution for powering AI applications. The analysis shows that, while powerful, choices like GPT-3 and GPT-4 from OpenAI incur high costs at more than $180 per hour to support 100 concurrent users.

Model / Cost item	GPT4 32K	GPT 3.5 Turbo 16k	Claude V2 100K or 12K	Claude Instant 100K	Falcon 40B on SageMaker (1 g5.12xlarge)	Falcon 40B on SageMaker (1 g5.48xlarge)	Falcon 40B on SageMaker (N instances g5.48xlarge with static batching)	Falcon 40B on SageMaker (N g5.48xlarge with continuous batching)
Input, per MM tokens	$60	$3	$11.02	$1.63	-	-	-	-
Output, per MM tokens	$120	$4	$32.68	$5.51	-	-	-	-
Input tokens per request	100	100	100	100	100	100	100	100
Output tokens per request	100	100	100	100	100	100	100	100
Number of instances	-	-	-	-	1	1	1	1
Max requests per minute	3,500	2,000	300	300	12	20	20	20
Max tokens per minute	350,000	180,000	150,000	150,000	-	-	-	-
Number of concurrent user sessions	100	100	100	100	100	100	100	100
Number of requests per user session per hour	100	100	100	100	100	100	100	100
At rate limit (max RPM)?	FALSE	FALSE	FALSE	FALSE	TRUE	TRUE	TRUE	FALSE
At rate limit (max tokens per minute)	FALSE	FALSE	FALSE	FALSE	No token limit	No token limit	No token limit	No token limit
cost per user per turn	$0.018000	$0.000700	$0.004370	$0.000714	-	-	-	-
per hour cost	$180.00	$7.000	$43.70	$7.14	$7.09	$20.36	$20.36	$20.36

FIGURE 1.9: Snapshot 1 of the cost calculator showing costs per hour for various model options based on input factors and how rate limits can be exceeded in certain cases

Model / Cost item	GPT4 32K	GPT 3.5 Turbo 16k	Claude V2 100K or 12K	Claude Instant 100K	Falcon 40B on SageMaker (1 g5.12xlarge)	Falcon 40B on SageMaker (1 g5.48xlarge)	Falcon 40B on SageMaker (N instances g5.48xlarge with static batching)	Falcon 40B on SageMaker (N g5.48xlarge with continuous batching)
Input, per MM tokens	$60	$3	$11.02	$1.63	-	-	-	-
Output, per MM tokens	$120	$4	$32.68	$5.51	-	-	-	-
Input tokens per request	100	100	100	100	100	100	100	100
Output tokens per request	100	100	100	100	100	100	100	100
Number of instances	-	-	-	-	14	1	9	1
Max requests per minute	3,500	2,000	300	300	168	20	180	190
Max tokens per minute	350,000	180,000	150,000	150,000	-	-	-	-
Number of concurrent user sessions	100	100	100	100	100	13	100	100
Number of requests per user session per hour	100	100	100	100	100	100	100	100
At rate limit (max RPM)?	FALSE	FALSE	FALSE	FALSE	FALSE	TRUE	FALSE	FALSE
At rate limit (max tokens per minute)	FALSE	FALSE	FALSE	FALSE	No token limit	No token limit	No token limit	No token limit
cost per user per turn	$0.018000	$0.000700	$0.004370	$0.000714	-	-	-	-
per hour cost	$180.00	$7.000	$43.70	$7.14	$99.26	$20.36	$183.24	$20.36

FIGURE 1.10: Snapshot 2 of the cost calculator showing costs per hour for various model options based on input factors, showing how vertical and horizontal scaling, dynamic batching can help satisfy request rate demands

More affordable options are needed, especially because models today have different capabilities, so it may be beneficial to consider multiple models and model providers to balance cost with performance. This is also exactly why companies like OpenAI and Anthropic provide multiple versions of models such as one cheaper, quicker version with decent performance (Claude Instant) and a more powerful but also more expensive version (Claude v2 100,000). Figures 1.9 and 1.10 show a clear difference in cost between larger and smaller models offered by these LLM API providers (GPT 4 versus GPT 3.5 Turbo, or Claude V2 versus Claude Instant).

Based on published rate limits, Claude Instant would allow 300 requests per minute across users, while Claude V2 increases this to 2,000 RPM. Both comfortably satisfy the 100 RPM per user estimate in our hypothetical scenario without hitting any usage limits, but Claude Instant is cheaper (as expected) at $7.14 per hour, so it seems like the obvious choice.

But can we find an even better option? Of course, we have overloaded the term *better* here. What is better for one use case may mean decent performance at lower cost, whereas for another use case, this necessarily means higher performance. Choosing Claude Instant or GPT 3.5 Turbo may mean less accuracy or fewer general capabilities to solve multiple complex use cases like their larger counterparts.

This cost-performance trade-off means that we need to look deeper into self-hosting, or shared-hosting options. Here's where cloud services like Amazon SageMaker and others show promise. Running the open-source Falcon 40B model leveraging SageMaker optimizations allows requests to be served at a very modest 12 RPM from a single compute instance based on static batching. With 100 users doing 100 requests per minute, this limit would be exceeded with only one g5.12xlarge instance. Vertical scaling is usually the next thing to think of when trying to scale up self-hosted LLMs (or any model for that matter).

Looking at Figure 1.10, we would need at least 14 instances costing about $100 per hour to satisfy our rate of incoming requests, in the ideal case. A larger instance, say an ml.g4.48xlarge can handle almost 1.6x the number of requests, but with only one instance and naïve static batching, this will still hit our rate demand constraint and cost a bit more. Using nine of these instances costs as much as one of the costliest models out there per hour, and the accuracy of results and general applicability of a central model may not be as great as GPT 4, for example. Not bad, but can further optimization be achieved?

It turns out we can use another trick: continuous batching. By dynamically batching requests before they are fed to the model, throughput increases dramatically. A 9.5x improvement is estimated based on the 512 token requests (see www.anyscale.com/blog/continuous-batching-llm-inference). This lets us fully utilize a single instance costing a modest $20 per hour to satisfy all requests. The big caveat is that the model used is a Falcon 40B; even though this ranks pretty high on the open-source leaderboard, we know that its performance lags behind more advanced models like GPT4.

While models like GPT 3.5 Turbo and Claude instant provide a simple, low-cost option, SageMaker with an open-source model unlocks higher-scale use cases with more flexibility on your LLM inference stack. You also have the option of considering a cost budget for a given level of expected performance as a factor in deciding your architecture in this case. With instance sizing and batching optimizations, SageMaker allowed a 100x increase in request capacity over Claude while cutting cost by more than 60%, assuming that the performance for that particular use case is equivalent. The comparison here uses the AWS service SageMaker to demonstrate the importance of knowing how to perform this benchmark but several other cloud providers and SaaS companies provide competitive options for self-hosting.

This is not meant to be a full benchmark study, but it highlights key considerations when evaluating LLMs for GenAI applications. Usage limits must be accounted for in addition to raw model pricing. Factors like batching, model compression or quantization, and instance or worker scale-out capacity play a crucial role. Testing different configurations using projected workload numbers helps find the sweet spot between cost, performance, and flexibility that works well for your particular team. There may be factors beyond what are explained here as technical indicators that may inform a choice. For example, deep expertise in Kubernetes-based stacks may be a huge motivation to build this entire stack on Kubernetes. Unlocking innovations like continuous deployment and batching and understanding the capabilities and constraints of modern LLMs transform the cost-performance landscape to enable solutions for delivering next-generation AI applications.

SUMMARY

This chapter introduced the concept of LLMs and GenAI, starting from the history of language models to the three-layer GenAI stack. We then took a sample application (a GenAI chatbot) and discovered the various components that may be necessary to build out this solution. Based on this blueprint, we covered various ways to benchmark important components of this architecture while balancing performance, cost, and accuracy.

2

Tuning Techniques for Cost Optimization

WHAT'S IN THIS CHAPTER?

➤ Fine-Tuning and Customizability

➤ Parameter-Efficient Fine-Tuning Methods

➤ Cost and Performance Implications of PEFT Methods

FINE-TUNING AND CUSTOMIZABILITY

LLMs such as BERT , GPT-3 , and PaLM have achieved state-of-the-art performance on a wide range of NLP tasks. However, the computational demands of training and deploying these massive models present significant challenges. LLMs rely on an enormous number of parameters, with models scaling up to hundreds of billions of parameters. For example, GPT-3 contains 175 billion parameters , while PaLM reaches 540 billion parameters. This massive scale enables them to learn rich representations of language from huge datasets during pre-training. However, it also leads to immense computational requirements.

Specifically, the memory footprint and floating-point operations (FLOPs) scale linearly with the number of parameters. This makes training and fine-tuning computationally infeasible without specialized hardware. Even the deployment of such models for inference can be prohibitively expensive. As models continue to grow in scale, these costs will only increase. For example, training GPT-3 was estimated to cost $12 million! Furthermore, full fine-tuning requires training a separate model instance for each new task, which is storage-intensive. The computational barriers restrict the wider adoption of LLMs and preclude many organizations from benefiting from their capabilities. Therefore, developing techniques to optimize the cost of using LLMs has become imperative. First, let's discuss why pre-training your own models from scratch is not always the best idea to start with.

Basic Scaling Laws You Should Know

Before we dive into how to make training and fine-tuning more efficient, first let's discuss how resource intensive these models can be. Since we are talking about training and fine-tuning (as opposed to inference), resource constraints are mostly related to memory, or more specifically GPU memory.

Several papers have talked about "scaling laws" for LLMs, but two papers stand out. First, in a paper from researchers at OpenAI titled "Scaling Laws for Neural Language Models," derive scaling laws governing the relationship between model performance and key training factors such as model size, dataset size, and compute budget for autoregressive transformer language models (https://arxiv.org/abs/2001.08361). Through extensive empirical analysis on models ranging from 100 million to 10 billion parameters, they found power law dependencies between the test loss and model parameters, training tokens, and training FLOPs. These scaling laws provide precise quantitative guidance on how to increase factors such as model size and training data to achieve better performance with more available compute. The study reveals that larger models are significantly more sample efficient and that the common practice of training to convergence is inefficient.

Researchers from DeepMind revisited the question of optimally trading off model size and training data given a fixed compute budget in 2022 in a paper titled "Training Compute-Optimal Large Language Models." Through training more than 400 transformer models, from 70 million to 16 billion parameters on up to 500 billion training tokens, they found that the model size and dataset size should be increased equally with more compute. They propose that compute currently used to train models such as Gopher could be better utilized to train smaller but sufficiently powered models on more data. As evidence, they trained Chinchilla, a 70 billion parameter model trained on 1.4 trillion tokens, which outperforms the 280 billion parameter Gopher model across evaluations despite using the same training compute. Their work emphasizes the growing importance of high-quality datasets in addition to model scale increases.

To summarize, here were the main takeaways:

Larger models require fewer samples to reach the same performance. Anecdotally, we have all been experiencing this. Bigger models perform better at a wide variety of tasks.

The optimal model size grows smoothly with the loss target and compute budget. This means that smaller models, when trained with more data, can theoretically reach the same loss. With smaller models, this translates to lower production costs when doing fine-tuning and inference.

Model and dataset size should be increased proportionally to the compute budget. If you start with a given compute budget (which translates to a dollar value you are willing to spend), the optimal model size and dataset size can be derived. In the paper from DeepMind mentioned previously, an "optimally sized," smaller 70-billion parameter model outperforms the 175-billion parameter GPT3, 280-billion parameter Gopher, and 530-billion parameter megatron models!

Great, but how do you actually use these scaling laws? Assume you are part of a team that has decided they want their own model. Furthermore, it is decided that 40-billion parameter models are a good bet given the good performance of this class of models. Let's start with the model size: N = 40 billion parameters.

To determine the compute budget, we use the following equation:

```
N ~ C α
```

where N is the number of model parameters, and C is the compute budget. The constant α = 0.46 and is empirically calculated based on experiments conducted in the paper.

Solving for C, provided for our model N is 40e9, gives this:

```
C_min ~ 40e9^(1/0.46) = 1.116e23 FLOPs = 1.116e8 PetaFLOPs
```

This estimate also matches another approach provided by the Chinchilla paper, as shown in Figure 2.1 (look for your model on the map!).

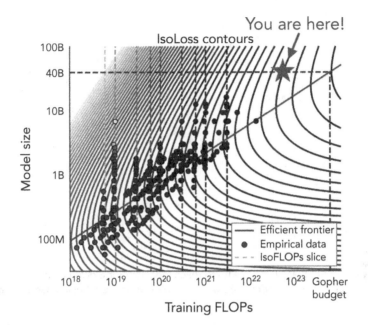

FIGURE 2.1: IsoLoss contours from the Chinchilla paper, which shows models size versus training FLOPs, with contour lines showing what is required for a model of a given size to achieve the same loss with varying resource budgets

Now, assume you have access to a training cluster with 256 A100 GPUs, with each GPU capable of providing about 150 TFLOPs/s of training throughput. This is a gross estimate and is found to be a good starting point for these kinds of high-level calculations. What this means is that with an ideal compute budget of 1.116e8 PFLOPs, you can complete training in (1.116e23 / (256*150e12))/(24*60*60) = 33 days. With an on-demand cost of $32.7726 per hour, a single training run of the model with a consolidated dataset will cost more than $830,000!

These quantitative estimates are based on several assumptions and can be considered a lower bound. The scaling laws allow us to compute budgets for planning but may not be granular enough compared to an actual, low-epoch benchmark. Although 256 A100 GPUs correspond to 32 P4D instances on EC2, this comes with an overhead of actual setting up, managing, and debugging what happens within the cluster. With a more managed service such as Amazon SageMaker, several such aspects of the ML life cycle is managed, for a slightly increased cost of $33.688 per hour for a single P4D instance, with a total cost of $955,000 for the 32 instances you need. This also means that to reach the ideal loss, you would need to train the model with at least 850 billion tokens, as shown in Figure 2.2. (the Gopher model estimate from the paper with a model size of around 63 billion parameters, trained with 1.4 trillion tokens is also shown for reference).

As we can see, few companies around the world, specifically LLM API providers, can justify the ROI in pretraining unique models and chat-ready versions of LLMs.

The rest of this chapter focuses on methods to enable efficient fine-tuning of LLMs to downstream tasks through cost optimization. We refer to these techniques collectively as *parameter-efficient fine-tuning*, or PEFT. The goal of PEFT is to tune only a small subset of parameters in the LLM instead of all parameters like in full fine-tuning. This provides substantial reductions in computation, memory, and storage without significantly impacting model performance.

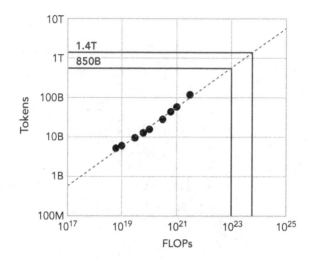

FIGURE 2.2:   Number of tokens to train with to reach ideal loss for a given compute budget and model size; the hypothetical 40-billion model is shown in comparison to a a 63-billion Gopher model from the original paper

We can organize PEFT methods into four main categories.

➤   Parameter-efficient modules such as adapters that introduce additional trainable parameters into the base LLM

➤   Prompt-based tuning that optimizes continuous prompt representations

➤   Sparse update techniques that select a subset of parameters to update

➤   Low-rank factorization methods that reparametrize weight updates

Through efficient use of resources, PEFT methods aim to alleviate the computational barriers and enable broader access to state-of-the-art LLMs. The chapter discusses the landscape of methods, analyzes their connections, and discusses practical considerations. Our goal is to guide researchers and practitioners toward more efficient use of LLMs in real-world systems. The next section will provide an in-depth discussion of parameter-efficient modules such as adapters, which encapsulate task-specific representations to reduce the optimization footprint during fine-tuning.

PARAMETER-EFFICIENT FINE-TUNING METHODS

As language models continue to scale exponentially in size, with models reaching hundreds of billions or even trillions of parameters, efficiently fine-tuning them on downstream tasks becomes increasingly challenging. The conventional approach of fine-tuning all the parameters on each new dataset is computationally wasteful and impractical.

Adapters offer an elegant solution that enables task-specific adaptation of massive pre-trained models with only a tiny fraction of trainable parameters. The key innovation of adapters is introducing small neural modules with new trainable weights into each layer of the pre-trained model. These adapter modules contain just thousands to millions of extra parameters—a tiny fraction of the billions in the full model. Only the adapter parameters are updated during fine-tuning, while the original model weights remain frozen. This allows extensive reuse of the pre-trained knowledge across tasks. Since adapters are small, encapsulated modules, they are forced to learn representations compatible with the surrounding unfrozen layers. This enables composing knowledge from multiple task-specific adapters in a modular way.

Adapters come in various forms and sizes, and the specific adapter architecture in use can also be customized by factors such as hidden dimensions, bottleneck size, and parameter sharing across layers. Placement of adapters can impact performance; prior work found the feedforward position works best in transformers. So, suffice it to say that every adapter architecture and implementation is very different and can be confusing when you look at a barrage of papers, GitHub links, and code.

While adapter architectures differ in their specifics, most follow a common framework.

➤ They introduce small modules with extra trainable parameters into each layer of a large pre-trained model such as BERT.

➤ Only the adapter parameters are updated during task-specific fine-tuning, while the original model weights remain frozen.

➤ Adapters transform the activations at each layer in a way that is compatible with subsequent frozen layers.

➤ Residual connections are used to combine the adapter outputs with the original pre-trained representations.

A key distinction exists between training adapters for a single task versus multiple tasks jointly.

➤ **Single-task adapters (ST-As):** With this approach, task-specific adapters are trained separately for each of N downstream tasks. The pre-trained model weights are frozen, and only the parameters in the adapter modules are updated per task. This allows easy parallelization across tasks.

➤ **Multitask adapters (MT-As):** With this setting, adapters for all N tasks are trained. MT-A enables sharing knowledge across tasks through both the base model and the adapter parameters. However, it requires simultaneous access to all datasets. Both ST-A and MT-A have been shown to perform close to full fine-tuning of the entire model, while introducing only a small percentage of extra trainable parameters in the adapter modules. In the next section, we dive deeper into adapter methods.

Adapters Under the Hood

As mentioned in the previous section, the key advantage of adapters is the significant reduction in optimization overhead. With most parameters frozen, less memory is needed for gradients and optimizer states. This means that models with billions of parameters can be fine-tuned on a GPU by updating only a few million adapter weights. But how does this exactly work? How is it implemented? Let's dive deeper.

> **NOTE** *This chapter aims to help you understand the plethora of adapters and PEFT methods that have already been studied. As noted, the predominant way to fine-tune models today is through PEFT methods because of the high enough performance and low cost to train. Recent state-of-the-art PEFT techniques achieve performance comparable to that of full fine-tuning. This means we need to start from an already existing LLM such as Falcon 40B or Llama2. These models are readily available in model hubs such as Hugging Face.*

To look under the hood of PEFT methods, the best place to start is the Hugging Face PEFT library (`https://huggingface.co/docs/peft/index`).

This library can be installed using `pip install peft`. The PEFT library includes implementations of the following methods:

- ➤ LoRA: https://arxiv.org/abs/2106.09685
- ➤ Prefix Tuning : https://arxiv.org/pdf/2110.07602.pdf
- ➤ P-Tuning: https://arxiv.org/abs/2103.10385
- ➤ Prompt Tuning: https://arxiv.org/abs/2104.08691
- ➤ AdaLoRA: https://arxiv.org/abs/2303.10512
- ➤ IA3: https://arxiv.org/abs/2205.05638
- ➤ MultiTask Prompt Tuning: https://arxiv.org/abs/2303.02861
- ➤ LoHa: https://arxiv.org/abs/2108.06098

To understand the various adapter methods, let's start with the basic decoder-only transformer block, which forms the core of model architectures such as GPT. Figure 2.3 shows how the raw input prompt gets converted to tokens and then into embeddings before getting passed into the decoder block. For a detailed explanation of transformer architecture and the GPT type decoder-only models, visit https://openai.com/research/language-unsupervised and https://arxiv.org/abs/2005.14165.

> **NOTE** *Encoder-only models are primarily employed in natural language understanding (NLU) tasks, such as text classification and named entity recognition (NER). These models are designed to calculate numerical representations of input text sequences. Their computations are based on both the left and right contexts of the text, which is often referred to as bidirectional attention. Examples of models falling into this category include BERT.*
>
> *On the other hand, decoder-only models find their utility in natural language generation (NLG) tasks. These models predict the most likely next word in an iterative manner, given an input sequence. The representations generated by these models are based solely on the left context, often known as causal or autoregressive attention. Models in the GPT family are representative examples of decoder-only models.*
>
> *Encoder-decoder models, as the name suggests, are versatile and can handle more complex tasks that involve both understanding and generating natural language. These tasks include machine translation and text summarization. Models such as BART and T5 are examples of encoder-decoder models.*

Prompt Tuning

As mentioned earlier, pre-training models from scratch, or fine-tuning models, will generally mean updating all the parameters of the model. This is an expensive exercise for LLMs with billions of parameters. Let's begin with one of the easiest (but most effective) ways to modify the module shown in Figure 2.3: prompt tuning. Prompt tuning introduces new parameters and learns "soft prompts" to condition frozen language models to perform specific downstream tasks. Looking back at Figure 2.3, when a model is presented with a sequence of N tokens, the initial step involves embedding these tokens. The embedding matrix X is a matrix of size $n \times e$.

To represent soft-prompts in prompt tuning, we can introduce a trainable matrix P of size $p \times e$, with p denoting the length of the tuned prompt for that task. The full embedding is a concatenated version of P and X with size $(p+n) \times e$. This combined matrix then proceeds through the decoder process in a standard manner. Figure 2.4 shows what this change looks like. As you can see, given the original architecture, a small change is introduced with the goal of training a parameter for a particular task. This small change shows that prompt tuning alone (with no intermediate-layer prefixes or task-specific output layers) is sufficient to be competitive with model tuning.

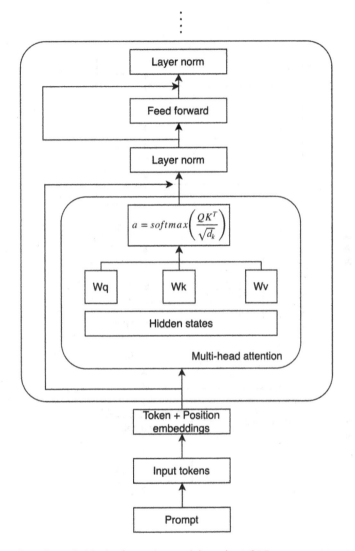

FIGURE 2.3: The basic decoder-only block of popular models such as GPT

Interestingly, the original paper for prompt tuning also discusses ensembling soft prompts for improved performance. By training N prompts on the same task, N separate prompt tuning adapters are created for a task, with the core language modeling parameters still shared throughout. To process one input prompt during inference, instead of computing forward passes of N different models, a single forward pass can be executed with a batch size of N, replicating the example across the batch and varying the prompt. This modification is shown in Figure 2.5.

In PyTorch code, for example, you can simply create an embedding like this:

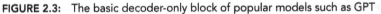

```
self.embedding = torch.nn.Embedding(number_of_virtual_tokens,token_dimension)
```

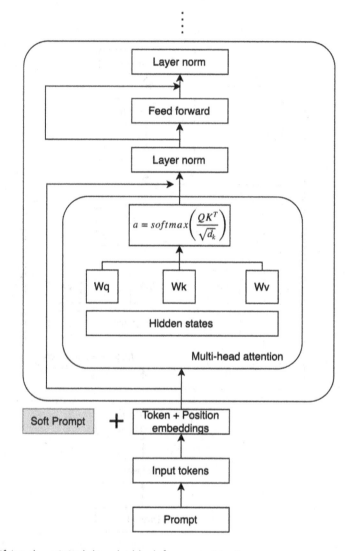

FIGURE 2.4:   Modifying the original decoder block for prompt tuning

You can then provide a forward pass function that looks like this:

```
def forward(self, indices):
    return self.embedding(indices)
```

That's it! You'll see that this forms the core parts of the implementation of the official prompt tuning adapter in the PEFT library: `https://github.com/w601sxs/peft/blob/main/src/peft/tuners/prompt_tuning/model.py`.

Prefix Tuning

Now that you understand how simple this version of an adapter is, let's discuss other adapter architectures, starting with prefix tuning. Inspired by the concept of prompting for language models, prefix tuning allows subsequent tokens to incorporate this prefix as if they were "virtual tokens," similar to prompt tuning. In the paper, prefix tuning was applied to GPT-2 for table-to-text generation and to BART for summarization.

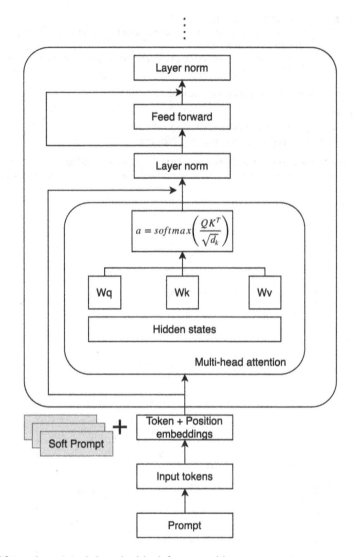

FIGURE 2.5: Modifying the original decoder block for ensemble prompt tuning

The results indicate that with modifications to just 0.1% of the parameters, prefix tuning achieves comparable performance in the full data setting, outperforms fine-tuning in low-data scenarios, and exhibits better extrapolation to examples with unseen topics during training! The key difference from prompt tuning is that unlike prompting, the prefix here consists entirely of free parameters, which do not correspond to real tokens, and it is not just the prefix that gets tuned, it is also the hidden representations of later layers. Specifically, prefix tuning prepends one tunable prefix vector to the keys and values of the multihead attention at every layer. Figure 2.6 shows what this looks like when we modify the original decoder block.

Note that the PEFT library does not add the matrices Pk and Pv as shown in Figure 2.6 to each layer. The implementation is similar to prompt tuning, with a fully connected projection matrix added to the main prompt prefix. In code, this would look like:

```
self.embedding = torch.nn.Embedding(number_of_virtual_tokens,token_dimension)
```

```
self.projection = torch.nn.Sequential(
              torch.nn.Linear(token_dim, encoder_hidden_size),
              torch.nn.Tanh(),
              torch.nn.Linear(encoder_hidden_size, 2*token_dim),
          )
```

You can then provide a forward-pass function that looks like this:

```
def forward(self, indices):
    prefix_tokens = self.embedding(prefix)
    return self.projection(prefix_tokens)
```

A full implementation similar to what is shown in Figure 2.6 can be found at `https://github.com/adapter-hub/adapter-transformers/blob/master/src/transformers/adapters/prefix_tuning.py`.

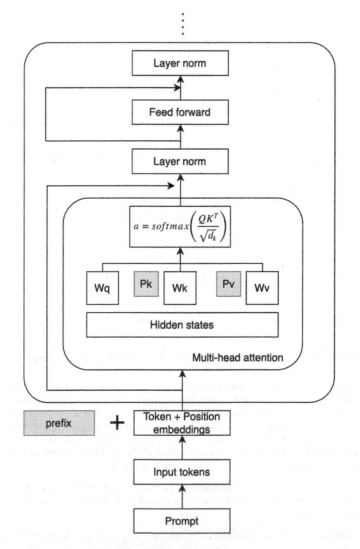

FIGURE 2.6: Modifying the original decoder block for prefix tuning

P-tuning

Let's keep going and discover newer methods of modifying the base decoder architecture to enable efficient fine-tuning. Next, we discuss P-tuning, a method that replaces the input embeddings of pre-trained language models with its differential output embeddings.

Before we can dive into P-tuning, let's first discuss what a prompt template is. A prompt template is a user-defined, structured format that serves as a starting point or framework for generating prompts for natural language processing models, such as language models or chatbots. It is designed to guide users or developers in crafting specific queries or commands for these models. The template typically includes placeholders or variables where users can insert specific information or context relevant to their task or query. By using a template, users can ensure that their prompts are well-structured, follow a consistent format, and include all the necessary information for the model to provide meaningful responses. For example, a prompt template for a language model might look like this:

```
Given the function name and source code, generate an English language explanation
of the function.

Function Name: {function_name}

Source Code:{source_code}

Explanation:
```

In the previous example, parts of the template that can be modified are the `function_name` and `source_code`. The rest of the prompt remains the same. You can see why this can be useful; passing in different texts for the two variables we see here will result in different prompts being passed into an LLM, which completes the text for the explanation and (ideally) does what the instructions are: to generate an explanation of the function. Manually creating these templates can be time-consuming and resource-intensive. Automatically "looking" for the right template to maximize the performance of the task from the large vocabular of the model is also intractable. This is where P-tuning helps.

A prompt template for the purpose of prompt tuning can be thought of a mix of changeable and fixed blocks of text or content. As shown in Figure 2.7, the same prompt template consisting of blocks with fixed portions of text (pseudo tokens and pseudo prompts)—and changeable portions (function name and source code)—is first converted to embeddings. Traditionally, every token (shown as small squares or boxes) is converted into embeddings based on learned embedding layer. This is also true in P-tuning, but only for the parts of the prompt template that can change. For the rest of the template, we are looking for better "filler material" so that the end task of generating English language explanations for code is more accurate. P-tuning uses trainable pseudo-tokens to come up with task-specific prompt templates that improve performance. What is interesting is that P-tuning connects a sequence of related tokens using a bidirectional long short-term memory network (LSTM), followed by a ReLU-activated two-layer multilayer perceptron (MLP). This enables P-tuning to find better continuous prompts as part of the prompt template, beyond what the original vocabulary of the model can express. In the original paper for P-tuning, the authors show that the method outperforms manual tuning and full model fine-tuning for models such as GPT2 and Megatron. Figure 2.8 modifies the original decode block to show how P-tuning works.

In code, we can first initialize a bidirectional LSTM and an MLP like this:

```
self.lstm_head = torch.nn.LSTM(
    input_size=input_size,
    hidden_size=hidden_size,
    num_layers=num_layers,
    dropout=True,
    bidirectional=True,
    batch_first=True,
    )
```

```
self.mlp_head = torch.nn.Sequential(
    torch.nn.Linear(self.hidden_size * 2, self.hidden_size * 2),
        torch.nn.ReLU(),
    torch.nn.Linear(self.hidden_size * 2, self.output_size),
    )
```

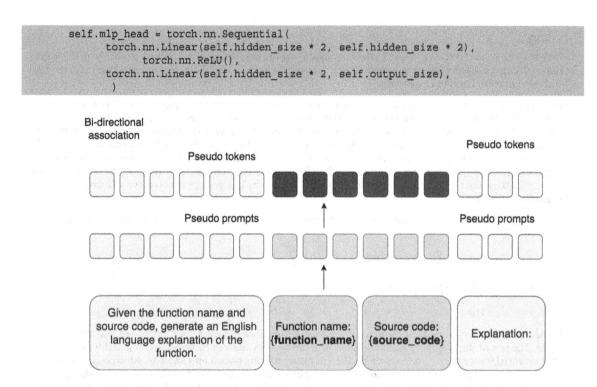

FIGURE 2.7: Prompt template being converted to pseudo-tokens for P-tuning

The forward pass in this case would look like this:

```
def forward(self, indices):
    input_embeds = self.embedding(indices)
    return self.mlp_head(self.lstm_head(input_embeds)[0])
```

The complete code for P-tuning can be found in the PEFT library here: `https://github.com/huggingface/peft/blob/main/src/peft/tuners/p_tuning/model.py`.

IA3

Before discussing IA3, let's understand another type of prompt template that is in practice today: few-shot prompting. Take a look at the following prompt:

```
Please unscramble the letters into a word, and write that word:

asinoc = casino,
yfrogg = froggy,
plesim = simple,
iggestb = biggest,
astedro =
```

If you are good with word jumbles, you probably guessed correctly: the desired output is "roasted." By providing examples of what good looks like, LLMs can be made to perform well at different tasks without any fine-tuning. This is suitable for simple tasks where a few examples are enough. However, in practice, while we can see that more examples are better, too many examples can make the model lose context. The order of examples provided has also been shown to influence the final output. Additionally, a large number of examples in your input prompt can introduce a higher cost per inference. With a high volume of inferences, you could in fact be spending more money than with fine-tuning.

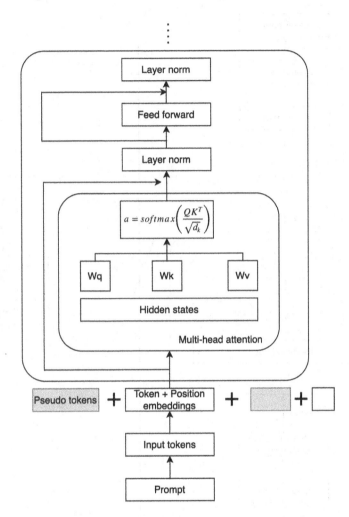

FIGURE 2.8: Modifying the original decoder block for P-tuning

This is the exact motivation of a paper called "Few-shot parameter efficient fine tuning is better and cheaper than in-context learning" (`https://arxiv.org/pdf/2205.05638.pdf`), which introduced Infused Adapter by Inhibiting and Amplifying Inner Activations (IA3). IA3 is a PEFT method that scales activations by learnable parameters similar to some of the methods shown so far. In addition, the method also modifies the loss function to reduce the likelihood of incorrect outputs. Figure 2.9 shows how the standard decoder block can be modified for IA3. As we can see in the figure, three parameters, Lk, Lv, and Lf, are added at various parts of every layer. Additionally, an adapter is added with Lf as a trainable weight.

Earlier in this section, we talked about ST-As and MT-As. So far, we have seen mostly how ST-A methods can be implemented; some ST-A methods can be repeated for multiple tasks, and in effect you can have an MT-A. However, can we implement this in an even better way? This is where multitask prompt tuning (MPT) comes in. MPT is a method that introduces both individual prompts per task as well as a shared prompt structure that encourages cross-task knowledge. Why is this important?

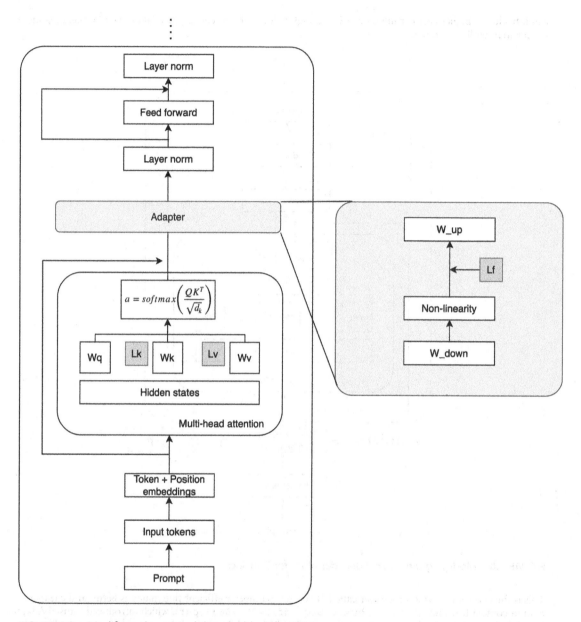

FIGURE 2.9: Modifying the original decoder block for IA3

Imagine you have adapters trained for two tasks: solving complex math problems and translating sentences from English to German. The adapter that makes your model really good at task 1 may not be good at task 2, and vice versa. Now what if you needed to solve complex math problems but respond in German? Cross-task knowledge sharing becomes important here.

As shown in Figure 2.10, MPT does this by introducing two new vectors: u and v. These vectors are multiplied to get a tensor W, which then get multiplied elementwise (Hadamard product) with the shared prompt to get a resulting soft prompt P, specific to a task.

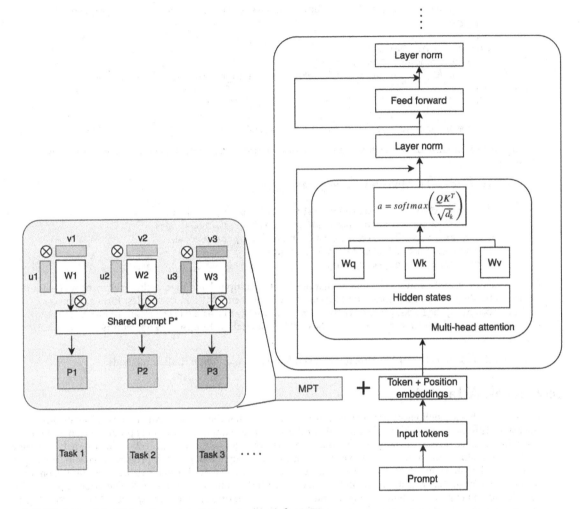

FIGURE 2.10: Modifying the original decoder block for MTP

In practice, however, the direct learning of these task-specific prompt decompositions from the multitask datasets (S) was observed to lead to the overfitting of the shared component (P*) to larger tasks. One way to solve this was knowledge distillation from source prompts that are trained separately. The process involves obtaining a teacher prompt P(teacher) for each source task through conventional prompt tuning that we covered in an earlier section. Then, a corresponding student prompt P(student) is initialized by combining the shared prompt P* with task-specific vectors (u and v).

It's worth noting that each student prompt shares the same P* but is equipped with its own unique set of task-specific vectors, as previously explained. Finally, the shared prompt matrix is enhanced through a distillation process via a custom loss function to transfer knowledge across tasks. This approach lets us get improved prompts that effectively capture the nuances of various tasks while mitigating the issue of overfitting to larger tasks in the context of multitask learning.

In code, we can first create the U and V parameters like so:

```
self.u = torch.nn.Parameter(
    torch.normal(mean=0,
```

```
                std=0.02, size=(self.num_tasks, total_virtual_tokens, self.num_ranks)
            )
        )
    self.v = torch.nn.Parameter(
        torch.normal( mean=0,
        std=0.02, size=(self.num_tasks, self.num_ranks, self.token_dim)
        )
    )

        prompt_embeddings = self.embedding(indices)
```

It is common to initialize these weights to a normal distribution. Then in the forward pass, we can do the following:

```
    def forward(self, indices, task_ids):

        task_cols = torch.index_select(self.u, 0, task_ids)
        task_rows = torch.index_select(self.v, 0, task_ids)
        task_prompts = torch.matmul(task_cols, task_rows)
        prompt_embeddings *= task_prompts
        return prompt_embeddings
```

Notice how we select the rows and columns that need to be multiplied and then multiply element-wise with the prompt embeddings. The PEFT library on Hugging Face implements MPT in its simplest form at `https://github.com/huggingface/peft/blob/main/src/peft/tuners/multitask_prompt_tuning/model.py`. For a full implementation, take a look at the materials at `https://zhenwang9102.github.io/mpt.html`.

Next, we will look at a class of PEFT methods called *low-rank Adaptation* (LoRA) methods.

Low-Rank Adaptation

Despite LLMs having billions of parameters, it is hypothesized that the models actually have a low intrinsic dimension. This means (roughly) only a portion of the weights are important for most predictions. Based on everything we have seen in the previous section, even small changes to the prompt embedding can help fine-tune an LLM with billions of parameters. However, so far, we were only looking at soft prompt variations. What if we could apply the same concept to every weight in the model? LoRA creates learnable matrices A and B from each weight matrix W so that W is approximately B times A, with the same dimensions of W. The original paper with more details and experimental tests can be found at `https://browse.arxiv.org/pdf/2106.09685.pdf`. The most important parameter in LoRA is "rank," or r, which is one of the dimensions of the A and B matrices. That is, B, being a matrix of dimensions d × r, is multiplied by A, a matric with dimensions r × k. This results in a matrix of size d × k, which is the same dimensions of the original weight matrix W.

Figure 2.11 shows how LoRA is implemented in a decoder block. There are, of course, more complex implementations of LoRA, but this illustrates the core concept.

The primary advantage of LoRA lies in the substantial reduction of memory and storage utilization, while still allowing deeper changes within the model versus just the prompt. When applied to an LLM, this approach can lead to a reduction of up to two-thirds in VRAM usage, particularly when the ratio r is less than the dimension d of the model (which is usually the case). This reduction stems from the fact that there's no need to store optimizer states for the frozen parameters. For instance, in the case of GPT-3, which is a 175-billion parameter model, the VRAM consumption during training drops significantly from 1.2TB to 350GB. When r = 4 and only the query and value projection matrices are adapted, the checkpoint size sees a remarkable reduction of approximately 10,000 times, plummeting from 350GB to a mere 35MB!

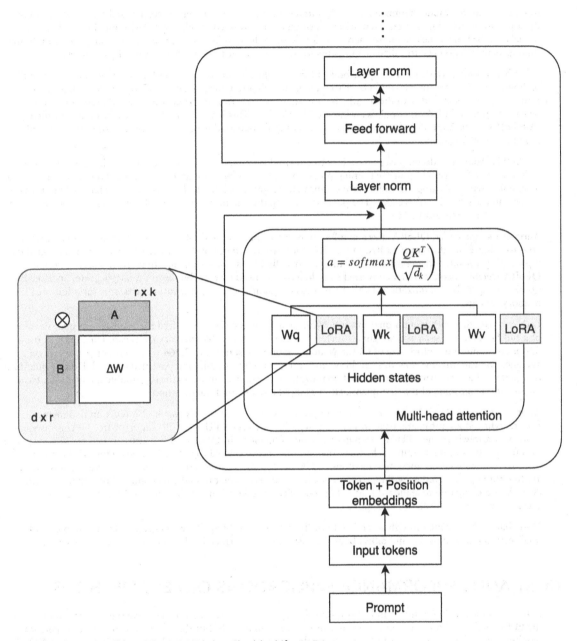

FIGURE 2.11: Modifying the original decoder block for LoRA

This substantial size reduction enables training with significantly fewer GPUs and eliminates I/O bottlenecks, even for very large LLMs. Another noteworthy benefit is the cost-effective task-switching capability when deployed. Much like the other methods discussed so far, this is achieved by merely swapping the LoRA weights, as opposed to replacing all the model parameters. This facilitates the creation of numerous customized models that can be dynamically switched in and out on machines storing the pre-trained weights in VRAM. Finally, smaller LoRA models can be trained faster, and so there is a significant reduction in cost per training job compared to full fine-tuning, as there's no need to calculate gradients for the vast majority of the frozen model parameters.

What if you were given a total compute budget (which translates to a parameter budget, as we have seen in the scaling laws)? This means we would have to intelligently choose which weights are important enough to have LoRA weights associated with them and which weights to leave frozen. Trying every possible combination of weights that have LoRA and don't is an intractable problem. This is where methods such as adaptive LoRA (AdaLoRA) help. AdaLoRA dynamically allocates compute budget during training by adjusting the ranks of individual LoRA matrices.

To do this, AdaLoRA decomposes the weight to a learnable version of SVD (since actually doing SVD for every weight update for every step in the training process would again be computationally intractable). The eigen values in singular matrix V can point to how important that weight matrix is, and this is used to retain only important weights in the set of LoRA weights. The paper describing this method can be found at `https://openreview .net/pdf?id=lq62uWRJjiY`.

Another method called QLoRA uses a combination of two methods—double quantization and paged optimizers—to achieve speedups over LoRA. In QLoRA, there are two types of data used: a low-precision storage data type, typically 4-bit, and a computation data type, usually BFloat16. This means that when working with a QLoRA weight tensor, it is first converted to BFloat16, followed by a 16-bit matrix multiplication. Specifically, QLoRA uses double quantization (DQ), the process of quantizing the quantization constants for additional memory savings.

Let's compare this with regular quantization. While a small block size is required for precise 4-bit quantization of a full float tensor (such as a weight tensor), it also has a considerable memory overhead. For example, using 32-bit constants and a block size of 64 for W, quantization constants add $32/64 = 0.5$ bits per parameter on average. You can imagine how this can blow up for a several hundred-billion parameter model. Double quantization helps reduce the memory footprint of quantization constants. More specifically, double quantization treats quantization constants of the first quantization as inputs to a second quantization.

Another aspect of QLoRA is the use of paged optimizers. Paged optimizers use the NVIDIA unified memory feature, which does automatic page-to-page transfers between the CPU and GPU for error-free GPU processing in the scenario where the GPU occasionally runs out of memory. In QLoRA, this feature is used to allocate paged memory for the optimizer states, which are then automatically evicted to CPU RAM when the GPU runs out of memory. In combination, these two methods can be used to increase the effective number of parameters that you are fine-tuning, while reducing the precision of each parameter. The original paper showed that there was no degradation compared to standard LoRA. For more details, take a look at the paper at `https://browse .arxiv.org/pdf/2305.14314.pdf`.

Now that we have gone through several state-of-the-art PEFT techniques, we will conclude this chapter with a final section that zooms out and talks about the cost and performance implications of using these methods.

COST AND PERFORMANCE IMPLICATIONS OF PEFT METHODS

Full pre-training or fine-tuning can be prohibitively expensive, and few companies have the budget. Not only are the PEFT methods a resource- and cost-efficient way to train models, but these models can in fact outperform baseline performance. Let's revisit the hypothetical scenario where you would like to pretrain your own 40-billion parameter LLM. Similar examples exist in the wild, such as the popular open-source LLM Falcon 40B.

According to the notes from the creators of Falcon 40B (`https://huggingface.co/tiiuae/falcon-40b`), the model was trained using 384 A100 GPUs (available on a 48-node cluster of P4d instances) on AWS, and training took approximately two months. Based on on-demand prices of a P4d instance per hour ($37.688), the total cost of training the Falcon 40B is approximately 60 days × 24 hours × 48 instances × $37.688 per hour, which is about $2.6 million.

The team also trained on a trillion tokens! Based on our initial section on "optimal" use of training resources and scaling laws, the cost of training with an ideal compute budget and ideal number of tokens (far less than a trillion), would be less than $1 million, and with fewer instances (32). Why are these numbers so different? The significant difference in training costs between the hypothetical ideal scenario and the real-world scenario for models such as Falcon 40B arises from several factors.

Resource availability and scale: In the ideal scenario, we consider an optimal compute budget, which means having access to the perfect amount of computational power and resources for training with various assumptions on linear scaling, zero overhead on training, perfect distributed training, etc. This is almost never true in practice.

Less efficient distributed training: The Falcon 40B was trained across 384 GPUs using the DeepSpeed family of optimizations to squeeze out as much performance as possible from these clusters. With each cloud node providing only eight A100 GPUs, a cluster containing hundreds of nodes can be created with the help of high-speed cross-node interconnects (such as Infiniband), providing a throughput of around 400GBps. Although Deep-Speed's ZeRO optimizations have been applied to various large models, they can still incur high data transfer overhead when training on many GPUs with small per-GPU batch sizes or on low-end clusters with limited cross-node network bandwidth. In such scenarios, ZeRO's efficiency can be constrained by communication challenges despite its transformative capabilities in optimizing large deep learning models. Teams such as DeepSpeed continue to make progress getting the real-world performance closer to the ideal performance (see www.microsoft.com/en-us/research/blog/deepspeed-zero-a-leap-in-speed-for-llm-and-chat-model-training-with-4x-less-communication).

Data volume: Training on a trillion tokens, as Falcon 40B did, requires significantly more data and computational resources than a smaller-scale training. The data acquisition, preprocessing, and storage costs can be substantial. While the scaling laws predict IsoLoss curves that can theoretically get you the same performance with smaller models and smaller amounts of training data, the capacity of the model as well as the actual amount of information contained in the data can vary. Most of the data used during the training of these models is far from clean or curated, high-quality data. We also see in practice that teams that spend time curating high-quality datasets can see significant performance gains, but curating these datasets is a costly endeavor with (costly) humans in the loop.

Additional costs: In practice, setting up, managing, and maintaining a large-scale training cluster even with fully managed services such as Amazon SageMaker involves substantial overhead. This includes configuring the cluster, handling hardware failures, debugging issues, and ensuring continuous operation. These tasks require skilled engineers and infrastructure, which adds to the overall cost.

In our discussion about PEFT methods so far, we have considered only one possible datatype (or dtype) of the parameters, float 32. This corresponds to the type of each number in the 40 billion numbers that represent the weights of this model. There are more efficient dtypes and associated techniques such as AMP (or automatic mixed precision) that one can use to further reduce the computational burden of training. We briefly saw this used in the QLoRA method earlier. Later chapters in this book will go into details of quantization, which is a method for reducing the size of a model, wherein it transforms the model weights from high-precision floating-point format into low-precision floating-point (FP) or integer (INT) formats, such as 16-bit or 8-bit representations. For now, let's continue our discussion with the understanding that smaller dtypes will give us lower overall memory utilization given the same number of full or LoRA parameters.

When making a choice about which GPU to use, it is good to research the ideal throughput provided by the GPUs in question, as well as the cost, availability, and ability to scale out to a cluster of GPUs, since it is conceivable that you may need multiple GPUs to train your models based on the desired setting. Table 2.1 shows a comparison of four different GPU choices: Nvidia A10, V100 (16 GB), V100 (32 GB), and A100. We can take the Falcon 40B model and use LoRA to train v2% of the total 40 billion parameters in the LoRA setting. In addition, we can see if quantization can further help reduce the computational requirements for fine-tuning.

TABLE 2.1: Comparing different GPUs for full and LoRA-based training on full and quantized versions of the Falcon 40B model

FALCON 40B	FLOAT32	FLOAT16	INT8	INT4
Total Size (GB)	153.87	76.93	38.47	19.23
Inference (GB)	184.64	92.32	46.16	23.08
Training using Adam (GB)	615.47	307.73	153.87	76.93
LoRA Fine-Tuning (GB)	192.57	100.25	54.09	31.01
Num A10 for full training	26	13	7	4
Num A10 for LoRA training	9	5	3	2
Num V100 (16GB) for full training	39	20	10	5
Num V100 (16GB) for LoRA training	13	7	4	2
Num V100 (32 GB) for full training	20	10	5	3
Num V100 (32 GB) for LoRA training	7	3	2	1
Num A100 for full training	16	8	4	2
Num A100 for LoRA training	5	3	2	1

First, notice how large the memory requirements are for full training or fine-tuning without LoRA for a 40-billion parameter model. Even though the full float model parameters are around 150GB in size, the total demand for the model as well as the optimizer states (there can be multiple states per parameter of the model) is around 615GB! Through model sharding, you can still practically do full fine-tuning, but the question is if you really have to. The int8 version of the model, for example, with LoRA will need only about 50GB of GPU memory for training. It is not surprising that memory requirements reduce as we go from higher to lower fidelity of weights such as Float 32, Float 16, Int 8, and Int 4.

As we can see from Table 2.1, the A100 GPU and the 32GB V100 version of the GPU are comparable in terms of memory requirements but vary greatly in terms of available TFLops. For example, with the new Tensor Float (TF) precision on A100s, the throughput can be 20 times more than V100s. So, it makes sense cost-wise to train on a larger instance, even though the per hour cost is lower on instances providing V100s.

While we are still in the early days of research around PEFT methods, you can expect more work in the areas around new methods, ways to combine existing methods, faster and purpose-built chips for training LLMs, and smaller models that are more capable than their larger counterparts.

SUMMARY

This chapter discussed how resource intensive and costly the training of LLMs can be. Parameter-efficient fine-tuning was introduced as a concept with deep dives into multiple state-of-the-art methods such as P-tuning and LoRA. Finally, we discussed some cost implications of deciding to train or fine-tune your own LLMs.

3

Inference Techniques for Cost Optimization

WHAT'S IN THIS CHAPTER?

➤ Introduction to Inference Techniques

➤ Prompt Engineering

➤ Caching with Vector Stores

➤ Chains for Long Documents

➤ Summarization

➤ Batch Prompting for Efficient Inference

➤ Model Optimization Methods

➤ Parameter-Efficient Fine-Tuning Methods

➤ Cost and Performance Implications

INTRODUCTION TO INFERENCE TECHNIQUES

Machine learning workflows involve various phases, from model training to deployment, each bearing its own set of costs. Among these phases, the inference phase is particularly significant as it's the point where the trained models are put to work to generate predictions on new data. The cost of inference is often overlooked during the model development phase; however, it becomes a focal point when models are deployed at scale in real-world applications. This cost is not merely financial but extends to computational resources and time, impacting the overall efficiency and effectiveness of machine learning solutions. Inference costs can make or break entire machine learning projects.

In the broader machine learning landscape, cost optimization during the inference phase is vital as it directly impacts the return on investment of machine learning applications. In a scenario where the use of machine learning as a service (MLaaS) is increasing, companies that provide general-purpose models such as object detectors and image classifiers need to optimize the costs to remain competitive and efficient. With the advent of cloud computing, inference workloads have shifted to the cloud, and as these workloads grow, so does the cost associated with them. Various strategies, such as cluster-level, instance- and runtime-level, and model-level optimizations, are employed to manage and reduce these costs.

Transitioning to our current topic of interest, large language models (LLMs), the narrative of cost optimization during inference gains an added layer of complexity. These models, because of their size and the extensive computational resources they require, present a unique set of challenges. The financial and computational costs can escalate quickly when deploying LLMs at a large scale, making cost optimization a crucial consideration.

This chapter delves into a multitude of techniques tailored toward optimizing the cost of inference, with a particular focus on LLMs. We start with an exploration of prompt engineering, a technique that can be used to tailor inference responses for cost while maintaining the same response accuracy. A better understanding of prompting impacts both performance in certain tasks and cost. As we move through the chapter, various facets of cost optimization, including caching, model optimization methods, and hyperparameter tuning, among others, are discussed in detail. The objective is to equip you with a comprehensive understanding and practical insights into managing and optimizing inference costs, thereby harnessing the true potential of LLMs in production in a cost-effective manner.

PROMPT ENGINEERING

Prompt engineering is a refined practice pivotal when interacting with LLMs. At its core, it's about crafting input queries or prompts in a way that guides the model to produce desired, accurate, and concise outputs. For instance, if the task is to translate a piece of text from English to French, a well-structured prompt would be: "Translate the following English text to French, ensuring accuracy and a formal tone: {text}."

Here, the added instruction of ensuring accuracy and maintaining a formal tone provides the model with additional guidance, helping it generate a more appropriate response. Similarly, for information extraction, instead of a vague prompt such as "Tell me about Barack Obama," a more precise prompt such as "Provide a brief summary of Barack Obama's political career, focusing on his presidency" can help in eliciting a more focused and relevant response from the model.

Another illustration could be extracting coding solutions; a detailed prompt such as "Provide a Python code snippet to open a file, read its contents, and print them to the console" will yield a more precise code snippet compared to a vague prompt such as "Code to read a file in Python."

Digging a bit deeper into the practice of prompt engineering, it's about understanding the behavior and tendencies of the model and tailoring the prompts to navigate these tendencies. For example, LLMs such as GPT-3 are known to be verbose and sometimes provide more information than necessary. Hence, crafting prompts that guide the model toward conciseness can be beneficial. It's also about the choice of words, the structure of the query, and even the formatting, all of which can influence the model's response. For example, asking "What are the benefits of exercising regularly?" might yield a different response compared to "List five benefits of regular exercise."

Impact of Prompt Engineering on Cost

The connection between prompt engineering, performance, and cost is quite straightforward yet significant. Each word or token in the prompt and the model's response incurs a cost. For instance, with OpenAI's GPT-3.5 Turbo, the pricing is structured as $0.0015 per 1,000 tokens for input and $0.002 per 1,000 tokens for output in a 4K context, and $0.003 per 1,000 tokens for input and $0.004 per 1,000 tokens for output in a 16K context. A verbose or off-topic response due to a poorly designed prompt could escalate costs quickly. Conversely, a well-crafted prompt that elicits a concise and accurate response can help manage and reduce these costs significantly.

Estimating the cost of interactions with LLMs beforehand can be done using tools such as `tiktoken`, a Python library from OpenAI. `tiktoken` helps count the number of tokens in a text string without making an API call. The process involves a few steps.

1. Install `tiktoken` using pip.

```
pip install --upgrade tiktoken
```

2. Import `tiktoken` in your Python script.

```
import tiktoken
```

3. Load the encoding used by the model you are interested in.

```
encoding = tiktoken.get_encoding("cl100k_base")  # For GPT-3.5 Turbo
```

4. Use the encode method to convert a text string into a list of token integers, and count the tokens by counting the length of the list returned by encode.

```
def num_tokens_from_string(string: str, encoding_name: str) -> int:
    encoding = tiktoken.get_encoding(encoding_name)
    num_tokens = len(encoding.encode(string))
    return num_tokens

num_tokens = num_tokens_from_string("your text here", "cl100k_base")
```

For example, let's take the paragraph preceding this code and calculate the number of tokens using this function:

```
num_tokens = num_tokens_from_string("Estimating the cost of interactions with LLMs
beforehand can be done using tools like `tiktoken`, a Python library from OpenAI.
`Tiktoken` helps count the number of tokens in a text string without making an API
call. The process involves a few steps", "cl100k_base")
```

Here we get the number of tokens as 56. With the number of tokens and the pricing details from OpenAI, you can estimate the cost by multiplying the number of tokens with the cost per token. For example, if your input prompt consists of 56 tokens and the model's response consists of 80 tokens, the total cost would be (56+80) tokens * $0.002 per token = $0.272 (assuming a 4K context).

Some APIs may provide the number of input and output tokens to help you with calculating and baselining your cost with an example, representative prompt. Utilizing OpenAI's API offers a straightforward method to interact with LLMs such as GPT-3.5 Turbo, and it conveniently provides token usage information in the response, which can be used to estimate the cost of a request. This method serves as an alternative to using the `tiktoken` library, especially when a library for token counting is not available for the model you are working with.

To interact with the OpenAI API, you'll need to install the official bindings for Python or Node.js, depending on your preference. Here's how you can install OpenAI's Python SDK:

```
pip install -U openai
```

Once installed, you will need to authenticate your requests using an API key. This key should be kept secret and never exposed in client-side code. It's recommended to route production requests through your backend server where your API key can be securely loaded from an environment variable or a key management service. Here's how you can authenticate your requests:

```
import os
import openai

# Set your OpenAI API key and (optionally) organization ID
openai.api_key = os.getenv("OPENAI_API_KEY")
openai.organization = "YOUR_ORG_ID"  # Optional
```

To generate text with OpenAI, you can use the completions API.

```
completion = openai.ChatCompletion.create(model="gpt-3.5-turbo", messages=[{"role":
"user", "content": "Say this is a test!"}])
print(completion.choices[0].message.content)
```

This is similar to doing a `curl` request.

```
curl https://api.openai.com/v1/chat/completions \
  -H "Content-Type: application/json" \
  -H "Authorization: Bearer $OPENAI_API_KEY" \
  -d '{
    "model": "gpt-3.5-turbo",
    "messages": [{"role": "user", "content": "Say this is a test!"}],
    "temperature": 0.7
  }'
```

The response from this request will look like this:

```
{
    "id": "chatcmpl-abc123",
    "object": "chat.completion",
    "created": 1677858242,
    "model": "gpt-3.5-turbo-0613",
    "usage": {
        "prompt_tokens": 13,
        "completion_tokens": 7,
        "total_tokens": 20
    },
    "choices": [
        {
            "message": {
                "role": "assistant",
                "content": "\n\nThis is a test!"
            },
            "finish_reason": "stop",
            "index": 0
        }
    ]
}
```

As you can see, the number of prompt tokens and completion tokens is returned. This can be used to directly calculate the cost for this request. If your request is representative of the many requests you will be making as part of your application, this is a good per-prompt-completion cost.

Estimating Costs for Other Models

Estimating costs related to other models available as APIs also generally comes down to either estimating tokens from appropriate tokenizer libraries if available, directly calculating cost when the number of tokens is returned as part of the response from APIs, or using a thumb rule to estimate tokens based on the words in your prompt text. A helpful rule of thumb from OpenAI (applicable to many other LLMs) is that one token generally corresponds to ~4 characters of text for common English text. This translates to roughly ¾ of a word (so 100 tokens is approximately 75 words).

When LLMs are not available as APIs, such as OpenAI's models, self-hosting becomes a viable option, with platforms such as Amazon SageMaker being a suitable choice for this purpose. Unlike the token-based pricing model of OpenAI, where the cost is based on the number of tokens processed, SageMaker adopts a different pricing structure. While self-hosting on SageMaker or similar platforms provides more control over the environment, it introduces a different set of cost considerations compared to using API-based LLMs such as OpenAI's GPT-3.5. On SageMaker, you are billed for the amount of time your machine learning model is running on a particular instance type, among other factors. The cost of SageMaker real-time endpoints is based on the per instance-hour consumed for each instance while the endpoint is running. Additionally, costs are incurred for the amount of provisioned storage (EBS volume) and the data processed in and out of the endpoint instance.

While APIs such as the one from OpenAI charge per token, implying a direct cost for each word or token processed, self-hosted models on SageMaker have pricing that is based on the duration and resources consumed during the inference process. Therefore, in a self-hosted scenario, optimizing the prompts to elicit precise and succinct responses can contribute to faster processing times, lower computational resource usage, and, consequently, a reduction in the overall cost of the inference operation. This alignment of prompt engineering with cost optimization elucidates the broad spectrum of considerations that come into play when maneuvering through the cost landscape of LLM inference, be it in an API-based or self-hosted environment.

As we delve into the various facets of prompt engineering in the subsequent subtopics, the aim is to equip you with the knowledge and tools to craft effective prompts that not only elicit accurate responses but also manage and optimize the cost of interactions with LLMs. From understanding the construction of clear and direct prompts, providing the right amount of context, and indicating the desired format to iterating and refining our prompts, each step is geared toward achieving cost-effective interactions with LLMs.

Clear and Direct Prompts

The technique of crafting precise prompts to guide LLMs toward generating desired outputs is termed *prompt engineering*. This practice emerged notably with the advent of GPT-3 in 2020, where initially prompts included task descriptions, user inputs, and examples to guide the model. These examples were crucial because of the LLMs' weak alignment ability, which refers to their capacity to accurately follow a given instruction. However, as LLMs evolved and enhanced their alignment ability, the requirement of examples in prompts diminished. Clear instructions, articulated in natural language, became sufficient to guide the model to produce the desired output.

Clear and direct prompts are pivotal in harnessing the optimal performance from LLMs. They help in articulating the task or question in a manner that is easily comprehensible by the model, thus increasing the likelihood of receiving accurate and relevant responses. Two fundamental principles underline good prompts: clarity and specificity. Clarity entails using simple, unambiguous language, avoiding jargon and overly complex vocabulary. Specificity, on the other hand, involves providing a detailed context or breaking down complex questions into smaller, manageable queries to guide the model accurately.

Adding Qualifying Words for Brief Responses

In most applications, when dealing with a capable LLM, writing clear instructions that describe the intended form and length of response lead to better outputs. For example, if you wanted to know about diabetes and prompted an LLM such as Claude with "tell me about diabetes," you may get a response similar to the following:

```
Here's a brief overview of diabetes:
Diabetes is a chronic disease that affects how the body processes blood sugar
(glucose). There are three main types of diabetes:

Type 1 Diabetes - The body's immune system attacks and destroys the insulin-
producing cells in the pancreas. It usually develops in childhood or young adult
hood and requires insulin injections to manage blood sugar levels.

Type 2 Diabetes - The body becomes resistant to the effects of insulin or doesn't
make enough insulin. It accounts for 90-95% of diabetes cases and often develops
later in adulthood. Risk factors include being overweight, inactive, family
history, and ethnicity. It can often be managed through lifestyle changes, oral
medications, and sometimes insulin.
```

```
Gestational Diabetes - Develops in some women during pregnancy when the body cannot
properly process the additional insulin required. It usually resolves after deliv-
ery but increases risk of developing type 2 diabetes later.

Some common symptoms of diabetes include increased thirst, frequent urination,
hunger, fatigue, blurred vision, and slow healing of cuts/bruises. If left uncon-
trolled, diabetes can lead to complications like nerve damage, kidney disease,
vision loss, stroke, and heart disease.

Diagnosis involves blood tests to check blood sugar levels. Early diagnosis and
treatment is important to prevent or delay complications. Treatment aims to keep
blood sugar levels within a healthy target range.

This is done through medications, insulin therapy, lifestyle modifications like
diet, exercise, and home blood sugar monitoring.

Let me know if you need any clarification or have additional questions!
```

Prompting with "Give me a brief overview of diabetes in 100 words or less" gives this:

```
Diabetes is a chronic condition where the body can't properly regulate blood sugar
levels. There are three main types - Type 1, Type 2, and Gestational. It's caused
by inadequate insulin production or insulin resistance. Common symptoms include
increased thirst and urination, hunger, fatigue, and blurred vision. If left
uncontrolled, diabetes can lead to serious complications like nerve damage, kidney
disease, blindness, stroke, and heart disease. Management focuses on keeping blood
sugar in a healthy range through medications, insulin, lifestyle changes, and blood
sugar monitoring.
```

While the number of output tokens has been reduced, it is unlikely you got what you needed from this interaction. With an LLM that is trained for chat applications, one can get better answers by breaking down the question manually. Instead of asking a broad or complex question such as "Tell me everything about diabetes," which might lead to an overwhelmingly verbose response or possibly an unclear or incomplete answer, breaking the questions down manually could be more effective and cost-efficient. In the broader context of chat-based LLMs, a similar approach could be taken to ensure that the model understands the task clearly from the get-go. By breaking down complex queries into simpler, direct prompts or using a chain of thought reasoning, users can guide the model through a logical pathway to arrive at the desired answer. This approach not only helps in getting accurate responses but also in managing the cost associated with the interaction, especially when the pricing model is based on the number of tokens processed.

Breaking Down the Request

Here's how the user might break down the request into a series of simpler, interconnected questions on the same diabetes topic seen earlier:

```
User: Briefly describe what diabetes is
LLM: Diabetes is a chronic condition characterized by high blood sugar levels due
to the body's inability to produce or effectively use insulin.

User: What are the types of diabetes?
LLM: There are primarily three types of diabetes: Type 1, Type 2, and Gestational
Diabetes. Type 1 is an autoimmune condition, Type 2 is more closely related to
lifestyle factors and genetics, while Gestational Diabetes occurs during pregnancy.
```

```
User: What are the common symptoms of Type 2 diabetes?
LLM: Common symptoms of Type 2 diabetes include increased thirst, frequent
urination, hunger, fatigue, and blurred vision.

User: How is Type 2 diabetes diagnosed?
LLM: Type 2 diabetes is diagnosed through various tests such as the A1C test,
fasting plasma glucose test, and the oral glucose tolerance test.

User: What are the treatment options for Type 2 diabetes?
LLM: Treatment for Type 2 diabetes includes lifestyle modifications, medication,
and sometimes insulin therapy. Monitoring blood sugar levels is crucial for manag
ing this condition.
```

By breaking down the original complex query into a series of simpler questions, the user is able to obtain precise and manageable responses from the LLM. Each question builds upon the previous answer, guiding the LLM through a logical sequence of information retrieval. This approach helps not only in getting accurate and detailed responses but also in controlling the length (and thus cost) of each interaction, as each prompt and response is focused and to the point.

Clear prompts help in guiding the model to provide the desired output efficiently without going through iterative or verbose dialogues. This is particularly important when dealing with models in a chat-based setting where the goal is to achieve a specific outcome or answer. A well-phrased prompt can reduce the number of tokens used in the interaction, which directly impacts the cost, especially in a pay-per-token model. Claude by Anthropic presents a vivid example of how precise prompt design can significantly influence the responses from the model. The guidelines provided in Claude's documentation emphasize the importance of clarity, simplicity, and a well-structured format when constructing prompts. For instance, a simple task may require only a few straightforward sentences to get the desired response. However, for more complex tasks or when dealing with a variety of inputs, a well-thought-out prompt is imperative to ensure consistent and accurate performance from the model.

Example of Using Claude for PII Removal

In a practical example provided in Claude's documentation, a task requiring the removal of personally identifiable information (PII) from a text was used to demonstrate the impact of prompt construction. A poorly constructed prompt resulted in inadequate processing of the text, while a more detailed and clearer prompt led to a more satisfactory output. The well-constructed prompt provided Claude with ample context, defined the terms clearly (what constitutes PII), and specified how Claude should accomplish the task. This well-phrased prompt not only guided Claude to perform the task accurately but also in a manner that is repeatable across a variety of inputs. Read more about this example at https://docs.anthropic.com/claude/docs/constructing-a-prompt.

Furthermore, the structure of the prompt, particularly in a conversational setting, plays a significant role. Claude utilizes a specific formatting with \n\n**Human**: and \n\n**Assistant** to differentiate between the user's instructions and the model's response. This structure helps in setting a clear dialogue flow, making it easier for the model to understand the task at hand and respond appropriately.

Additionally, understanding the model's behavior and adjusting the prompt accordingly can also aid in cost optimization. For instance, if a model tends to provide verbose or off-topic responses to certain types of prompts, refining the prompt to be more direct and to the point can help reduce the verbosity and, consequently, the associated cost.

If the model's behavior is to hallucinate, it will provide answers for any question you pose. For example, when asking Claude "How heavy is Jupiter?" we get this response:

```
Jupiter is the largest planet in our solar system and has a tremendous mass.
Specifically:

- Jupiter's mass is about 318 times greater than Earth's.
```

```
- Jupiter's equatorial radius is 71,492 km, over 11 times Earth's radius.

- Jupiter's volume is large enough to fit 1,321 Earths inside it.

- Jupiter's mass is 2.5 times the mass of all the other planets in the solar
system combined.

- Jupiter weighs in at 1.898 x 10^27 kg. That's equivalent to 318 Earths.

- Jupiter is composed primarily of gases like hydrogen and helium. Its dense core
likely contains heavier materials like iron and rock.

- The force of gravity on Jupiter's visible "surface" (its cloud tops) is 2.5 times
Earth's gravity.

So in summary, Jupiter is extremely massive and heavy compared to Earth and the
other planets. Its huge size and weight contribute to its role as the dominant
planet in our solar system. Jupiter's mass alone accounts for over 70% of the total
mass of all the planets.
```

However, we have no reason to believe that these "fact-based" answers are correct. Many LLM API providers will provide a disclaimer that these model answers need to be verified. Providing a better prompt, such as "Answer the following question only if you know the answer or can make a well-informed guess; otherwise tell me you don't know it. How heavy is Jupiter?" gives us this:

```
Jupiter is the largest planet in our solar system, but its precise mass in kilo-
grams or other units is not something I can calculate or definitively state without
speculating.
```

Much better! In fact, this is a best practice to be followed even with the popular retrieval augmented generation (r RAG) approach when dealing with QnA over documents. We will cover RAG approaches in more detail in later chapters. For now, let's return to how prompt engineering can give you better performance at lower costs.

Consider this application of finding PII information from a conversation:

```
Identify PII information from the following transcript:

Agent: Hi, thank you for calling us today. Whom do I have the pleasure of speaking
with today?
Caller: Hello, my name is John Stiles.

Agent: Hi John, how may I help you?
Caller: I haven't received my W2 statement yet and wanted to check on its status.
Agent: Sure, I can help you with that. Can you please confirm the last four digits
of your Social Security number?
Caller: Yes, it's 1111.

Agent: Ok. I'm pulling up the status now. I see that it was sent out yesterday, and
the estimated arrival is early next week. Would you like me to turn on automated
alerts so you can be notified of any delays? Caller: Yes, please.

Agent: The number we have on file for you is 555-456-7890. Is that still correct?
Caller: Yes, it is. Agent: Great. I have turned on automated notifications. Is
there anything else I can assist you with John?

Caller: No, that's all. Thank you.
Agent: Thank you, John. Have a great day.
```

In response from the LLM, we get the following:

```
Based on the transcript, the following information can be considered PII
(Personally Identifiable Information):

- Full name of caller: John Stiles
- Last 4 digits of Social Security number: 1111
- Phone number: 555-456-7890

Other details like the request about the W2 status and the conversation about
setting up automated alerts do not contain sensitive or identifiable personal
information. Providing just the first name (John) alone would not be con-
sidered PII.

The agent should be careful about asking for and confirming personal details like
full name, Social Security number, phone number, etc. over the phone. This informa
tion should be adequately protected and only made accessible to authorized individ
uals due to privacy considerations.
```

Being more specific with the instruction and including a desired output format works better. For example, when prompted with "Identify PII information from the following transcript and output in JSON format. For example {"name_of_pii_field_1_key": "value," ...}," we get the following:

```
{
  "full_name": "John Stiles",
  "last_4_ssn": "1111",
  "phone_number": "555-456-7890"
}
```

Not only is this output shorter (and therefore more cost efficient), but it is also accurate and directly usable in a downstream application that can ingest this JSON output. This is important to note: we do not intend to make answers shorter at the cost of accuracy. To illustrate this, let's look at an example. Prompting LLMs with "One word answer if the statement is True? The odd numbers in this group add up to an even number: 15, 32, 5, 13, 82, 7, 1" on GPT4 gives the following:

```
"Yes"
```

This in fact is a false statement since the odd numbers add up to 41, which is an odd number, so the statement is false. Let's change the question a bit to "One word answer if the statement is False? The odd numbers in this group add up to an even number: 15, 32, 5, 13, 82, 7, 1."

```
"False"
```

How do we interpret this? The answer is false, or if the answer to the preceding question "is the statement False" is false, which means the answer is true! This is short but confusing and unusable.

Let's try improving the prompt to "The odd numbers in this group add up to an even number: 15, 32, 5, 13, 82, 7, 1. Only answer with a choice below, do not say anything else: A: True B: False."

```
"False"
```

Great! This means that we can expect a short answer, which is also accurate. But not so fast! Are we sure this prompt is robust? Let's switch the order of choices to "The odd numbers in this group add up to an even number: 15, 32, 5, 13, 82, 7, 1. Only answer with a choice below, do not say anything else: A: False B: True."

```
"True"
```

This shows that, for some reason, even a really capable model such as GPT4 (arguably the most capable model as of writing this book) picks the last option whether it is correct or wrong. How do we then make this prompt lead to accurate but short answers? One trick to use is encouraging "chain of thought reasoning" by adding statements such as "Let's think step by step" to the prompt—"The odd numbers in this group add up to an even number: 15, 32, 5, 13, 82, 7, 1. Let's think step by step." GPT 4 responds with this:

```
Okay, let's break this down step by step.

First, we need to identify the odd numbers in the given group:

Numbers given: 15, 32, 5, 13, 82, 7, 1

From the above numbers, the odd ones are: 15, 5, 13, 7, 1

Next, let's add these odd numbers together to check if their sum is even:

15 + 5 + 13 + 7 + 1 = 41

The sum of the odd numbers is 41, which is an odd number.

Thus, the statement "The odd numbers in this group add up to an even number" is
incorrect for the given group of numbers.
```

This is accurate! But the response is also wordy. With more complicated problems that your business might come up with, the answer may be even more detailed. Let's try "The odd numbers in this group add up to an even number: 15, 32, 5, 13, 82, 7, 1. Explain your thinking and answer in one short sentence." and try the same query multiple times. For each of the five trials with the same prompt, we get this:

```
The sum of odd numbers 15, 5, 13, 7, and 1 is 41, which is odd; therefore, the
statement is false.
The sum of the odd numbers 15, 5, 13, 7, and 1 is 41, which is an odd number, so
the statement is incorrect.
The sum of the odd numbers 15, 5, 13, 7, and 1 is 41, which is an odd number.
The sum of the odd numbers is 15 + 5 + 13 + 7 + 1 = 41, which is odd, so the
statement is incorrect.
The sum of 15, 5, 13, 7, and 1 is 41, an odd number; hence, the statement is false.
```

We see from several runs of the same input prompt that our answer is short and cost effective, as well as accurate. For a business application, consider testing various prompts with typical examples.

Another way to increase the accuracy of actual answers while maintaining an output "format" is to provide few-shot examples. Consider this version of the prompt:

```
Take a look at the examples below and answer the ? accurately and in the same
format. Do not say anything else.

The odd numbers in this group add up to an even number: 4, 8, 9, 15, 12, 2, 1.
A: The answer is False.

The odd numbers in this group add up to an even number: 16,  11, 14, 4, 8, 13, 24.
A: The answer is True.

The odd numbers in this group add up to an even number: 15, 32, 5, 13, 82, 7, 1.
A: ?
```

This prompt returns (for GPT4) "A: The answer is False." Providing examples has helped the model be both accurate and succinct while following a suggested answer format. This is called *in-context learning*.

> **NOTE** *In-context learning (ICL) is a phenomenon whereby LLMs can learn to perform a task after being presented with only a few examples, without undergoing specific training for that task. This ability arises because large models encompass smaller, simpler linear models within them, which can be trained to tackle a new task using the information already encapsulated in the larger model. Essentially, ICL is an emergent behavior in LLMs where the model performs a task merely by conditioning on input-output examples, without the need for optimizing any parameters.*
>
> *The core principle behind in-context learning is to "learn from analogy." It necessitates a few examples to form a demonstration context, often laid out in natural language templates. These examples guide the model in making decisions during the task at hand. This is similar to the last odd-number example we explored. The effectiveness of in-context learning heavily relies on the quality of the chosen examples for forming this context. This form of learning is particularly beneficial for knowledge-intensive natural language processing (NLP) tasks and has been identified as one of the significant contributors to the success of LLMs. Furthermore, the recursive improvement of in-context learning abilities within large language models has been explored, indicating a meta-learning aspect within in-context learning.*
>
> *In-context learning is viewed as a promising avenue, especially for LLMs, because of their training on vast datasets that likely encompass similar examples or scenarios they might encounter during inference. This, in turn, enables them to perform various tasks based on just a few input-output examples provided at the time of inference. Besides, efforts are being made to overcome the context window limitation often faced by large language models, such as the introduction of parallel context windows (PCWs) to enhance the in-context learning capabilities.*

Conclusion

In summary, clear and direct prompts form the cornerstone of effective interaction with LLMs, playing a pivotal role not only in achieving the desired output but also in managing and optimizing the inference cost. Through well-constructed prompts, users can guide the model in a structured manner, making the interaction more efficient and cost-effective.

Providing Context

Providing context in prompts is akin to laying down a foundation upon which LLMs can build accurate and coherent responses. Context can be defined as the additional information provided in a prompt that helps guide the LLM toward understanding the user's requirement more precisely. It may encompass such things as background information, related concepts, or specific instructions that lead the model toward generating a desired response. The essence of providing context lies in eliminating ambiguities and presenting a clearer picture of the user's query to the model.

LLMs, while exceptionally proficient in handling vast amounts of information, can sometimes falter in generating relevant responses if the prompt lacks sufficient context. A well-contextualized prompt can significantly enhance the model's ability to provide accurate, relevant, and insightful responses, thereby improving the user experience. For instance, a user querying a medical LLM about a specific condition would receive a more insightful response by providing a brief background of the symptoms they are experiencing, as opposed to a vague query.

Furthermore, context plays a crucial role in scenarios where the conversation involves a sequence of interconnected questions or a follow-up to a previous query. In such cases, retaining the context from previous interactions is indispensable for ensuring that the responses remain coherent and relevant throughout the conversation.

Examples of Providing Context

In certain domains such as healthcare or legal, the queries may inherently be complex, and providing context can assist in ensuring that the model's responses are accurate and meaningful. The necessity of context provision is rooted not only in obtaining better answers but also in reducing the chances of misinterpretation, which could lead to incorrect or misleading information being provided. This aspect is particularly crucial in domains where accuracy and precision are paramount, such as medical, legal, or financial advising. Let's look at this example:

```
User: What is termination for convenience?
LLM: Termination for convenience refers to a clause that may be included in a
contract that allows one party to terminate the contract without having to provide
a cause or reason, usually under specified conditions.

User: Is it allowed in healthcare contracts?
LLM: Termination for convenience clauses can indeed be included in healthcare
contracts, but their enforceability and implications may be subject to the laws and
regulations governing healthcare contracts in a specific jurisdiction.

User: What are the implications in New York?
LLM: In New York, termination for convenience clauses in healthcare contracts may
allow a party to terminate the contract without cause, but there are certain legal
and regulatory considerations to be aware of, which may impact the enforceability
and implications of such clauses.
```

We see that the user interactively dives deeper into the conversation across three turns with the LLM. Now let's look at an equivalent example that provides the full context up front:

```
User: In New York healthcare contracts, what does termination for convenience mean
and what are its implications?
LLM: In New York, termination for convenience in healthcare contracts refers to a
clause that allows one party to terminate the contract without providing a cause or
reason, usually under specified conditions. The enforceability and implications of
such clauses are subject to New York's laws and regulations governing healthcare
contracts. For instance, there might be specific notice requirements or conditions
under which such termination is permissible, and parties might need to adhere to
these requirements to ensure the termination is carried out legally.
```

In the first example, the user had to engage in three separate turns to obtain the desired information about termination for convenience in New York healthcare contracts. This multiturn interaction requires three separate computational inferences, potentially leading to higher costs and time spent. On the other hand, in the second example, by providing the jurisdiction and domain context initially, the user obtains the desired information in a single interaction. This is more cost-effective and efficient, demonstrating the importance of providing context, especially in domains with complex or nuanced terminologies and regulations.

Note that the cost of inference is connected to the interactions we went through in the earlier example as well. In the first scenario, the user may need to engage in additional interactions to obtain the desired information, thus consuming more computational resources and time, increasing the cost. In contrast, in the second scenario, by providing context initially, the user obtains the desired information in a single interaction, which is more cost-effective and efficient. The more direct and contextualized the prompt, the more likely the user is to receive the desired information without needing additional clarifying questions, thus managing the cost of inference better.

RAG and Long Context Models

The practice of providing context has also seen a shift with the advent of models capable of maintaining a longer conversation history. Earlier models with limited context window sizes struggled to maintain context in extended interactions, but newer models with expanded context windows can better retain and utilize information from earlier parts of the conversation to provide more accurate and contextual responses. Claude from Anthropic can accept a context length of up to 100,000 tokens, which is approximately 75,000 words and longer than many books.

Retrieval augmented generation (RAG), on the other hand, refers to augmenting LLMs with a retriever to provide relevant context from a large collection of documents. These two concepts are connected. The more context an LLM can handle, the more source documents you can retrieve and append to the context of your question. This allows focusing the LLM's attention on the most relevant snippets rather than all available context. In RAG, a stand-alone retriever first retrieves the most relevant context passages from a large document collection based on the input query. These relevant passages are then provided as input context to the LLM to generate the output. Figure 3.1 shows the sequence diagram of how a typical RAG system works.

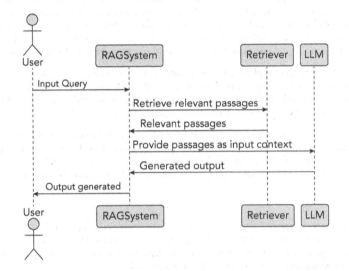

FIGURE 3.1: Sequence diagram for typical RAG systems

The earlier sequence diagram depicts the interaction between the user, the RAG system, the retriever, and the LLM. The user initiates the process by providing an input query to the RAG system. The RAG system then communicates with the retriever to retrieve relevant passages. The retrieved passages are provided as input context to the LLM, which generates the output. Finally, the RAG system delivers the generated output back to the user.

For example, for a question-answering task, the retriever would retrieve relevant passages from a corpus based on the question. The LLM would then attend only to these retrieved passages, rather than all documents, to generate the answer. The retriever allows rapidly focusing on pertinent context, while the LLM models interactions between this context to produce the output. RAG combines the efficiency and scalability of sparse retrieval with the reasoning and generalization capabilities of large LLMs. The retriever performs fast nearest neighbor search to identify relevant context, which is more efficient than the LLM having to attend to all context. This provides a way to scale up contextual modeling without having to expand the LLM's context window itself. At the same time, the LLM can powerfully model the retrieved context to generate accurate outputs. Recent work has shown RAG provides strong performance on many tasks while requiring fewer computational resources compared to simply expanding an LLM's context window. As long context window models are becoming more common, which model do you use when?

Recent Work Comparing RAG with Long Content Models

A recent paper from NVIDIA, "Retrieval Meets Long Context Large Language Models" by Xu et al., begins to answer this question by providing insights into the interplay between retrieval augmentation and extending the context window size of LLMs. The authors compare these two techniques for handling long context using two state-of-the-art LLMs—a proprietary 43 billion parameter GPT model and the publicly available 70 billion parameter LLaMA 2 model.

Recent advances have enabled expanding the self-attention context window of LLMs directly to lengths such as 16,000 or 32,000 tokens, and even to 100,000 tokens such as with Claude v2. The study finds that RAG with LLMs using even a 4K context window can achieve comparable performance to 16K context window LLMs on several long-context tasks. Surprisingly, combining retrieval with 16K or 32K context window LLMs can further enhance performance over just using a long context window.

The results indicate that RAG provides strong long context modeling capability efficiently, without requiring extensive fine-tuning to expand an LLM's context window. At the same time, retrieval continues to boost performance even for large context window LLMs. The choice between RAG and long context LLMs depends on factors such as task performance needs, inference latency constraints, and compute resources. For many practical applications, RAG provides a compelling solution by retrieving task-specific context efficiently while requiring fewer computational resources during inference compared to expanding an LLM's context window.

However, note that for certain complex tasks, long context LLMs may be better suited to model intricate contextual dependencies over very long sequences. Combining RAG and long context LLMs can offer complementary benefits—retrieval provides relevant context efficiently while the expanded context window better models long-range dependencies. This is because every RAG system depends on retrieval.

Practitioners can draw on these insights to make informed choices between RAG versus expanding an LLM's context window for their specific use-case needs. The findings highlight that both techniques provide viable solutions for long context modeling, with their own trade-offs. Testing different combinations on domain-specific data can further elucidate the ideal approach based on aspects such as task accuracy, latency needs, and available compute.

Conclusion

The exploration of context provision's evolution showcases its importance and the continuous effort in the field to leverage context for better interaction with LLMs. As models evolve, the methods and extent of context provision are also advancing, aiming at more intuitive and fruitful interactions between users and LLMs. The following section will illustrate some limitations of providing context to LLMs.

Context and Model Limitations

Despite diligent provision of context in prompts, there can still be limitations to an LLM's understanding or its response generation capacity. These limitations arise from several inherent and external factors that affect the model's performance.

First, the training data of the LLM plays a crucial role in its ability to understand and respond accurately to a prompt. If the model hasn't been trained on relevant or updated data concerning the topic in question, it may produce incorrect or outdated responses. For instance, in rapidly evolving fields such as law or medicine, where regulations and guidelines may change frequently, an LLM might not be up to speed with the latest developments if its training data doesn't encompass the most recent information.

Second, the intrinsic design of LLMs, including their size and architecture, can also contribute to their limitations. For example, even with an extensive context provided, the model might not fully grasp highly specialized or nuanced topics, especially if such topics require a level of expertise or understanding beyond what the model has learned during training. The model's capacity to retain and utilize the provided context effectively throughout a lengthy or complex interaction can also be a challenge.

Moreover, external factors such as the length of the prompt, the clarity of the language used, and the complexity of the question posed can further exacerbate these limitations. A verbose or convoluted prompt might confuse the model or lead to irrelevant or overly general responses. On the other hand, a too brief or ambiguous prompt may not provide enough information for the model to generate a meaningful response, even if the model has the capacity to understand the underlying topic.

Lastly, despite well-articulated context, LLMs may still exhibit biases or produce inappropriate responses based on the biases inherent in their training data. This necessitates careful review and possibly manual intervention to ensure the accuracy and appropriateness of the LLM's responses, particularly in sensitive or critical domains.

Therefore, while providing context significantly enhances the interaction with LLMs, being aware of these limitations and preparing for possible inaccuracies or misunderstandings is crucial. It's also beneficial to have strategies in place to verify the information provided by LLMs, especially in professional or critical use-case scenarios. This awareness and preparedness contribute to a more effective and reliable utilization of LLMs in various domains.

Indicating a Desired Format

Guiding LLMs to generate responses in a particular format is a crucial aspect of prompt engineering. This is where indicating the desired format in your prompts comes into play. By specifying the format, you not only streamline the interaction but also potentially save on computational resources, which is crucial for cost optimization.

For instance, if you are utilizing an LLM to extract specific data from a set of documents, indicating the desired format could mean the difference between receiving a neatly organized table or a verbose paragraph. Suppose you are working on a project that requires the extraction of financial data from company reports. A prompt such as "Extract the revenue, profit, and loss figures from Company X's 2023 Annual Report" is fairly straightforward but leaves the format open-ended. The LLM might return a verbose paragraph describing the figures, which then requires additional time and resources to parse. However, if you refine the prompt to "Extract and tabulate the revenue, profit, and loss figures from Company X's 2023 Annual Report," there's a higher likelihood of receiving the data in a tabular format, which is easier to work with and more efficient in terms of both time and cost.

Example of Formatted Extraction with Claude

Let's try this example with Claude V2. Claude allows users to attach long PDFs and ask questions based on the attached context. Figure 3.2 shows a snapshot of the PDF (Amazon's 10-K from 2022 is an 81-page file).

FIGURE 3.2: Snapshot of the first page of the 2022 Amazon 10-K filing

Trying the prompt "Extract the revenue, profit, and loss figures from Amazon's 2022 Annual Report" on Claude gives the following:

```
Here are the key revenue, profit, and loss figures from Amazon's 2022
Annual Report:

Revenue:
- Total net sales: $513.9 billion, increased 9% compared to prior year
- By segment:
    - North America net sales: $315.9 billion
    - International net sales: $118.0 billion
    - AWS net sales: $80.1 billion

Profit:
- Operating income: $12.2 billion, decreased 51% compared to prior year
- Net loss: $2.7 billion, compared to net income of $33.4 billion in prior year

Loss per share:
- Basic and diluted loss per share: $0.27, compared to earnings per share of $3.24
in prior year
```

Improving the prompt to "Please provide a markdown table with details of revenue, profit, and loss figures from Amazon's 2022 Annual Report" gives the response in the desired format, as shown in Figure 3.3.

Please provide a markdown table with details of revenue, profit, and loss figures from Amazons's 2022 Annual Report

Here is a markdown table containing detailed revenue, profit, and loss figures from Amazon's 2022 Annual Report:

Category	2021	2022
Net sales:		
- North America	$279,833 million	$315,880 million
- International	$127,787 million	$118,007 million
- AWS	$62,202 million	$80,096 million
- Consolidated	$469,822 million	$513,983 million
Operating income (loss):		
- North America	$7,271 million	$(2,847) million
- International	$(924) million	$(7,746) million
- AWS	$18,532 million	$22,841 million
- Consolidated	$24,879 million	$12,248 million
Total non-operating income (expense)	$13,272 million	$(18,184) million
Benefit (provision) for income taxes	$(4,791) million	$3,217 million
Equity-method investment activity, net of tax	$4 million	$(3) million
Net income (loss)	$33,364 million	$(2,722) million
Earnings (loss) per share:		
- Basic	$3.30	$(0.27)
- Diluted	$3.24	$(0.27)

Copy Retry

FIGURE 3.3: Claude response for the improved prompt

Let's look at another example. Consider a scenario where you are employing an LLM to retrieve specific information from a dataset of research papers. The goal is to extract the names of authors and the titles of papers published in 2021 from a particular journal. Without specifying the desired format, a vague prompt such as "List the authors and titles of papers from Journal X published in 2021" could lead the LLM to generate a verbose narrative, perhaps describing each paper and its author(s) in separate sentences or paragraphs. This verbosity not only deviates from the desired concise listing but also increases the number of tokens generated, thereby increasing the cost of the query based on a pay-per-token pricing model.

Now, let's refine the prompt to indicate a desired format: "Provide a JSON list of authors and titles of papers on Neural Network advancements published in 2021." This prompt sets a clear expectation for a JSON format, guiding the LLM to structure the information more concisely and directly. Here's a hypothetical comparison of the responses from the LLM for both prompts.

➤ **Vague prompt response:**

```
Paper 1: "Advancements in Convolutional Neural Networks" by Alice Johnson and
Bob Smith. This paper explores the latest developments in Convolutional Neural
Networks and their applications in image recognition... Paper 2: "Recurrent
Neural Network Optimization" by Charlie Brown and Dana Williams. A comprehensive
study on the optimization techniques used in Recurrent Neural Networks, shedding
light on... ...
```

➤ **Formatted prompt response:**

```
[ { "Authors": "Alice Johnson, Bob Smith", "Title": "Advancements in
Convolutional Neural Networks" }, { "Authors": "Charlie Brown, Dana Williams",
"Title": "Recurrent Neural Network Optimization" }, ... ]
```

In the first example, the LLM veers off into a verbose narrative, generating a lengthy response that also includes undesired information about the paper's content. This verbosity results in more tokens being generated, increasing the cost of the query. Moreover, the unstructured response necessitates further post-processing to extract and organize the required information, incurring additional time and possibly cost. On the other hand, the response to the formatted prompt is structured, concise, and directly provides the needed information in a JSON format. This structured response is not only more aligned with the user's goal but is also directly usable in downstream applications and more cost-effective as it generates fewer tokens, thus lowering the cost of the query. Furthermore, since the JSON format eliminates the need for further post-processing, it saves on additional development time and resources.

Moreover, specifying the format can be crucial when dealing with numerical data or calculations. For example, if you are using an LLM to perform a complex calculation, indicating whether you want the answer in decimal, fraction, or percentage can save additional back-and-forth interactions. A prompt such as "Calculate the percentage increase in sales from 2019 to 2020" is more likely to get you the desired output in one go compared to a vague prompt such as "Calculate the increase in sales from 2019 to 2020."

In scenarios where the desired output format is complex or unconventional, providing an example within the prompt can be highly beneficial. This is somewhat akin to few-shot learning, where you provide the model with examples of the desired output format alongside the prompt. For instance, if you need the LLM to generate code based on a natural language description, including an example of how the code should be structured could guide the LLM to produce more accurate and appropriately formatted code.

We saw through examples that indicating the desired format is beneficial in controlling the length of the responses, which directly impacts the cost, especially when the pricing model is based on the number of tokens processed. A more concise and to-the-point response generated because of a well-formatted prompt will be more cost-effective compared to a verbose and unstructured response that requires further interaction or post-processing. However, there are practical challenges and considerations that come into play.

Trade-Off Between Verbosity and Clarity

One of the paramount considerations is the trade-off between verbosity and clarity. While being verbose may sometimes aid in elucidating complex information, it could also lead to higher costs. Furthermore, the model's capacity to accurately interpret and adhere to the language direction is contingent on its training and the clarity of the instructions provided. There may be instances where despite clear language direction, the model may not fully grasp the desired tone or format, which underscores the importance of designing prompts that are unambiguous and well-articulated. In summary, language direction is a pivotal facet of prompt engineering, contributing substantially to optimizing the cost of inference. Through effective language direction, users can significantly enhance the quality of interaction with the model, making the interaction not only more meaningful and engaging but also cost-effective.

In summary, indicating the desired format in your prompts is a straightforward yet effective technique to ensure that the interaction with the LLM is efficient, accurate, and cost-effective. It minimizes the need for further clarification or post-processing, thereby optimizing the costs associated with the inference process. Each component of prompt engineering complements the other, collectively contributing to an optimized interaction with the model.

CACHING WITH VECTOR STORES

Caching is a well-established technique to expedite data access by storing frequently used or computed data temporarily in a high-speed storage layer. When dealing with LLMs, caching becomes a crucial tool to curtail redundant computations, thus saving both time and resources. This efficiency is particularly pronounced when a model encounters recurring queries or needs to access previously computed information.

What Is a Vector Store?

Vector stores come into play as a specialized form of caching that is suited for the needs of LLMs. They are data structures designed to handle and store vectors efficiently, allowing for rapid lookups and similarity searches. In the context of LLMs, vector stores can cache the embeddings of frequently accessed data, significantly reducing the lookup time for this information. The cached data in vector stores can be anything from text embeddings to the embeddings of more complex data structures. This caching mechanism is a step toward making interactions with LLMs more cost-effective and efficient.

How to Implement Caching Using Vector Stores

Implementing caching via vector stores in LLMs involves storing the vector representations of data that the model interacts with frequently. When a query is made, the system first checks the vector store to see if the requested information or a similar representation is already cached. If a match is found, the system retrieves the cached data, bypassing the need for a more computationally intensive retrieval or computation. This streamlined access to previously computed data not only accelerates the response time but also optimizes the cost by reducing the computational load on the LLM. Figure 3.4 shows the sequence diagram of this pattern.

In a scenario where multiple LLMs are in play, the system can be designed to have a shared vector store that caches data common to or used by all the LLMs. This way, the vector store acts as a centralized cache, serving multiple models and ensuring consistency and efficiency across the board. Figure 3.5 is a revised diagram to illustrate this setup.

Here, the user specifies the target LLM along with the query. The system first checks the vector store for cached data. If a match is found, it retrieves the cached data and responds to the user. If a match isn't found, it directs the query to the specified LLM. The designated LLM then generates the response and stores the query and response in the vector store for future reference, and the system sends the response to the user. This way, the setup maintains the efficiency of caching across multiple LLMs while accommodating the user's choice of LLM.

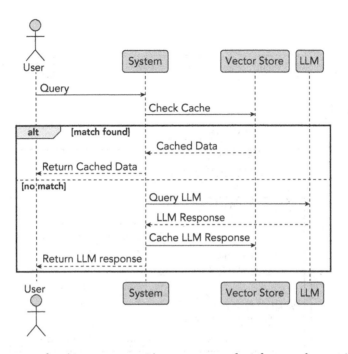

FIGURE 3.4: Basic pattern of caching requests with a vector store for inferences from an LLM

HOW DOES THE VECTOR STORE FIND A MATCH FOR THE USER QUERY HERE?

This is central to both the basic setup with one LLM and the more advanced setup with a central cache in front of multiple LLMs. Let's look at an example in a healthcare setting. Suppose a medical researcher is looking for information regarding a specific drug interaction between Drug A and Drug B. They input the query "What are the interactions between Drug A and Drug B?" into the system.

In this scenario, the system first directs the query to the vector store to check for a match. Each previously answered query has been converted into a vector using text encoding techniques and stored in the vector store. Now, the vector store computes the vector for the new query and compares it with the vectors of previously answered queries using cosine similarity to determine semantic closeness.

Suppose in the past, another user had asked, "Tell me about the interactions of Drug A with Drug B." This query has been processed by the LLM, and its vector representation is stored in the vector store along with the LLM-generated response. Because of the high semantic similarity between the new query and the stored query, as determined by a high cosine similarity score, the vector store identifies a match. If multiple users have asked similar questions, the response with the highest score is matched. Also, one can usually configure a threshold of when to receive cached responses (for example, retrieve cached responses only when the similarity score is greater than 90%).

The system finally retrieves the cached response associated with the matched vector, which details the interactions between Drug A and Drug B, and presents this information to the medical researcher without having to reprocess the query through the LLM. This not only provides a quick answer to the researcher but also saves computational resources and costs associated with processing the query afresh through the LLM.

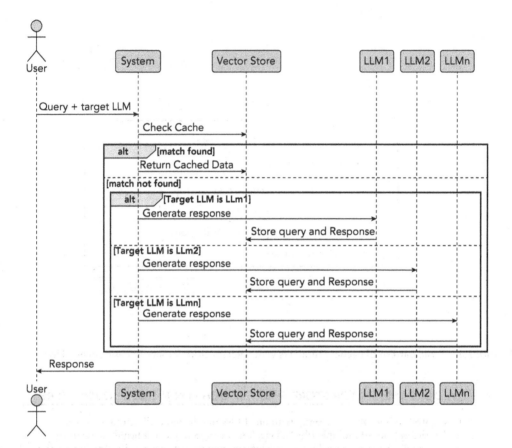

FIGURE 3.5: Caching requests when there are multiple LLMs behind the scene

The cost-effectiveness of caching with vector stores is a cornerstone for optimizing the inference cost in LLMs, whether you have a single LLM or many LLMs in production. By reducing the need for recalculating identical or similar queries, vector stores diminish the computational resources required, directly impacting the cost in a pay-per-use or pay-per-compute environment. For instance, in a scenario where an LLM is used to provide real-time recommendations, caching the vector representations of frequently asked queries in a vector store can significantly reduce the cost of providing these recommendations. Furthermore, manually curated FAQs can be high-quality responses that are returned when the match score is high, and this may overall be better than completely relying on the LLM to respond. Lastly, similar questions and answers can be used as few-shot examples for in-context learning with the actual user query.

Real-world implementations of caching with vector stores in LLMs are burgeoning as the benefits are more widely recognized. Companies and researchers are leveraging vector stores to optimize the cost of inference, making the deployment of LLMs more financially viable. The positive impact on both response times and cost efficiency has made caching with vector stores an appealing option for those looking to optimize their interaction with LLMs. However, implementing caching with vector stores is not without challenges. The accuracy of cached data, the eviction policies of the cache, and the overhead of maintaining the vector store are among the considerations that need to be addressed. Moreover, the trade-off between the freshness of data and the efficiency gained through caching is a consideration that requires careful deliberation.

Conclusion

In conclusion, caching with vector stores presents a promising avenue for optimizing the cost of inference in LLMs. By efficiently handling frequently accessed or computed data, vector stores provide a pathway to not only improve the performance of LLMs but also make their deployment more cost-effective. The ongoing advancements in this domain hint at an exciting trajectory toward more efficient and cost-effective LLM interactions.

CHAINS FOR LONG DOCUMENTS

Handling long documents can be a challenging task for LLMs because of their token limit constraints. While some LLMs have a relatively high token limit, such as GPT-3.5 with 8,192 tokens, it still may not be sufficient for processing extensive documents in their entirety. This limitation necessitates the development of techniques to manage long documents efficiently, ensuring accurate and meaningful inference while keeping costs under control. One such technique is the use of chains.

What Is Chaining?

The concept of chains revolves around breaking down a long document into smaller, manageable chunks, each of which can be processed independently by the LLM. This division can occur at various levels, such as paragraphs, sections, or even sentences, depending on the document's structure and the LLM's token limit. Once segmented, each chunk is processed sequentially, with the LLM's output from one chunk used as an input, alongside the next chunk, for subsequent processing.

This chaining of chunks enables the LLM to handle the document in a piecemeal fashion, ensuring that the analysis or other desired processing occurs accurately across the entire document. For example, consider a legal document spanning 20,000 tokens that needs to be analyzed for specific legal references. Utilizing a chaining technique, this document could be divided into smaller sections of 2,000 tokens each. The LLM could then process each section sequentially, using the output from one section as an input alongside the next section, to maintain contextual understanding across the document. Moreover, chaining can potentially optimize costs. By breaking down the document, it's possible to parallelize the processing of individual chunks, leveraging concurrent processing capabilities to reduce the total inference time.

Additionally, by processing only relevant sections of the document based on the outputs of previous chunks, it's possible to avoid unnecessary processing, further optimizing costs. However, there are challenges and considerations to address. The segmentation of the document must ensure that the division points do not disrupt the contextual understanding necessary for accurate processing. Also, the management of chains, including the storage and retrieval of intermediate outputs, could introduce additional complexity and potential costs. The chaining technique represents a pragmatic approach to managing the challenges associated with processing long documents in LLMs. Through careful planning and implementation, it's possible to optimize both the accuracy and cost-effectiveness of inference processes involving extensive documents.

Implementing Chains

In addressing the topic of chains for long documents in the context of optimizing inference when working with LLMs, it's critical to dive into how this technique operates and why it's crucial for cost efficiency. When dealing with extensive texts, processing the entirety of the content in one go can be computationally intensive and expensive. This is where the concept of "chaining" comes into play, serving as a method to break down the process into smaller, more manageable, and cost-effective steps.

Chaining involves segmenting a long document into smaller portions, which are then processed sequentially or in a manner that ensures coherence and completeness in the derived insights or responses. Each segment or "chain" is processed individually, with the output of one potentially serving as an input or reference for the processing of the subsequent segments. This sequential or structured approach allows for the distributed handling of extensive text data, ensuring that the LLM can manage the content effectively without being overwhelmed by its size or complexity.

Example Use Case

Take, for instance, the scenario where a legal firm intends to utilize an LLM to review a collection of lengthy case law documents to extract and summarize key legal precedents. Given the extensive nature of these documents, processing them in their entirety could result in prohibitive costs and computational demands. However, by employing a chaining approach, each document can be segmented into smaller sections, each of which can be processed individually to extract the relevant information. The insights derived from one segment can then be utilized to guide or inform the processing of subsequent segments, ensuring a coherent and comprehensive analysis.

In implementing a chaining approach, several factors need to be considered to ensure effectiveness and cost-efficiency:

Segmentation strategy: Determining how to segment the long document is crucial. This could be done based on natural breaks in the text, such as chapters or sections, or through a more systematic approach, such as fixed-length segmentation.

Overlap: Including some overlap between segments can ensure that context is not lost across segment boundaries, which is crucial for maintaining coherence in the derived insights.

Sequential processing: Processing the segments in a structured or sequential manner ensures that the insights derived are coherent and complete. This might involve using the output of one segment as input for the next, ensuring a continuous flow of context and information.

Parallel processing: In cases where the segments are independent, parallel processing could be employed to expedite the processing, reducing the time and potentially the cost involved.

State management: Maintaining a state across the segments ensures that context and insights are carried forward effectively.

Efficient Summarization: Utilizing summarization techniques on each segment to reduce the amount of text that needs to be carried forward can also contribute to cost efficiency.

A practical example of chaining can be found in the domain of financial analysis. Suppose an analyst is tasked with reviewing a decade's worth of a corporation's annual reports to extract trends and key financial metrics. Each report is a lengthy document, and reviewing them all at once would be computationally demanding. By segmenting each report into individual sections (e.g., balance sheet, income statement, cash flow statement, etc.) and processing each section sequentially, the analyst can obtain a comprehensive understanding of the financial trends over the decade without overwhelming the LLM.

Let's look at some ways we can actually implement this for getting insights from long documents. For processing long documents with LLMs, two primary workflows exist: sequential and parallel processing. Each workflow requires a set of common components that interact to process and extract insights from extensive text data effectively.

Common Components

At the core of both workflows are several key components: the input handler, segmentation module, chain processor (be it sequential or parallel), LLM chain, summary module, state management, and the compiled insights database. The input handler is the initial point of contact, receiving the document from the user. The segmentation module then takes over, breaking down the lengthy document into manageable segments. The LLM chain is tasked with processing these segments, applying the model's capabilities to extract valuable insights. The summary module is responsible for condensing the insights into more digestible content, while state management ensures that information is carried over from one segment to the next effectively. Finally, the compiled insights database is where all the insights are stored and eventually presented to the user.

In the sequential processing workflow (see Figure 3.6), the document is processed one segment at a time. The segmentation module sends each segment to the sequential chain processor, which then forwards it to the LLM chain. Insights are generated for each segment individually and summarized before being sent to state management, where they're temporarily stored. This process is repeated for each segment until the entire document has been processed. The final step involves compiling all insights into a comprehensive overview, reflecting the document's full scope.

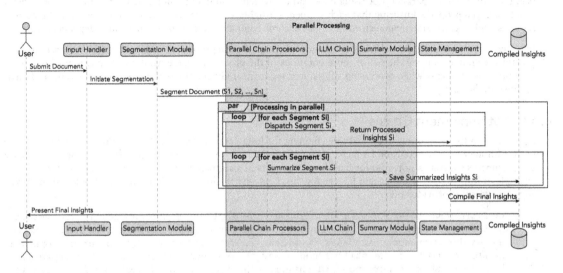

FIGURE 3.6: Sequential processing workflow diagram for long documents

Conversely, the parallel processing workflow processes multiple segments simultaneously. Figure 3.7 below shows what a parallel processing workflow might look like. After segmentation, the parallel chain processor dispatches segments to multiple instances of the LLM chain. As insights are generated, they are concurrently summarized and stored, significantly speeding up the process. This method takes full advantage of the LLM's capabilities and computing resources to handle numerous segments at once, reducing the overall time needed for processing. Parallel processing is inherently more efficient than sequential processing. By handling multiple segments at once, it cuts down the total processing time and makes better use of computational resources. This is particularly beneficial when dealing with extremely long documents where time efficiency is paramount. The ability to summarize and process in parallel also mitigates information bottlenecks, allowing for a faster synthesis of the final insights.

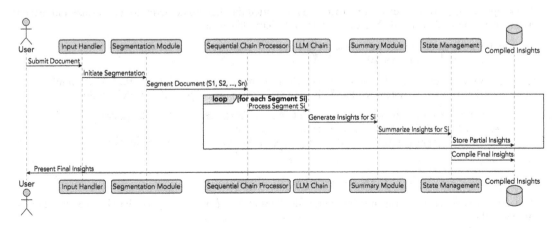

FIGURE 3.7: Parallel processing workflow diagram for long documents

However, parallel processing is not without its limitations. When the number of segments is excessively high, it can lead to computational strain and resource contention. Each segment requires processing power, and there's a limit to how many parallel operations can be executed effectively before the system's performance begins to degrade. Furthermore, parallel processing may lead to challenges in maintaining coherent context across segments if not managed properly. Ensuring that each segment's insights are integrated correctly into the overall picture requires sophisticated state management and can become complex if the segments have interdependencies.

In general, the chaining approach can be enhanced through the integration of vector stores as discussed in the previous section. By storing the vector representations of the processed segments, the system can quickly reference previous segments when processing subsequent segments, reducing the redundancy in processing and further optimizing the cost.

Tools That Implement Chains

In terms of software solutions that facilitate chaining for long documents, Langchain could potentially serve this need. Although specific details on Langchain's functionality in this regard are not available, its role in summarizing documents suggests a potential for handling large texts in a segmented or chained manner. Let's look at an example of how to use the Langchain library for this. Consider the long 2022 letter to shareholders from Amazon. An excerpt is provided here:

```
As I sit down to write my second annual shareholder letter as CEO, I find myself
optimistic and energized by what lies ahead for Amazon. Despite 2022 being one of
the harder macroeconomic years in recent memory, and with some of our own operating
challenges to boot, we still found a way to grow demand (on top of the unprece-
dented growth we experienced in the first half of the pandemic). We innovated in
our largest businesses to meaningfully improve customer experience short and long
term. And,

...

As these equations steadily flip—as we're already seeing happen—we believe our
leading customer experiences, relentless invention, customer focus, and hard work
will result in significant growth in the coming years. And, of course, this doesn't
include the other businesses and experiences we're pursuing at Amazon, all of which
are still in their early days. I strongly believe that our best days are in front
of us, and I look forward to working with my teammates at Amazon to make it so.
```

For simplicity, assume some upstream process has converted the shareholder letter to text format and made it available to you in a local path. You can then read the letter like this:

```
with open(path_to_shareholder_letter, "r") as file:
    letter = file.read()
```

Earlier, it was mentioned that the chunk size and the amount of overlap are huge factors in determining how a general retrieval or search system works. With Langchain, these are easily configurable as follows:

```
from langchain.text_splitter import RecursiveCharacterTextSplitter
text_splitter = RecursiveCharacterTextSplitter(
    separators=["\n\n", "\n"], chunk_size=4000, chunk_overlap=100
)

docs = text_splitter.create_documents([letter])
```

Now, the variable docs is a list containing individually split docs from the original shareholder letter. Let's look at one of these:

```
Document(page_content='There have also been times when macroeconomic conditions or
operating inefficiencies have presented us with new challenges. For instance, in
```

the 2001 dot-com crash, we had to secure letters of credit to buy inventory for the holidays, streamline costs to deliver better profitability for the business, yet still prioritized the long-term customer experience and business we were trying to build (if you remember, we actually lowered prices in most of our categories during that tenuous 2001 period). You saw this sort of balancing again in 2008-2009 as we endured the recession provoked by the mortgage-backed securities financial crisis. We took several actions to manage the cost structure and efficiency of our Stores business, but we also balanced this streamlining with investment in customer experiences that we believed could be substantial future businesses with strong returns for shareholders. In 2008, AWS was still a fairly small, fledgling business. We knew we were on to something, but it still required substantial capital investment. There were voices inside and outside of the company questioning why Amazon (known mostly as an online retailer then) would be investing so much in cloud computing. But, we knew we were inventing something special that could create a lot of value for customers and Amazon in the future. We had a head start on potential competitors; and if anything, we wanted to accelerate our pace of innovation. We made the long-term decision to continue investing in AWS. Fifteen years later, AWS is now an $85B annual revenue run rate business, with strong profitability, that has transformed how customers from start-ups to multinational companies to public sector organizations manage their technology infrastructure. Amazon would be a different company if we'd slowed investment in AWS during that 2008-2009 period.\n\nChange is always around the corner. Sometimes, you proactively invite it in, and sometimes it just comes a-knocking. But, when you see it's coming, you have to embrace it. And, the companies that do this well over a long period of time usually succeed. I'm optimistic about our future prospects because I like the way our team is responding to the changes we see in front of us.\n\nOver the last several months, we took a deep look across the company, business by business, invention by invention, and asked ourselves whether we had conviction about each initiative's long-term potential to drive enough revenue, operating income, free cash flow, and return on invested capital. In some cases, it led to us shuttering certain businesses. For instance, we stopped pursuing physical store concepts like our Bookstores and 4 Star stores, closed our Amazon Fabric and Amazon Care efforts, and moved on from some newer devices where we didn't see a path to meaningful returns. In other cases, we looked at some programs that weren't producing the returns we'd hoped (e.g. free shipping for all online grocery orders over $35) and amended them. We also reprioritized where to spend our resources, which ultimately led to the hard decision to eliminate 27,000 corporate roles. There are a number of other changes that we've made over the last several months to streamline our overall costs, and like most leadership teams, we'll continue to evaluate what we're seeing in our business and proceed adaptively.')

Based on the way we chunked the original shareholder letter, this represents one document segment from the entire shareholder letter. Now, let's look at how we can analyze one of these documents. To do this, we create a generic prompt template in Langchain as follows:

```
from langchain.prompts import PromptTemplate
from langchain.output_parsers import XMLOutputParser, PydanticOutputParser
from langchain.output_parsers.json import SimpleJsonOutputParser
from langchain.schema.output_parser import StrOutputParser


xml:parser = XMLOutputParser(tags=['insight'])
str_parser = StrOutputParser()

prompt = PromptTemplate(
```

```
        template="""

    Human:
    {instructions} : \"{document}\"
    Format help: {format_instructions}.
    Assistant:""",
    input_variables=["instructions","document"],
    partial_variables={"format_instructions": xml:parser.
get_format_instructions()},
)
```

Here, we use the high level `PromptTemplate` class, define some boilerplate text that will be useful for interacting with Claude (note the `Human/Assistant` notation and the use of XML tags), and also use some helper functions for parsing the output. Now, to create a "chain" in Langchain, we use the following pipe-separated syntax as defined in the documentation for Langchain Expression Language (`https://python.langchain.com/docs/expression_language`):

```
insight_chain = prompt | model | StrOutputParser()
```

It's as simple as that! What this says is that the `insight_chain` (or the chain that analyzes insights from a single document segment) takes in a prompt, formats it based on the prompt template, passes this preprocessed input prompt to the model (which in this case in Claude V2), and then parses the output using a standard output parser provided by Langchain. We can use the invoke function attached to the chain and get the final output.

To apply this to all segments or chunks created, we can write a simple `for` loop that stores the insights from each document in a list.

```
insights=[]
for i in range(len(docs)):
    insights.append(
        insight_chain.invoke({
        "instructions":"Provide Key insights from the following text",
        "document": {docs[i].page_content}
    }))
```

A single insight item looks like this:

```
Here are the key insights from the text formatted as XML:
```xml
<insights>
    <insight> During tough economic times, Amazon balanced cost cutting with
long-term investments that proved successful, like continuing to invest in AWS
during the 2001 dot-com crash and 2008-2009 recession.
    </insight>

<insight> Amazon embraces change and sees it as an opportunity, rapidly innovating
and entering new businesses like AWS, which was still small in 2008 but now generates $85 billion in revenue.
    </insight>

    <insight> Recently, Amazon evaluated all businesses on long-term profitabil-
ity, leading to closing some like physical stores and ending free grocery delivery,
while still investing in other areas.
    </insight>
```
```

```
        <insight> Hard choices like workforce reductions help focus resources on the
most promising businesses. Amazon continually evaluates their strategy and makes
changes adaptively.
        </insight>
</insights> ```
```

Take a look at the full document that was printed earlier to make sure that key insights are being captured. Also take note of the output XML format. This clearly organizes separate insights from a single doc and makes it easier to post process later.

Now that we have all of the individual insights from documents, we can pass this in to an LLM through another chain to finally get a concise summary. To do this, we define a new chain, as shown here:

```
str_parser = StrOutputParser()

prompt = PromptTemplate(
    template="""

    Human:
    {instructions} : \"{document}\"
    Assistant:""",
    input_variables=["instructions","document"]
)

summary_chain = prompt | model | StrOutputParser()
```

Then, we use this summary chain's `invoke` command to generate a summary using all of the individual segment specific insights.

```
print(summary_chain.invoke({
        "instructions":"You will be provided with multiple sets of insights.
Compile and summarize these insights and provide key takeaways in one concise
paragraph. Do not use the original xml tags. Just provide a paragraph with your
compiled insights.",
        "document": {'\n'.join(insights)}
    }))
```

The output we get when running this chain is as follows:

```
Amazon continuously evolves and adapts its strategy based on changing macroeconomic
conditions, emerging technologies, and new market opportunities. Despite challenges, Amazon maintains investments in long-term priorities like AWS, advertising,
international expansion, grocery, healthcare, and satellite broadband access.
Amazon aims to build customer trust through relevant advertising, cost optimizations, and new capabilities like generative AI. Amazon believes it is still early
in its potential growth, with significant room to expand core businesses like
retail and AWS as more commerce and computing shifts online. Amazon's culture
embraces invention, customer obsession, and long-term thinking, which gives confi-
dence that the company's best days lie ahead. Key future growth drivers include
advertising, grocery, healthcare, international markets, new retail initiatives
like Buy with Prime, and transformational technologies like machine learning and
satellite broadband access.
```

That looks great! An alternative way to do this is to use the map reduce pattern for summarization in Langchain. To do this, we use:

```
from langchain.chains.summarize import load_summarize_chain
summary_chain = load_summarize_chain(llm=model, chain_type="map_reduce",
verbose=False)
print(summary_chain.run(docs))
```

The output of the earlier chain run is as follows:

> Amazon CEOs remain confident in long-term growth despite current economic chal-
> lenges. They continue investing in emerging opportunities like cloud computing,
> advertising, healthcare, and satellite internet that leverage Amazon's strengths.
> Though optimizing for efficiency and managing costs in the near-term, Amazon's
> focus stays on customer-centric innovation and expanding into large addressable
> markets. Amazon has successfully navigated major transitions before, evolving from
> just books to diverse retail and web services. The company culture values inven-
> tion, taking risks on new ideas that could unlock big markets. Experience shows
> patience pays off as fledgling businesses like AWS become highly successful. Amazon
> will keep adapting its strategy while maintaining its customer obsession and
> long-term orientation.

Comparing Results

Now, how do we know which method produced a better result? One way is to manually compare the two summaries, involve multiple stakeholders, and take a majority vote on which summary better captures the insights
from the original stakeholder letter. Or, you could ask an LLM to compare these summaries by saying "Here are
two summaries of the 2022 Amazon shareholder letter. Which one do you think is better and why?" According
to Claude:

> Summary 1 provides a more comprehensive and balanced overview of the key points
> made in Amazon's 2022 shareholder letter. Here's why I think it's better:
>
> - It highlights Amazon's strategic agility and willingness to adapt based on
> changing conditions. This shows Amazon is not rigid but rather thoughtful and
> dynamic in its strategy.
>
> - It covers a wider range of Amazon's priorities and growth drivers, including
> advertising, grocery, healthcare, international expansion, AWS, and new initiatives
> like Buy with Prime. This gives a better sense of the breadth of Amazon's business.
>
> - It notes how Amazon aims to maintain customer trust and optimize costs, showing
> Amazon balances long-term vision with near-term execution.
>
> - It reflects Amazon's optimism about future potential growth in core businesses
> like retail and AWS. This provides a forward-looking perspective.
>
> - It touches on Amazon's culture and values around invention, customer obsession
> and long-term thinking. This provides important context on the company's
> philosophy.
>
> In contrast, Summary 2 focuses more narrowly on leadership confidence and emerging
> opportunities. While still hitting some key points, Summary 1 gives a more nuanced
> overview across Amazon's strategic priorities, operating context, growth drivers,
> and cultural values. The additional details and balance make Summary 1 a stronger
> summary in my assessment.

Do you agree with Claude's assessment? Using an LLM to evaluate outputs and compare them is in fact one of
the leading ways to do this at scale even with cutting-edge research papers (as of this writing).

Conclusion

The essence of chaining for long documents lies in its ability to break down a complex, resource-intensive task
into smaller, more manageable steps. By doing so, it not only makes the task achievable but also significantly optimizes the cost of inference, which is a critical consideration when working with LLMs, especially in a business
setting where cost-efficiency is a priority.

SUMMARIZATION

In the previous section, you saw an example of how to use chains to build summaries of very long documents. Summarization is not just an end application but can also be used as intermediate steps for many GenAI applications. Summarization in the context of LLMs and GenAI serves as a critical technique both for enhancing the efficiency of processing large datasets and for optimizing the storage of information. This goes beyond the traditional view of summarization as merely a tool for creating abridged versions of text for end users.

Summarization in the Context of Cost and Performance

Let's delve into its role in cost and performance optimization.

Efficiency in Data Processing

LLMs and GenAI systems often deal with vast amounts of data, which can be computationally expensive to fully process. Summarization can distill this data into its most salient points, allowing the model to operate on a condensed version of the dataset. This reduction in data volume can lead to significant computational savings, as less information needs to be processed in subsequent steps. For instance, in a pipeline where an LLM is used to answer questions from a large corpus of documents, summarization can first shrink the corpus to the most relevant content, thus reducing the computational load for the LLM.

Cost-Effective Storage

Storing massive datasets can be costly. Summarization reduces the amount of data that needs to be stored without losing the essence of the information. When intermediate data is summarized, it occupies less storage space, which translates directly into cost savings, especially when using cloud services where storage costs are a consideration.

Enhanced Downstream Applications

Summarized data can serve as a valuable input for downstream applications. For example, in a multistage AI system where an initial model processes raw data and a secondary model performs further analysis, providing the secondary model with summarized data can speed up inference times and reduce resource utilization.

Improved Cache Utilization

In systems that employ caching to reuse previously computed inferences, storing summaries instead of full-length documents can optimize cache space and improve retrieval times. This is especially relevant for vector stores used in semantic search or recommendation systems, where a cache of summarized vectors can facilitate quicker and more efficient similarity computations.

Summarization as a Preprocessing Step

Before fine-tuning LLMs on specialized tasks, summarization can be used to preprocess the training data, ensuring that models learn from the most relevant features of the datasets. This can lead to more accurate models that require less fine-tuning and iteration, further optimizing the inference costs.

Enhanced User Experience

From a user experience perspective, even when summarization is not the end application, it contributes to creating more concise and relevant outputs from LLMs, which can be crucial for applications where user engagement is dependent on the brevity and relevance of the information provided.

Conclusion

Summarization acts as a multipurpose tool in the optimization of LLMs and GenAI, enhancing cost-effectiveness, computational efficiency, and overall performance of these systems. By processing and storing only what is necessary for the task at hand, summarization ensures that resources are allocated judiciously, thus optimizing both the cost and the performance of inference tasks.

BATCH PROMPTING FOR EFFICIENT INFERENCE

In the previous sections, we discussed various techniques to optimize the performance and cost of LLMs. Building on that knowledge, we now turn our attention to a technique known as *batching*. In general, batching is the process of sending in multiple inputs to a model. In this section, we will discuss two versions of batching that are relevant to inference workloads: batch inference and batch prompting.

Batch inference and batch prompting are sometimes used interchangeably, but they are in fact very different concepts. Let's dive deeper into this topic in the next two sections.

Batch Inference

Batch inference is a method of performing inference on a batch of observations all at once, rather than one at a time. It's often used when you have a large dataset, and you don't need immediate responses to your model predictions. This method can be more efficient than traditional inference, as it aggregates multiple inference requests into a single request to the ML/DL framework, reducing the computational overhead of inference. Let's walk through an example. First, start with loading an LLM. Here, we load the GPT Neo model (which is a modest 1B parameter model):

```
from transformers import pipeline

# Initialize a text generation pipeline using GPT-2
generator = pipeline("text-generation", model="EleutherAI/gpt-neo-1.3B", device=0)
generator.tokenizer.pad_token_id = generator.model.config.eos_token_id
```

The `generator` object can now be used to do predictions. Let's first create an array of inputs.

```
N=1000
# List of prompts for story generation
story_prompts = [
    "Deep in the Amazon rainforest, "
]*N
```

The list `story_prompts` now holds 1,000 replicas of the string "Deep in the Amazon rainforest." The intention is to see how the GPT Neo model we are using can come up with 1,000 variations or completions based on the same input sentence.

The naive way of doing this is, of course, writing a `for` loop and predicting the outputs one by one. Let's implement this in code and time it:

```
%%time
for s in story_prompts:
    out = generator(s, max_length=50, batch_size=1)
```

The `%%time` command in a notebook times the wall time of the code following it. Note that we are generating up to 50 tokens and forcing the batch size to be 1. We immediately notice a warning from the `transformers` library.

```
/opt/conda/lib/python3.10/site-packages/transformers/pipelines/base.py:1101:
UserWarning: You seem to be using the pipelines sequentially on GPU. In order to
maximize efficiency please use a dataset
```

The end-to-end wall time for the earlier code is 12 minutes and 14 seconds when run on a G5.2xlarge instance on AWS (https://aws.amazon.com/ec2/instance-types/g5). The 12 minutes of wall time seems excessive for only 1,000 input sequences! Let's now try batch inference by specifying a batch_size of 100.

```
%%time
# Generate text for each prompt in the batch
stories = generator(story_prompts, max_length=50, batch_size=100)
```

Going through the 1,000 stories now takes only 11.7 seconds! Just to make sure this actually generated all 1,000 story completions, we can take a look at the last 10 outputs.

Deep in the Amazon rainforest, and a short distance from the coast of Nicaragua, is an area of jungle that is untouched by human activity — the Amazonian Rainforest. The Amazonian Rainforest is also called the?

Deep in the Amazon rainforest, ichneumon mites are an unusual kind of arthropod, with their body plan consisting of a head and back and only a single pair of legs. In the rainforest, these mites live in

Deep in the Amazon rainforest, monkeys live in a lush landscape of large trees, rivers, lakes, and lush jungles. They live in a place where the forest is at its most dense and the animals that live there are at their most

Deep in the Amazon rainforest, a team of researchers are using drones to monitor the health of the ecosystem. Scientists from the University of Washington and the International Atomic Energy Agency have spent months deploying a drone that flies over the Amazon rainforest

Deep in the Amazon rainforest, ive seen the tiniest thing in my head and it turned out to be huge, over 5 feet tall and it was very black. It was in a tree next to my house, but i had no

Deep in the Amazon rainforest, away from the busy streets of Rio, an exclusive hotel in a lush, tropical setting in the town of Uatim lies to the south of the sprawling city. As we pulled the car into our hotel's

Deep in the Amazon rainforest, a group of scientists have uncovered a treasure trove of dinosaur bone fossils, with the oldest, the largest, and the most complete of all known dinosaur fossils ever found. But it's a discovery that could

Deep in the Amazon rainforest, ichneumon washes can turn into an insect plague that kills hundreds every year. In this picture taken on February 20, 2013, two researchers set up a trap for the ichneumon wasps,

Deep in the Amazon rainforest, illsome forests are slowly being cleared for the building of new palm oil plantations. And in the forest, you can still find living indigenous people who have been displaced and displaced, often in the

Deep in the Amazon rainforest, ichneumon is the largest insect in the world. The larva feeds on the leaves of several species of cacti. The larvae live in the hollow of the cactus stalk.

Experimental Results

In practice, we can continue to increase the batch size until we see diminishing returns. For example, we see the following times when we consecutively increase the batch size:

➤ Batch size 100, time to complete is 11.7 seconds

➤ Batch size 200, time to complete is 8.49 seconds

➤ Batch size 300, time to complete is 14.2 seconds

➤ Batch size 500, CUDA out-of-memory error

What we see from the observations earlier is that the optimal batch size for batch inference for this particular use case is around 200, beyond which the inference actually becomes slower. Beyond a point, the entire batch of inputs cannot fit into GPU memory and may error out. These results are model, instance, and batch-specific, so you should definitely use the same playbook to test the model that you plan to use. As we can see earlier, the optimum batch size should be used in production.

Now, we were able to find the optimum batch size for batch inference with the earlier model we tested (GPT Neo 1.3B) since it completely fit into GPU memory. But what if the model does not entirely fit into memory of a single GPU? This is where libraries such as accelerate help (https://huggingface.co/docs/accelerate/index). Table 3.1 shows various models, with the size demanded from memory in gigabytes.

TABLE 3.1:   Estimated model size in GBs

MODEL	SIZE (FP 32)	SIZE (FP 16)	SIZE (INT 8)
EleutherAI/gpt-neo-1.3B	4.91 GB	2.46 GB	1.23 GB
Tiiuae/Falcon-7B	25.79	12.89	6.45
Tiiuae/Falcon-40B	153.87	79.93	38.47
WizardLM/WizardLM-70B-V1.0	256.29	128.15	64.07

The GPU memory on the G5 instance type we used in the previous example is 24 GB, with one NVIDIA A10G GPU. All other instances of the same family have a maximum of 24GB of memory per GPU. One notable instance type within the G5 family is the G5.12xlarge, which has four GPUs. Other GPU instances on AWS (P2, P3, and G4 types) have a maximum of 16GB of memory per GPU. Thus, there is a need to shard (or partition) a model that is larger than the per GPU limit across multiple GPUs. The other important resource to use is the much larger CPU memory that is available in each of these instances. The accelerate library intelligently makes use of available GPU memory, CPU memory, and disk to perform inference on any size model. This includes the large Falcon 7B, Falcon 40B, and Wizard LM 70B mentioned in the table and beyond. The accelerate library can run any size model as long as the largest layer of the model can fit in GPU memory.

To load a model from the hub using accelerate, you can use device_map= 'auto'.

```
from transformers import AutoModelForSeq2SeqLM
model = AutoModelForSeq2SeqLM.from_pretrained("bigscience/T0pp", device_map="auto")
```

Some models are available as a sharded checkpoint (one that is already split into multiple files). You can download an example sharded model here (GPT2 XL), with the following code:

```
from huggingface_hub import snapshot_download
checkpoint = "marcsun13/gpt2-xl-linear-sharded"
weights_location = snapshot_download(repo_id=checkpoint)
```

Finally, you can also save a model that you are training in a format that `accelerate` can handle using the following:

```
accelerator.save_model(model, save_directory, max_shard_size='10GB')
```

This will result in model shards that look like the following set of files for WizardLM that we saw in Table 3.1: `https://huggingface.co/WizardLM/WizardLM-70B-V1.0/tree/main`.

Using the accelerate Library

With any of these versions of saved models, you can now use the `accelerate` library to load the model using this:

```
from accelerate import load_checkpoint_and_dispatch

model = load_checkpoint_and_dispatch(
    model, checkpoint=weights_location, device_map="auto",
no_split_module_classes=['Block']
)
```

The `accelerate` library will then determine automatically where to put each layer of the model depending on the available resources (GPU memory, CPU memory, disk). You can then use the model with the standard prediction APIs.

```
model.generate( your_inputs )
```

Read more about doing inference with LLMs using the `accelerate` library in the documentation on Hugging Face (`https://huggingface.co/docs/accelerate/usage_guides/big_modeling`).

Using the DeepSpeed Library

DeepSpeed-Inference is another library that can be used for large model inference (`www.deepspeed.ai/inference`). DeepSpeed-Inference offers a range of features to optimize the performance of transformer-based PyTorch models during inference. It employs model parallelism (MP) to accommodate large models within the constraints of GPU memory and also uses MP to enhance the speed of smaller models. In addition, DeepSpeed-Inference introduces specialized kernels tailored for inference, aimed at further reducing latency and operational costs. A unique method called MoQ is also part of its toolkit, designed to both compress the model size and lower inference costs in a production environment.

DeepSpeed also boasts an effortless inference mode compatible with models trained using its own framework, as well as those from Megatron and HuggingFace. This mode requires no alterations to the model, such as exporting or creating different checkpoints. When running inference on multi-GPU setups with compatible models, users simply need to specify the degree of model parallelism and provide checkpoint information or a preloaded model. DeepSpeed handles the rest, automatically partitioning the model, integrating high-performance kernels, and managing communication between GPUs. For a comprehensive list of models compatible with these features, users are directed to consult the relevant information provided by DeepSpeed. Take a look at the inference tutorial from DeepSpeed at `www.deepspeed.ai/tutorials/inference-tutorial`.

> **NOTE** *As LLMs typically have a substantial GPU memory footprint and high compute costs, optimizing their inference is crucial, especially since serving these models often dominates the compute cost in real-world applications. Traditional approaches have primarily focused on internal model changes such as quantization or custom CUDA kernels. However, system-level optimizations, particularly in batching, can yield substantial improvements in efficiency.*

Continuous batching, also known as dynamic batching or batching with iteration-level scheduling, offers a novel approach to this challenge. Unlike traditional batching, which processes a fixed batch size at once, continuous batching dynamically adjusts batch sizes and schedules them at the iteration level. This method has shown remarkable results, including up to 23x throughput improvement using continuous batching-specific memory optimizations and 8x throughput over naive batching. This is achieved by leveraging the unique characteristics of LLMs, particularly their iterative output generation and memory-bound nature, rather than being compute-bound.

The basis of continuous batching lies in the inherent structure of LLM inference. The initial ingestion of a prompt, known as the prefill phase, is time-consuming as it pre-computes some inputs of the attention mechanism that remain constant throughout the generation. Since these inputs can be computed independently, this phase efficiently utilizes the GPU's parallel compute capabilities. Recognizing that LLM inference is memory-IO bound, continuous batching optimizes memory usage, increasing throughput by enabling larger batch sizes to fit into the high-bandwidth GPU memory.

Continuous batching stands out because it doesn't necessitate modifications to the model weights for optimization. It enhances memory efficiency of LLM generation without altering the model itself, unlike strategies like model quantization. This aspect of continuous batching makes it a powerful and accessible tool for optimizing LLM inference, especially for applications where model modifications are not feasible or desirable.

Take a look at the following resources if you are interested in learning more about continuous batching: Hugging Face (`https://huggingface.co/`
`text-generation-inference`*), Anyscale (*`www.anyscale.com/blog/`
`continuous-batching-llm-inference`*), and Deci (*`https://deci.ai/blog/`
`infery-llm-inference-sdk-for-llm-deployment-redefining-state-`
`of-the-art-in-llm-inference`*).*

With larger models, the budget for larger than one batch size is limited. More testing is required before you decide on the final, optimum configuration for inference. Generally, use the available GPU resources completely using appropriate libraries and then test various batch sizes to find the optimum size for batch inference.

Now that we have talked about batch inference, let's switch gears and talk about a batch prompting.

Batch Prompting

The batch prompting approach to LLM inference groups multiple prompts into a single request, potentially lowering both the computational load and the costs associated with using these models. Batch prompting is especially relevant when dealing with a large number of related inference inputs, where processing requests one by one can be inefficient. By consolidating requests, batch prompting can save time and resources while maintaining the accuracy and quality of the model's responses.

This section will explore how batch prompting works, the scenarios where it's most effective, and the implications for those who use LLMs regularly. We'll look at concrete examples and data from recent studies, giving a clear picture of how batch prompting can be a valuable addition to your LLM toolkit. As we move forward, keep in mind the balance we've discussed between cost and performance—batch prompting is another tool to help strike that balance effectively.

Imagine you have 10 related questions you want an LLM to answer. With standard prompting, you would send each question to the LLM separately, wait for a response, and then send the next one. This means 10 separate prompts and 10 separate API calls. With batch inference, you batch the input questions and find an optimal batch size as discussed in the previous section, but each question passes through the model independently. With batch prompting, Instead of sending these questions one by one, you group them all into a single prompt and send all 10 questions at once, in an effective "batch" of inferences to the LLM. The LLM then processes all of them in a single go and generates responses for each question in that batch. This approach reduces the API calls saving on the computational resources and time needed for processing each individual prompt.

Example of Using Batch Prompting

To construct a batch prompt for a set of arithmetic reasoning questions (similar to what you would find from the GSM8K dataset) using the batch prompting method, follow these steps:

1. Start by providing a set of exemplars (questions and answers) in a structured format. These are few-shot examples with correct answers. For example:

```
Q[1]: There are 8 apples and you buy 4 more. How many apples do you have?
A[1]: You would have 8 + 4 = 12 apples.
Q[2]: If you have 10 cookies and eat 2, how many do you have left?
A[2]: You would have 10 - 2 = 8 cookies left.
```

2. Next, provide a batch of new questions without answers, formatted similarly to the exemplars.

```
Q[3]: You find 5 seashells at the beach and your friend gives you 3 more. How
many seashells do you have?
Q[4]: There are 7 cars in the parking lot and 5 leave. How many cars are left in
the parking lot?
```

3. The model is expected to use the structure of the provided exemplars to answer the new batch of questions.

```
A[3]: You would have 5 + 3 = 8 seashells.
A[4]: You would have 7 - 5 = 2 cars left in the parking lot.
```

The paper titled "Batch Prompting: Efficient Inference with Large Language Model APIs" explores this approach (https://arxiv.org/pdf/2301.08721.pdf). The results show batch prompting can significantly reduce the tokens consumed as well as the number of expensive LLM API calls needed. On 10 diverse datasets for commonsense QA, arithmetic reasoning, and natural language inference, batch prompting achieved comparable or even improved accuracy over standard prompting, while decreasing token costs by up to 5x and time costs by up to 5x (with six samples batched). Further analysis reveals the number of samples per batch and complexity of tasks can impact performance. Overall, batch prompting offers an effective drop-in replacement to standard prompting that retains strong performance while providing substantial efficiency gains, enabling more affordable large-scale LLM applications.

MODEL OPTIMIZATION METHODS

The goal of model optimization is to reduce the computational and memory footprint of models without significantly impacting their accuracy. Popular techniques include pruning, which removes redundant weights; distillation, which trains a smaller model to mimic a larger one; and quantization, which uses lower precision numbers to represent weights and activations. Additional methods such as tensor decomposition, compact network architectures, and dynamic execution engines have also been proposed. Among these, quantization has emerged as one of the most effective strategies for optimizing the inference efficiency of large language models. By compressing models into lower bitwidths, quantization enables faster and cheaper inference.

Quantization

Quantization refers to techniques for compressing the high-precision representations of weights and activations in neural networks into lower-precision integer values. For example, weights that are 32-bit floating-point numbers may be quantized to 8-bit integers. This conversion reduces the storage and memory bandwidth needed for models, allowing more efficient inference.

Quantization typically involves two steps: first, determining a mapping that represents the floating point values with integers, and second, actually converting the weights and activations to integers during inference. Common mappings include linear and logarithmic quantization to uniformly space integers over the value range.

Deploying gigantic language models with hundreds of billions of parameters poses a major challenge for inference efficiency and cost. To address this issue, quantization has emerged as a popular approach that compresses the floating-point weights and activations of models into low-precision integers such as INT8 or INT4. This section will discuss five major types of quantization techniques that have been explored to optimize the inference efficiency of large language models.

Decomposition: One method called *mixed-precision decomposition* handles the outlier values in activations by decomposing features into two groups: one quantized in low precision like INT8, while the other retains higher precision like FP16 for dimensions containing outliers. This avoids aggressive quantization of outliers but still benefits from INT8 quantization for the majority of activations. Studies show this method works well for large models where outliers start emerging.

Fine-grained quantization: Instead of quantizing the entire tensor, fine-grained quantization performs quantization at a more granular level like token or channel. For instance, weights can be quantized in groups of 128, while activations use token-wise quantization. This provides more flexibility to balance precision across tensor dimensions than coarse methods. Fine-grained quantization has been shown to effectively minimize the quantization error.

Layerwise quantization: This method quantizes each layer separately by directly minimizing the layerwise reconstruction error between full-precision and quantized models. Compared to fine-tuning the entire model, layerwise quantization offers a more efficient approach for large models. Techniques like fixed quantization order and Cholesky reformulation are used to make the optimization feasible for models with hundreds of billions of parameters.

Other quantization methods aim to balance the difficulties of quantizing weights and activations by incorporating techniques like scaling transformations. For instance, SmoothQuant migrates the quantization difficulty from activations to weights through a learnable scaling factor. This makes weights slightly harder but activations easier to quantize for better overall accuracy.

Quantization-aware training: In contrast to the post-training methods, quantization-aware training incorporates fake quantization operations during model training itself. This approach can achieve better accuracy but requires full model retraining with quantization baked in. For large models, hybrid strategies such as using efficient adapters or distillation are often needed to make this feasible. In summary, many quantization techniques have been proposed to optimize the inference efficiency of large language models.

Code Example

Continuing with our code examples from the previous section, let's take a look at how you can quantize a model. Here we will be using a combination of the `transformers` library and the `autoawq` library that implements an algorithm called *activation-aware weight quantization* (AWQ). For more information, see `https://arxiv.org/abs/2306.00978`. Quantizing reduces the model's precision from FP16 to INT4, which effectively reduces the file size by about 70%. First, install the `autoawq` library:

```
pip install autoawq
Then, to quantize the Falcon 7B model, you can do this:

from awq import AutoAWQForCausalLM
from transformers import AutoTokenizer

model_path = 'tiiuae/falcon-7b'
quant_path = 'falcon-7b-v1.5-awq'
quant_config = { "zero_point": True, "q_group_size": 64, "w_bit": 4, "ver-
sion": "GEMM" }
```

```
# Load model
model = AutoAWQForCausalLM.from_pretrained(model_path, **{"low_cpu_mem_
usage": True})
tokenizer = AutoTokenizer.from_pretrained(model_path, trust_remote_code=True)

# Quantize
model.quantize(tokenizer, quant_config=quant_config)

# Save quantized model
model.save_quantized(quant_path)
tokenizer.save_pretrained(quant_path)
```

Now you have a 4-bit quantized version of Falcon 7B! Note that this took 17 minutes in the G5 instance. Finally, we end this section by talking about a recent and popular quantization technique called GPTQ.

Recent Advancements: GPTQ

The GPTQ method introduces an efficient layerwise quantization approach that leverages approximate second-order information to quantize massive generative pretrained transformer (GPT) models with hundreds of billions of parameters. GPTQ reformulates the standard layerwise quantization objective into a least squares problem and utilizes the Hessian matrix to determine the optimal quantization and update of weights.

To make this computationally feasible for huge models, GPTQ employs techniques such as arbitrary quantization order, lazy batch updates, and Cholesky reformulation of the Hessian. This allows GPTQ to quantize models such as OPT-175B and BLOOM-176B to just 3 to 4 bits per weight in only a few GPU hours while preserving accuracy. In the paper on GPTQ, the method enabled reduced the precision inference of massive 175 billion parameter models on a single GPU for the first time. Experiments showed GPTQ consistently outperformed naive round-to-nearest quantization across various perplexity benchmarks and zero-shot tasks. The paper also demonstrated practical speedups of 3x to 4x during sequence generation using custom quantized kernels. Overall, GPTQ provides an efficient and accurate quantization framework to optimize large language model inference. You can read more about the GPTQ method in the original paper at https://arxiv.org/pdf/2210.17323.pdf.

PARAMETER-EFFICIENT FINE-TUNING METHODS

In Chapter 2, we covered parameter-efficient fine-tuning (PEFT) methods in depth, examining how they revolutionize the fine-tuning process of LLMs by optimizing a subset of parameters instead of the entire model. This section takes the discussion further, focusing on the application of PEFT in inference. Building upon the foundational understanding of PEFT methods, we'll explore how these techniques, once used for training adapters, significantly enhance the efficiency and effectiveness of LLMs during the inference stage. This not only includes improvements in computational efficiency and storage but also highlights the flexibility offered by PEFT in deploying models for various tasks and domains. With the growing need for more agile and resource-efficient models in practical applications, understanding the role of PEFT in inference becomes crucial, especially as we look toward the use of multiple adapters to handle diverse and complex tasks.

Companies with several LLM use cases are now doubling down with a common strategy: train multiple PEFT adapters (such as LORA models) for multiple use cases and then deploy this base model along with multiple adapters in production. With the growing size of LLMs, full fine-tuning becomes impractical, particularly on consumer hardware. Additionally, storing and deploying fine-tuned models for each task is costly, as they are as large as the original pretrained models. Similarly, doing inference with full fine-tuned versions of the base model is even more impractical.

Recap of PEFT Methods

PEFT methods allow for the creation of small, efficient model checkpoints, which are just a few megabytes in size, in contrast to the large storage requirements of fully fine-tuned models. These small, trained weights from PEFT are added to the pretrained LLM, enabling the use of the same base model for multiple tasks by simply adding these lightweight adaptations. In practice, when a model trained using PEFT methods is ready for inference, the process involves saving only the incremental PEFT weights that were trained, resulting in significantly smaller file sizes. For example, a model such as bigscience/T0_3B tuned using a PEFT method such as LoRA for a specific dataset can be stored with just a couple of files, including the adapter configuration and the trained model weights, with the latter being remarkably small in size. This adaptability offered by PEFT is also notable during inference, as it enables the use of the same base model for various tasks by adding lightweight, task-specific adaptations. This approach is particularly beneficial for models deployed in resource-constrained environments or applications requiring quick adaptation to new tasks. Additionally, the fact that PEFT methods do not introduce additional inference latency is crucial, as it ensures that the enhanced efficiency and flexibility do not come at the cost of response time or output quality.

Figure 3.8 shows how you can use multiple PEFT models in production.

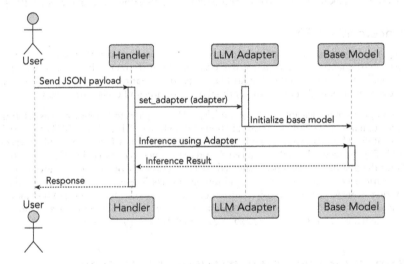

FIGURE 3.8: How to dynamically use multiple adapters in inference

The user sends in a JSON payload and the name or path to an adapter. Assume you already have a folder of saved adapters and a base model such as Falcon 7B. The folders contain `adapter_config.json` files and adapter weights for each saved adapter. The process shown in the sequence diagram involves loading the base model and then dynamically setting and switching adapters based on the provided adapter name or path. Assume that the handler receives a JSON payload with the "prompt" and the "adapter" that needs to be used for prediction. With this set up, adapters are dynamically loaded and used for prediction based on the task. For example, you can have one adapter that identifies PII information, another one that generates a one-line summary, another one that translates the input to French, and so on.

Code Example

With this understanding, you can now write a function that can set a new adapter in runtime and do a prediction.

```
from transformers import AutoModelForCausalLM, AutoTokenizer

# Load base model and tokenizer

model = AutoModelForCausalLM.from_pretrained(model_name)
tokenizer = AutoTokenizer.from_pretrained(model_name)
```

```
def set_adapter(model, adapter_name, tokenizer):
    """
    Sets the specified adapter for the model.

    Args:
    model: The pre-loaded LLM model instance.
    adapter_name: Name of the adapter to be used for inference.
    tokenizer: The tokenizer associated with the model.

    Returns:
    A function to perform inference with the specified adapter.
    """

    # Set the specified adapter for the model
    model.set_adapter(adapter_name)

    # Function to perform inference
    def perform_inference(prompt):
        inputs = tokenizer(prompt, return_tensors="pt").to("cuda")
        outputs = model.generate(**inputs, max_new_tokens=64, do_sample=True,
top_k=50)
        return tokenizer.decode(outputs[0], skip_special_tokens=True)

    return perform_inference

# Usage example

adapter_inference = set_adapter(model, json_payload["adapter"], tokenizer)

result = adapter_inference(json_payload["prompt"])
print(result)
```

In many cases, the actual adapter for a specific task is not known beforehand. In these cases, the prompt may contain some context that points to the adapter required to complete the task. In these situations, the user is expected to only provide a prompt, and the adapter is inferred using another model. In Figure 3.9, we modify the previous diagram to include an "Adaptor predictor" component. This can be a separate zero-shot model, a specifically trained model, or a set of rules.

COST AND PERFORMANCE IMPLICATIONS

Over the past several sections we have talked about many inference optimization techniques along with balancing cost and performance and how important this is in production. When optimizing LLMs for inference, striking a balance between cost and performance is crucial. Techniques such as prompt engineering and summarization directly impact performance by refining inputs and outputs to reduce computational load, enhancing both efficiency and accuracy. Meanwhile, caching with vector stores and batch prompting offer substantial cost savings by minimizing redundant computations and leveraging efficient resource utilization.

Model optimization methods such as quantization, in-flight batching, and tensor parallelism further enhance this balance. Quantization reduces model size and speeds up inference, while in-flight batching and tensor parallelism optimize resource usage for parallel processing. These methods collectively contribute to reducing operational costs while maintaining or even improving inference performance.

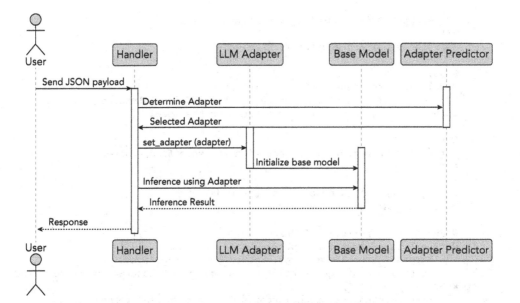

FIGURE 3.9: An adapter predictor component is introduced to automatically select the adapter for inference

However, implementing these optimizations requires careful consideration of their implications. For instance, while prompt engineering and iterative refinement can significantly improve output quality, they demand more upfront effort and expertise. Similarly, model optimization techniques such as quantization might introduce a trade-off between performance accuracy and efficiency. Thus, the choice of methods should align with specific use-case requirements, considering factors such as model size, available resources, response time requirements, and desired output quality.

Overall, the key to effective inference optimization in LLMs lies in a holistic approach that judiciously combines various techniques. By understanding and leveraging the strengths of each method, it's possible to achieve an optimal balance of cost and performance, ensuring that LLMs are not only powerful and accurate but also economically viable for a wide range of applications.

SUMMARY

In this chapter, we explored a spectrum of inference optimization techniques for large language models, delving into strategies such as prompt engineering, caching, and batch prompting to enhance efficiency. We examined various model optimization methods, including quantization and tensor parallelism, and discussed the importance of hyperparameter tuning. The chapter highlighted the intricate balance between cost and performance, offering insights into how these methods can be judiciously combined for optimal results in production.

REFERENCES

Huggingface accelerate for inference, `https://huggingface.co/docs/accelerate/usage_guides/big_modeling`

Deepspeed for inference, `www.deepspeed.ai/inference`

Batch prompting, `https://arxiv.org/pdf/2301.08721.pdf`

GPTQ paper, `https://arxiv.org/abs/2210.17323`

4

Model Selection
and Alternatives

WHAT'S IN THIS CHAPTER?

➤ Introduction to Model Selection

➤ The Role of Compact and Nimble Models

➤ Domain-Specific Models

➤ The Power of Prompting with General-Purpose Models

INTRODUCTION TO MODEL SELECTION

In the rapidly evolving field of artificial intelligence and machine learning, the selection of appropriate models has become a pivotal aspect of successful implementation in various applications. This chapter delves into the intricacies of model selection, focusing on the trade-offs between compact, nimble models and their larger counterparts, the emergence of domain-specific models, and the criticality of inference hyperparameter optimization.

The landscape of AI models has expanded dramatically, offering a spectrum from compact, nimble models to massive, complex ones. Each model type presents unique advantages and challenges, making the selection process critical for efficiency, cost-effectiveness, and performance optimization. This diversity in model choices allows for tailored solutions across different domains and applications, from mobile applications requiring low latency to large-scale data analysis demanding high computational power.

MOTIVATING EXAMPLE: THE TALE OF TWO MODELS

To illustrate the importance of model selection, consider the contrasting scenarios of a startup developing a mobile health application and a large corporation analyzing vast amounts of financial data. The startup might opt for a compact model due to limited resources and the need for real-time analysis, whereas the corporation could leverage a larger, more complex model to extract nuanced insights from extensive datasets.

In briefly exploring the contrasting scenarios and thought processes of the startup developing a mobile health application and a large corporation analyzing financial data, we can uncover the nuanced decisions involved in selecting small-language models (SMLs) versus large-language models (LLMs).

A startup, constrained by resources, may naturally gravitate toward experimenting with SLMs. These smaller models are not only cost-effective, requiring less data and less powerful hardware, but also offer greater efficiency, a key for startups operating with limited budgets. The customization potential of SLMs is particularly valuable for a health application startup, enabling them to tailor their model to specific medical datasets or cohorts. This ensures more accurate and relevant health diagnostics or recommendations, aligning closely with their specific business objectives and industry needs. Furthermore, the enhanced safety and security provided by smaller models that can possibly run on the edge, with a controlled training data environment and simpler risk assessments, are vital in healthcare applications where patient privacy and data sensitivity are paramount.

A large financial institution, handling copious amounts of complex data, would naturally lean toward utilizing large language models like GPT-4, capable of processing vast and intricate datasets. These models are not just proficient in deep financial analysis and generating insightful reports, they are also instrumental in content creation and information retrieval, serving critical functions such as financial market analysis and enhancing customer interactions.

The sheer cost of developing and maintaining these advanced models can be formidable. Yet, large financial entities have the means to not only invest in the initial pretraining of language models on petabytes of data but also in establishing centralized "GenAI platforms." Such platforms harness LLMs at their core, providing various internal teams with powerful tools for fine-tuning and applying these models to specific end-use cases. This level of investment and infrastructure allows these institutions to mitigate the risks and fully leverage the strengths of LLMs for their complex data environments. BloombergGPT, for example, was trained with internal and publicly available financial data using 1.3 million GPU hours! Large corporations with more substantial resources are in a better position to manage these models, overcoming the challenges associated with their scale and complexity.

Comparing these two scenarios, we see that (some) startups may prioritize cost-effective and domain-specific solutions like SLMs, while large corporations can leverage the broad applicability and deep analysis capabilities of LLMs. This doesn't mean that LLMs can be used only by large organizations with deep pockets. The choice between SLMs and LLMs is influenced by factors such as the organization's size, resource availability, specific needs of the industry, the nature of the data being processed, and the actual use case in question. In this illustrative tale of two models, the focus of a startup building the mobile health application is on efficient, accurate, and secure processing of sensitive health data. In contrast, a financial corporation would utilize the comprehensive data processing power of LLMs to glean insights from large volumes of financial data and empower multiple internal use cases, despite the higher costs and potential challenges. Both models have their unique place in the AI landscape, with startups and large corporations finding different value propositions in each. The selection of an AI model is a balancing act, weighing factors such as cost, performance, accessibility, and environmental impact. It's not merely a choice between small and large models but an intricate decision influenced by the specific requirements and constraints of each project.

This chapter will guide the reader through the complexities of model selection. We first discuss the development and application of compact and nimble models, emphasizing their importance in certain contexts. We then explore domain-specific models, highlighting how tailoring models to specific industries can enhance performance and relevance. Finally, we delve into the optimization of inference hyperparameters, a crucial step in refining model performance regardless of size.

THE ROLE OF COMPACT AND NIMBLE MODELS

Despite the allure of large models, companies that lead the GenAI race today like OpenAI and Anthropic continue to offer smaller models. This makes us wonder—why offer these smaller models?

When examining the performance and cost efficiency of small versus large language models, research indicates that smaller models, while perhaps less capable in terms of raw power and versatility, offer substantial benefits in certain contexts. Smaller models like OpenAI's GPT 3.5 Turbo and Anthropic's Claude Instant are tailored for specific tasks where quick, real-time interaction is essential, providing a more practical solution for applications such as mobile apps, chatbots, and interactive customer service tools.

Cost-wise, smaller models are significantly less expensive to train and deploy. Their reduced complexity means they can operate effectively on less powerful hardware, translating to lower infrastructure investments and maintenance costs. This economy extends to the environmental aspect as well; smaller models are inherently more energy-efficient, which not only lowers operating costs but also aligns with the increasing corporate emphasis on sustainability.

The reduction in training data requirements for smaller models further contributes to cost efficiency. Since they are often fine-tuned on specific datasets rather than the vast swaths of Internet text that large models like GPT-3 or GPT-4 require, the costs and time associated with the data gathering and cleaning processes are minimized. This also leads to performance benefits in specialized applications; a smaller model trained on domain-specific data can outperform a larger, more generalized model because of its targeted understanding.

However, large models remain unparalleled in their ability to generate nuanced and complex content, understand and generate human language accurately, and handle a broad range of AI tasks. The trade-off between size and performance is most evident in the balance between the depth of capability provided by large models and the agility and cost efficiency offered by smaller models. In practice, the choice between them often comes down to the specific use case at hand, with smaller models providing an accessible entry point or specialized tool in many scenarios and large models serving as powerhouse solutions for high-stakes or highly complex applications.

In summary, both small and large language models have their place in the AI ecosystem, and their performance and cost must be evaluated in the context of the following:

➤ **Resource efficiency:** Smaller models require less computational power, making them more accessible and cost-effective, especially for startups or projects with limited budgets.

➤ **Latency and real-time processing:** Compact models offer lower latency, crucial for applications requiring real-time processing like mobile apps or interactive systems.

➤ **Energy consumption:** Larger models have a significant environmental impact due to higher energy consumption. Compact models are more sustainable, aligning with growing environmental concerns.

➤ **Accessibility and democratization:** Smaller models democratize AI, allowing broader access and experimentation across diverse sectors.

EXAMPLES OF SUCCESSFUL SMALLER MODELS

In this section, we will go through some recent advancements in smaller models, with a focus on how their performance compares to models that are several times larger in terms of number of parameters. There are two main ways of getting to a smaller, powerful "small-language" model:

➤ Use post-training techniques to compress a larger model.

➤ Train or fine-tune a smaller model from scratch.

First, let's study some recent techniques on quantization, which is an important and practical technique to compress existing models. We briefly discussed quantization in Chapter 3, but here, we will use a new perspective of looking at these techniques creating smaller models that are equivalent in performance.

Quantization for Powerful but Smaller Models

Quantization refers to the process of constraining an input from a large set to output in a smaller set. In the context of neural networks, it typically involves reducing the precision of the numbers used to represent model weights and activations such as transforming floating-point representations into lower-bit-width formats like int8 or int16. This transformation not only decreases the memory footprint of the model but also potentially speeds up its computations, particularly on specialized hardware designed for low-precision arithmetic.

Quantization typically involves the conversion of floating-point representations (such as 32-bit or 64-bit floats) into lower-bit-width integers (like 8-bit or 16-bit). This process can be applied to different aspects of a neural network:

Weight quantization: Reduces the precision of the weights of the model. Since weights are fixed, once the model is trained, this is often the primary focus of quantization.

Activation quantization: Involves quantizing the activation outputs of each layer. This is more challenging than weight quantization as activations are dynamic and change with every input.

The quantization process can be either uniform, where the step size between quantized values is constant or non-uniform. Though non-uniform quantization is more complex, it can sometimes yield better accuracy as it can be tailored to the specific distribution of values. Quantizing a model effectively reduces its size. For instance, converting 32-bit floats to 8-bit integers cuts the model's size by roughly 75%, significantly lowering memory requirements and storage. This reduction enables the deployment of complex models on devices with limited memory, like smartphones and IoT devices.

However, quantization can introduce errors due to the reduced precision, which might affect the model's performance. We don't want a smaller model that is not as accurate or useful as the larger model. The art of quantization lies in balancing the trade-off between model size, computational efficiency, and accuracy. In the next section, we will briefly explore how advanced quantization techniques like AWQ, GPTQ, and LLM.Int8() address these challenges, ensuring minimal loss in performance while significantly reducing the model size.

Before moving on, let's first discuss three recent techniques that are being used for quantization:

➤ **Adaptive weight quantization (AWQ):** AWQ is a method that focuses on optimizing the quantization process according to the specific characteristics of the model's weights. AWQ adapts to the distribution of weights, allowing for more effective quantization that minimizes performance degradation. It has been particularly effective in various language modeling, commonsense QA, and domain-specific benchmarks, showing better generalization and good quantization performance across different model families such as LLaMA, OPT, and visual language models like OpenFlamingo-9B and LLaVA-13B.

➤ **Generative pre-trained transformers quantization (GPTQ):** GPTQ is a post-training quantization technique tailored for generative pre-trained transformers. This method emphasizes maintaining the accuracy of the quantized model, focusing on large-scale language models like BLOOM and OPT families. GPTQ stands out in its ability to compress models to 3 and 4 bits per weight while maintaining minimal loss in performance, especially in challenging language generation tasks. It has been particularly effective with very large models, such as BLOOM-176B and OPT-175B.

➤ **LLM.Int8():** LLM.Int8() is a quantization approach that focuses on 8-bit matrix multiplication, enabling the compression of multibillion-parameter transformers. Unique in its approach, LLM.Int8() uses mixed-precision decomposition to manage large magnitude features effectively, thereby preserving the performance of large-scale models. It has been shown to maintain full 16-bit performance across a range of transformer sizes up to 175B parameters, marking a significant advancement in model quantization and efficiency.

As mentioned earlier, one of the most notable challenges in quantization is maintaining the model's performance after reducing precision. Let's look at these performance efficiencies in some more detail for these three methods:

➤ AWQ, for example, applies low-bit weight quantization, significantly reducing the model size. Performance-wise, it improves WikiText-2 perplexity across various model sizes and bit-precisions, and on the COCO captioning dataset, it notably reduced quantization degradation in various shot settings.

➤ **GPTQ**, tailored for generative pre-trained transformers, also shows remarkable results. When applied to the OPT-175B model, it reduces the memory requirement to about 63GB, including components maintained at FP16 precision. Performance metrics such as WikiText-2 perplexity remain close to the baseline, indicating minimal loss in model effectiveness despite the substantial reduction in size.

➤ **LLM.Int8()**, focusing on 8-bit matrix multiplication significantly downsizes models without sacrificing performance. It maintains full perplexity across transformer sizes ranging from 125M to 13B parameters, demonstrating no loss in performance compared to the original 32-bit float models. This method is especially effective in preserving performance in zero-shot tasks for models up to 175 billion parameters, marking a notable achievement in the field of model quantization.

Overall, these quantization methods represent a crucial development in the field of AI and machine learning. They enable the deployment of small yet powerful AI models, particularly in environments where resources are limited, without compromising on their core functionality and effectiveness.

Next let's look at smaller models that are not a result of post-training techniques like quantization.

Text Generation with Mistral 7B

Mistral 7B, developed by Mistral AI, represents a significant advancement in the realm of large language models. This 7 billion parameter transformer model is a testament to the rapid evolution and growing capabilities of neural networks in natural language processing (NLP) applications. It stands out not only for its size but also for its exceptional performance, offering a blend of efficiency and power that allows it to outperform even larger models like Meta's Llama 2 13B and Llama 1 34B in various benchmarks.

> **NOTE** *Note that the "B" in 7B stands for the number of billions of parameters, if you haven't caught on to that already! The actual number of parameters may not be exactly 7 billion but is close to this in most cases.*

Mistral 7B is a decoder-based language model incorporating cutting-edge features such as Sliding Window Attention. Trained with a context length of 8000 and a fixed cache size, Mistral 7B achieves a theoretical attention span of 128,000 tokens. This architectural choice underpins the model's efficiency and its ability to handle extensive data sequences, a critical factor in complex NLP tasks.

Mistral 7B has been rigorously benchmarked against other models, particularly the Llama models. It significantly outperforms the Llama 2 13B model across all metrics and is on par with the Llama 34B model. In terms of specific benchmarks, Mistral 7B excels in commonsense reasoning, world knowledge, reading comprehension, math, and coding tasks. It demonstrates superior performance in code and reasoning benchmarks, illustrating its dual capability in handling natural language and technical tasks. An interesting aspect of its performance is in the cost/performance ratio. On reasoning, comprehension, and STEM reasoning benchmarks (MMLU), Mistral 7B performs equivalently to a Llama 2 model that would be more than three times its size. This efficiency translates into memory savings and increased throughput, a crucial factor in real-world applications. It is also important to note that Mistral 7B largely outperforms the Llama 2 13B on all evaluations, except on knowledge benchmarks, where it is on par. This exception is likely due to its limited parameter count, which restricts the amount of knowledge it can compress. Interestingly, Mistral 7B also approaches the coding performance of Code-Llama 7B, which is a specialized model for generating code, without sacrificing performance on other tasks.

During inference, Mistral 7B demonstrates its efficiency in handling requests and maintaining low latency under various loads. For instance, with an A100 40GB GPU, the best response time at 1 user is 4.6 seconds, and the model maintains this performance up to 0.8 requests per second (RPS) before experiencing significant latency increases. Similarly, with an A10 24GB GPU, the best response time is 18 seconds, maintaining performance up to 0.4 RPS. When using a different configuration, the best response time can be as low as 2.3 seconds, with performance holding steady up to 2.8 RPS. These metrics indicate the model's robustness in processing requests efficiently across different hardware setups. For more information, you can visit `https://mistral.ai`.

Mistral 7B is a great choice for real-world applications such as AI assistants (try it out on `https://huggingface.co/spaces/w601sxs/mistral-chat-fast`), specialized reasoning tasks, and general-purpose natural language tasks such as PII redaction, legal clarification, summarization, and classification into categories. The Mistral 7B is also a starting point to develop other small yet powerful models like the Zephyr 7B from Huggingface. We will dive deeper into this model in the next section.

Zephyr 7B and Aligned Smaller Models

Zephyr 7B, a language model developed by Hugging Face, is built upon the foundation laid by Mistral 7B. Mistral 7B, known for its efficiency and capability to deliver enhanced performance with less computational demand, has paved the way for the development of even more powerful models like Zephyr 7B. Specifically, Mistral 7B's efficiency in instructional tasks allowed it to excel on platforms such as Hugging Face, competing closely with models nearly double its size. This success led to the development of Zephyr 7B, which demonstrates the potential of fine-tuned smaller models like Mistral 7B to surpass larger chat models in some tasks, even rivaling GPT-4 in certain aspects.

A key aspect of Zephyr 7B's development is the use of *knowledge distillation*. This technique involves training a smaller "student" model on the complex patterns learned by a larger "teacher" model, thus enhancing its accuracy without sacrificing language modeling capabilities. Zephyr 7B's development employed distilled supervised fine-tuning (dSFT) and distilled direct preference optimization (dDPO), using AI feedback from an ensemble of larger teacher models as preference data. This approach significantly reduced the time and resources needed for training while maintaining high-quality interaction and understanding.

KNOWLEDGE DISTILLATION

Knowledge distillation is a process in machine learning where knowledge from a complex, large model (teacher) is transferred to a smaller, simpler model (student). This technique allows the student model to perform tasks nearly as accurately as the complex model, but with greater efficiency and less computational demand. The core idea is to use the soft probabilities (logits) generated by the teacher model as "soft targets" to train the student model in addition to the usual class labels. This approach provides more information per training case than hard targets alone.

In knowledge distillation, different knowledge types, distillation strategies, and teacher-student architectures play crucial roles. The most popular form of knowledge distillation is response-based, where the student model mimics the logits of the teacher model predictions, and Kullback-Leibler divergence is commonly used for the distillation loss to align the student model with the teacher model(s).

Knowledge distillation has been used in various models, with early applications focusing on creating smaller, more efficient models for deployment on devices with limited resources. Some examples include DistilBERT, which is a distilled version of BERT, and TinyBERT, optimized for size and speed for mobile or edge devices.

In terms of performance, Zephyr 7B is comparable to much larger 70 billion parameter models. It excels in academic benchmarks and conversational capabilities, validated through rigorous testing across benchmarks like MT-Bench and AlpacaEval. These benchmarks assess conversational abilities in both single and multi-turn contexts. Zephyr 7B established new benchmarks for 7B models in these evaluations and showed competitive performance against larger models, proving the effectiveness of its training approach. The model's strengths and weaknesses across various task categories such as writing, reasoning, STEM, coding, and math have been identified through these evaluations. As you can see from the radar chart in Figure 4.1, Zephyr 7B beats a 10 times larger Llama-chat 70B model and comes close to the performance of leading models such as GPT-4 and Claude!

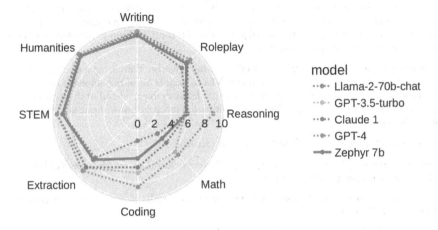

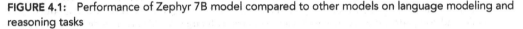

FIGURE 4.1: Performance of Zephyr 7B model compared to other models on language modeling and reasoning tasks

The development of Zephyr 7B underscores the evolving landscape of language models, demonstrating that the distillation of conversational capabilities from a large language model onto a smaller model can be achieved effectively. By leveraging the strong foundation of Mistral 7B, Zephyr 7B sets a new benchmark for 7B parameter chat models, showcasing the potential of smaller, open-source models to understand and respond to user intent effectively.

> **NOTE** *A variant of Zephyr called Notus 7B is another efficient 7 billion parameter model that performs better than several larger models on some benchmarks. Notus 7B is fine-tuned using direct preference optimization (DPO) and AI feedback. Using the same dataset (the Ultrafeedback dataset) as Zephyr, the only difference between Zephyr and Notus is the way this dataset is preprocessed. The dataset consisted of example responses, their scores as rated by GPT-4, and a rationale for this critique. While the Zephyr model used the critique scores directly, Notus used the mean of preference ratings for each of the different preference aspects, namely, helpfulness, honesty, instruction-following, and truthfulness. This led to an even better model, Notus 7B, which performed as well as the Llama 2 Chat 70B model, GPT 3.5 Turbo, and Claude 2.*

CogVLM for Language-Vision Multimodality

Visual language models (VLMs) have emerged as a promising approach for multimodal AI systems that can process and reason about images and text together. VLMs are pretrained on large datasets of image-caption pairs to acquire commonsense knowledge about the visual world and how to describe it in natural language. These models are then fine-tuned on downstream tasks such as visual question answering, image captioning, and visual grounding.

Leading VLMs like BLIP, FLAVA, and Oscar have demonstrated impressive performance, but they scale poorly due to reliance on extensive compute resources. As models grow ever larger with trillions of parameters, there is a need for more efficient model architectures that can achieve strong multimodal understanding without the same massive parameter count.

CogVLM, developed by researchers from Tsinghua University and Zhipu AI, demonstrates that smaller visual language models can outperform much larger models on various tasks. With "only" 17 billion parameters, CogVLM significantly outperforms the 55 billion parameter PaLI-X model and even the 84 billion parameter PaLM-E model on benchmarks like VQA, image captioning, and visual grounding. Of the 17 billion parameters, 10 billion are visual parameters, and 7 billion are language parameters.

The key to CogVLM's efficiency lies in its novel visual expert (VE) modules. Rather than using a shallow alignment to fuse vision and language features, CogVLM adds trainable VEs to each layer of the language model. These VEs transform the image features to deeply align with the textual features in each head of the attention mechanism. As a result, CogVLM enables much richer fusion of multimodal information without sacrificing performance on language-only tasks.

These are some key results demonstrating CogVLM's state-of-the-art efficiency:

➤ On VQA datasets like VizWiz QA and Science QA, CogVLM outperforms the much larger PaLI-X and PaLM-E models, while matching an 80 billion parameter model.

➤ Across visual grounding datasets, CogVLM sets new state-of-the-art results, significantly outperforming comparable models like PaLI-17B.

➤ For image captioning on Flickr30K, CogVLM achieves a 94.9 CIDEr score, far surpassing the 85.8 score from the 1.4 billion parameter Qwen-VL model. Note that Qwen-VL is smaller than the CogVLM model and still performs extremely well. Comparisons with larger VLMs are included here: https://arxiv.org/pdf/2308.12966.pdf.

You can see that the CogVLM model outperforms models that are multiple times its size. Smaller models also do this, but the main takeaway here is that the goal is to balance size and performance versus trying only to minimize size. Additionally, Figure 4.2 is an interesting plot showing how the 17 billion CogVLM outperforms several models, including popular (and large) models such as BLIP2 and PalmE (84B parameters) on various benchmarks.

By innovating model architecture rather than simply scaling up parameters, CogVLM points to a promising direction for efficient yet powerful visual language modeling, enabling broader applications on edge devices. For example, CogVLM is a great model to test if you need a multimodal chat application. Imagine taking a picture of an image from a textbook and asking CogVLM to explain the concept in a simple way. Another application could be technical troubleshooting using an automated service professional via a chat interface. To learn more about CogVLM, visit https://github.com/THUDM/CogVLM.

Prometheus for Fine-Grained Text Evaluation

LLMs like GPT-4 have shown promising capability as text evaluators, with the potential to match the depth of human assessment. For instance, when given an appropriate prompt and reference materials, GPT-4 can provide numerical scores and detailed feedback on machine-generated text based on customizable rubrics specified by the user. These rubrics may evaluate dimensions such as creativity, cultural sensitivity, child-safety, logical consistency, and more based on the application.

As an example from the Prometheus paper, the user could provide a rubric checking if a response is "formal enough to send to my boss," along with a reference answer exemplifying appropriateness. When given a candidate machine-generated response, GPT-4 can then output critical feedback focused on formality and professionalism, along with a 1-to-5 suitability score. The feedback rationalizes the scoring decision, evaluating relevant aspects such as tone, word choice, conciseness, etc., in light of the rubric and reference.

By accounting for subjective, nuanced criteria, this LLM evaluation approach aims to better replicate detailed human assessment than generic metrics like BLEU or ROUGE. However, reliance on proprietary models like GPT-4 raises issues of transparency, reliability, and access limitations that open-source alternatives like Prometheus aim to address.

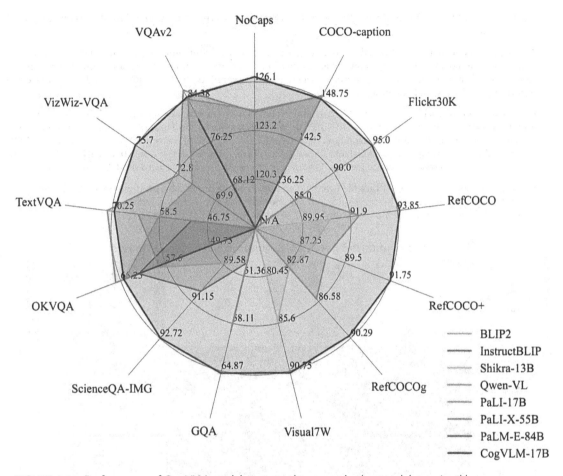

FIGURE 4.2: Performance of CogVLM model compared to several other models on visual language modeling tasks

Prometheus, from KAIST and NAVER AI Lab, shows smaller, open-source models can match GPT-4 evaluation with appropriate reference materials. With 13 billion parameters, Prometheus significantly outperforms models like 7B Llama and GPT-3.5 Turbo for customized rubrics.

Prometheus leverages the Feedback Collection, a new rubric dataset with reference answers, and GPT-4 feedback. For each rubric, there are 20 instructions with 5 responses scored 1-to-5 and corresponding feedback per instruction. This comprises 100,000 training instances. By sequentially generating feedback then scores during fine-tuning, Prometheus learns detailed critical assessment focused on text quality improvement.

The Prometheus model builds off the Llama series of models but is specially trained to induce strong text evaluation capabilities with just 13 billion parameters. In experiments, base Llama models with 7 billion, 13 billion, and even 70 billion parameters struggled to effectively evaluate customized rubrics, with Pearson correlation to GPT-4 assessments on the order of 0.5 or less. This shows that simply scaling up model size does not reliably confer stronger evaluation skills.

In contrast, by leveraging the Feedback Collection dataset and associated training approach, the 13 billion parameter Prometheus model consistently achieved correlations greater than 0.85 with GPT-4 assessments based on unseen rubrics. This far surpasses the base 13B Llama's 0.44 correlation, while even outperforming the much larger 70B Llama. Qualitatively, Prometheus generates more critical, meaningful feedback compared to all Llama variants.

The superior performance of Prometheus over larger Llama models highlights that specialized training is more impactful than model scale for inducing strong evaluation capabilities. With an order of magnitude fewer parameters, Prometheus matches proprietary models where base Llama falters, enabling accurate and affordable evaluation for the wider research community.

Results show Prometheus achieves 0.897 Pearson correlation with human scores on new rubrics, on par with even GPT-4 (0.882) and far surpassing GPT-3.5 Turbo (0.392), as shown in Figure 4.3. In pairwise comparisons, human annotators preferred Prometheus' feedback over GPT-4 58.62% of the time. Across Vicuna Bench, MT Bench, and Flask Eval datasets, Prometheus shows higher correlation to GPT-4 scores than GPT-3.5 Turbo and 70B Llama. On preference accuracy metrics, Prometheus outperforms other reward models.

By open-sourcing an accurate, affordable evaluator model, Prometheus enables progress on customizable criteria beyond coarse preferences for progress on reliability and transparency. For more information on Prometheus, please read the detailed research paper at `https://arxiv.org/pdf/2310.08491.pdf`.

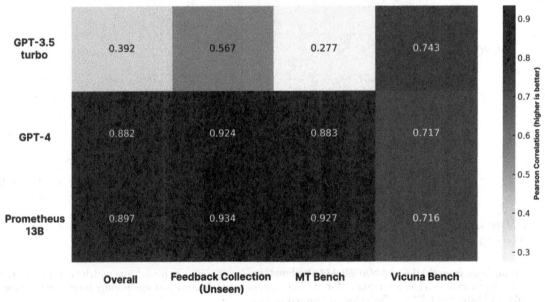

FIGURE 4.3: Pearson correlation between human annotator scores and those from GPT-3.5-Turbo, Prometheus, and GPT-4 across 45 custom rubrics. Prometheus achieves a high 0.897 correlation, similar to GPT-4 (0.882) and significantly higher than GPT-3.5-Turbo (0.392).

Orca 2 and Teaching Smaller Models to Reason

Developed by Microsoft, Orca 2 is a smaller-scale language model, designed to exhibit advanced reasoning abilities often associated with much larger models. It builds on the foundation of its predecessor, Orca, a 13 billion parameter model, but with notable enhancements in its methodology and performance. The original Orca paper can be found at `www.microsoft.com/en-us/research/publication/orca-progressive-learning-from-complex-explanation-traces-of-gpt-4`, and the latest Orca 2 paper can be found at www.microsoft.com/en-us/research/publication/orca-2-teaching-small-language-models-how-to-reason.

Orca 2 is presented in two versions, one with 7 billion and the other with 13 billion parameters. Both are derived from the Llama 2 base models and have been fine-tuned with high-quality, tailored synthetic data. This approach is crucial in teaching the model various reasoning techniques including step-by-step processing, recall then generate, recall-reason-generate, extract-generate, and direct answer methods. The model is trained to adapt its strategy depending on the task, a flexibility not typically seen in smaller models.

The training data for Orca 2 is sourced from responses generated by a more capable teacher model, such as GPT-4. This approach ensures that Orca 2 learns not just the final responses but also the underlying strategies and reasoning processes. The detailed instructions and multiple calls used to obtain the teacher's responses play a significant role in shaping Orca 2's capabilities.

Such a training methodology marks a departure from traditional models, where smaller models often lag in complex reasoning tasks. By focusing on teaching diverse reasoning techniques and the ability to select optimal strategies for various tasks, Orca 2 bridges the gap in performance usually observed between small and large models. This approach underscores the effectiveness of using carefully crafted synthetic data to enhance the reasoning capabilities of smaller models, positioning them closer to their larger counterparts in terms of performance.

Orca 2's performance is a pivotal aspect of its development, particularly when compared to larger models. This comparison was conducted using a comprehensive set of 15 diverse benchmarks, encompassing approximately 100 tasks and more than 36,000 unique test cases in zero-shot settings. These benchmarks covered various aspects including language understanding, commonsense reasoning, multistep reasoning, math problem solving, and reading comprehension.

The results of these evaluations are definitely noteworthy. Orca 2, in both its 7 billion and 13 billion parameter versions, not only matched but often surpassed the performance of much larger models, including models 5 to 10 times its size. This was particularly notable in zero-shot reasoning tasks, where Orca 2 demonstrated capabilities comparable to, or even better than, those of its larger counterparts.

These findings signify a major leap in the development of smaller language models. They showcase that with the right training and data, smaller models like Orca 2 can achieve levels of reasoning and performance that were previously thought to be exclusive to larger models. This success also highlights the potential of smaller models in scenarios where computational efficiency and high capability need to be balanced.

Orca 2, developed on the LLaMA 2 model family, shares its predecessor's limitations and those common to large language models, including biases from training data that could result in unfair or biased outputs, limited real-world understanding leading to inaccuracies, and a lack of transparency, often described as a "black-box" effect, which complicates understanding the model's decision-making process. The model may generate harmful content, and its susceptibility to hallucination, where it fabricates content, is a concern, especially as it's unclear if smaller models might be more prone to this because of reduced memorization capacities. Furthermore, Orca 2 could be misused for creating disinformation, and its performance heavily depends on the data it was trained on, potentially limiting its effectiveness in less-represented areas like math and coding. The model's responses vary with system instructions and are nondeterministic due to stochasticity. While strong in zero-shot settings, Orca 2 does not show the same improvement in few-shot learning as larger models. Its training on synthetic data, though benefiting from safety measures and guardrails within the Azure OpenAI API, necessitates further study to fully understand the associated risks. Currently, Orca 2 is intended for research only, as it has been tested solely in such settings and requires additional analysis to evaluate potential harm or bias in practical applications. This, of course, applies to many other models, large and small, discussed in this book.

While Orca 2 has these limitations, its development marks a significant step in diversifying the applications and deployment options of language models. The research on Orca 2 opens new possibilities for improved reasoning, specialization, control, and safety in smaller models.

Breaking Traditional Scaling Laws with Gemini and Phi

The scaling laws that we used in Chapter 1, like any other man-made law, fit an equation to observations or data. In this specific case, scaling laws like the Chinchilla Scaling laws predict that performance scales up proportionately to the number of parameters in a model, and/or the amount of compute you use to train the model. These laws are useful only so long as they successfully predict the performance at various scales. For example, Newton's laws of motion cannot successfully predict behavior at very large cosmic scale or very small quantum scale. A simplified version of the Chinchilla scaling law for our discussion is shown here:

$$L(N,D) = \frac{A}{N^\alpha} \quad + \quad \frac{B}{D^\beta} \quad + \quad E$$

The performance L, according to this scaling law, is a function of N the number of parameters in the model, and D, the amount of data (or for LLMs, the number of tokens) used to train the model. The value E is an irreducible (or best achievable loss). Let's ignore the other coefficients and focus on N and D for now (if you are interested, take a look at the Chinchilla paper at `https://arxiv.org/abs/2203.15556`). What the equation indicates is that (as expected) the more training data you have and the larger the model, the better your final performance is. More concretely, the loss value calculated is lower as N and D increases. However, this equation does not include a term for the quality of data, which can be a critical factor in model performance. High-quality data can significantly enhance a model's ability to generalize from its training and perform well on benchmarks. The absence of such a quality indicator means the equation does not capture scenarios where smaller models, like Phi, might outperform larger ones, such as Llama 2, on certain benchmarks. This is particularly noticeable in cases where the smaller model is trained on high-quality curated data, which can lead to it achieving better performance than a larger model trained on a more extensive, but lower-quality, dataset. The quality of data could potentially outweigh sheer volume or complexity, an aspect not considered in the current model, highlighting the importance of incorporating data quality into performance prediction equations. With this background, let's look at the Phi line of models next.

Phi 1, 1.5, and 2 B Models

Microsoft's Phi series of models challenges the conventional belief that larger model sizes are necessary for advanced capabilities. Instead, these models demonstrate that strategic choices in training and data selection can enable smaller models to achieve comparable, if not superior, performance. The Phi series, particularly Phi 2, underscores the importance of training data quality. Microsoft's approach focuses on using "textbook-quality" data, comprising synthetic datasets designed to imbue the model with commonsense reasoning and general knowledge, ranging from science to daily activities and theory of mind. This approach is complemented by a meticulous selection of web data, ensuring educational value and content quality. Such strategic data curation, combined with innovative scaling techniques, allows Phi models to break conventional language model scaling laws. Table 4.1 summarizes the compute effort for each of the three Phi models (Phi 1, 1.5, and 2), the number of A100 GPUs used, and the number of tokens in the training dataset.

TABLE 4.1: Compute effort for the Microsoft Phi series of models

MODEL	DAYS	A100 GPUS	TRAINING SIZE
Phi	4	8	54 B
Phi 1.5	8	32	150 B
Phi 2	14	96	1.4 T

You can see that the Phi models are small (less than 2 billion parameters) but are trained with significant compute resources and lots of data. Phi 2 specifically used 1.4 trillion tokens of high-quality data. This takes us back to the short discussion about the lack of a quality indicator in the scaling laws. Let's take a look at where Phi 2 stands with respect to very large models in Figure 4.4.

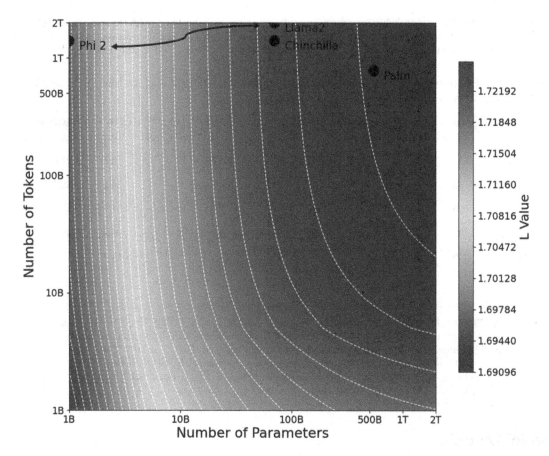

FIGURE 4.4: Visualizing the contours of the Chinchilla scaling laws with A = 406.4, B = 410, E = 1.69, a = 0.46, b = 0.54 in log 10 scale

The training data for Phi 1.5 is a composite of Phi 1's training data, consisting of 7 billion tokens, and newly developed synthetic "textbook-like" data, approximately 20 billion tokens, aimed at instilling commonsense reasoning and broad world knowledge in areas such as science and daily activities. This novel synthetic data was generated from 20,000 carefully chosen topics, using samples from web datasets to enhance diversity. It's important to note that the only nonsynthetic portion of Phi 1.5's training data includes the 6 billion tokens of filtered code dataset from Phi 1's training. The experience from developing the training data for both Phi 1 and Phi 1.5 underscores that creating a robust and comprehensive dataset demands more than sheer computational power; it requires thoughtful iterations, strategic topic selection, and a nuanced understanding of knowledge gaps to guarantee the quality and diversity of data. It's anticipated that synthesizing datasets will soon emerge as a vital technical skill and a key research area in AI.

The training corpus is further augmented with selectively curated web data, filtered to ensure high educational value and content quality. Innovative scaling techniques are employed, beginning with the 1.3 billion parameter model, Phi 1.5, and integrating its knowledge into the larger 2.7 billion parameter Phi 2 model. This method of scaled knowledge transfer not only hastens the training convergence but also significantly enhances the benchmark scores of Phi 2. Let's take a look at some extreme comparisons next.

The Chinchilla model, a 70 billion parameter model trained with 1.4 trillion tokens comes close to PaLM (540 billion parameters, 780 billion tokens). Llama 2 is a 70 billion parameter model trained with 2 trillion tokens and outperforms other larger models because it was trained with more data. But Phi 2, with the model's 2.7 billion parameters, comes close to the performance of very large models like the Llama 2 in tasks such as commonsense reasoning, language understanding and math, and it outperforms the Llama 2 70B in coding (see Table 4.2)!

TABLE 4.2: Performance of Phi 2 model compared to larger models such as Mistral 7B and Llama 7B, Llama 13B, and Llama 70B

MODEL	SIZE	BBH	COMMONSENSE REASONING	LANGUAGE UNDERSTANDING	MATH	CODING
Llama 2	7B	40.0	62.2	56.7	16.5	21.0
	13B	47.8	65.0	61.9	34.2	25.4
	70B	66.5	69.2	67.6	64.1	38.3
Mistral	7B	57.2	66.4	63.7	46.4	39.4
Phi-2	2.7B	59.2	68.8	62.0	61.1	53.7

> **NOTE** *In Table 4.2, the benchmarks span several categories, namely, Big Bench Hard (BBH) (3 shot with CoT), commonsense reasoning (PIQA, WinoGrande, ARC easy and challenge, SIQA), language understanding (HellaSwag, OpenBookQA, MMLU (5-shot), SQuADv2 (2-shot), BoolQ), math (GSM8k (8 shot)), and coding (HumanEval, MBPP (3-shot)). The original blog can be accessed at* www.microsoft.com/en-us/research/ blog/phi-2-the-surprising-power-of-small-language-models.

Gemini Models

Google's Gemini model series represents a significant leap in multimodal AI, encompassing the Ultra, Pro, and Nano models, each designed for specific complexity and operational needs. While Ultra and Pro have exhibited their prowess across a wide spectrum of benchmarks, the Nano models, particularly Gemini Nano, are remarkable for their efficiency and on-device applicability.

Across a comprehensive suite of more than 50 language understanding benchmarks, the Gemini Ultra and Pro models demonstrate state-of-the-art performance, including surpassing all other models on standardized exams, math, commonsense reasoning, coding, and translation tasks. On the Microsoft Math Language Understanding (MMLU) exam benchmark comprising multiple choice questions across 57 academic subjects (https:// github.com/hendrycks/test), Gemini Ultra achieves 90.04% accuracy, exceeding human expert performance of 89.8% for the first time. It also shows top results on mathematical reasoning across the GSM8K grade-school math benchmark (94.4% accuracy) (https://github.com/openai/grade-school-math) and high school and even university-level math problem sets like the MATH benchmark (53.2% accuracy). Additionally, Gemini models set new records on HumanEval coding tasks (74.4% accuracy) and multiple translation benchmarks like WMT23 covering high, mid, and low-resource languages (74.4 average BLEURT score). However, careful analysis reveals that many benchmarks may have train/test data leakage issues that can artificially inflate scores. As such, the team evaluated Gemini on strict decontaminated settings of benchmarks like HellaSwag (87.8% accuracy) and additionally tested performance on new held-out datasets like Math-AMC 2022-2023 problems to rigorously measure capabilities. The benchmark results underscore Gemini's versatility while highlighting the need for more robust evaluations.

Glossary

Here is a glossary of some terms used in the previous paragraph. These abbreviations are integral in the context of AI research and development, indicating various benchmarks and datasets used to measure the capabilities and progress of AI models.

➤ **MMLU:** Stands for Massive Multi-task Language Understanding. It's a comprehensive test designed to evaluate a text model's multitask accuracy in zero-shot and few-shot settings, covering 57 subjects like mathematics, history, computer science, and law. It assesses the model's world knowledge and problem-solving ability.

➤ **GSM8K:** Refers to Grade School Math 8K. This is a dataset consisting of 8,500 high-quality grade school math problems, created to evaluate the mathematical reasoning abilities of AI models.

➤ **BLEURT:** Stands for Bilingual Evaluation Understudy with Representations from Transformers. This is a metric for evaluating the quality of text generated by AI models, particularly in translation tasks. It's an advanced machine learning model trained to predict human judgments of translation quality.

➤ **WMT23:** Stands for Workshop on Machine Translation 2023. This is an event where advancements in machine translation are presented and evaluated. It's a significant conference in the field of computational linguistics focusing on machine translation technologies.

➤ **HumanEval:** Refers to coding tasks used to evaluate AI models, particularly in their ability to generate code. It's a benchmark for assessing the programming capabilities of language models.

➤ **Math-AMC 2022-2023:** Refers to problems from the American Mathematics Competitions for the years 2022–2023. It implies using these competition problems to test the capabilities of AI models in solving advanced mathematical problems.

The Gemini models release comprises three main sizes to support diverse applications. Gemini Ultra is the most capable variant, designed to push the frontier of performance on highly complex reasoning and multimodal tasks. On the other end of the spectrum, Gemini Nano is engineered specifically for on-device deployments where latency and memory constraints are critical.

Two Nano versions were developed, with 1.8 billion and 3.25 billion parameters, targeting low and high memory mobile devices, respectively. Despite their diminutive size compared to other Gemini variants, the Nano models demonstrate surprisingly strong competencies. When evaluated on an extensive suite of more than 50 language benchmarks spanning factual knowledge, reasoning ability, creativity, and other metrics, Gemini Nano 1 and 2 exhibited normalized scores between 0.4 to 0.9 times the much larger Gemini Pro model (see Figure 4.5).

For the Gemini nano models, particularly high relative performance was achieved on factual knowledge tasks such as Boolean question answering and summarization. More surprisingly, the Nano models also showed respectable aptitude on STEM exams, coding problems, multimodal tasks, and even non-English benchmarks when measured versus Pro. The efficiency optimizations applied to develop this new caliber of tiny yet mighty models open up an exciting frontier. Bringing such broad intelligence and multimodal understanding to ubiquitous mobile devices unlocks new on-device applications powered by Gemini Nano's versatility. At the same time, the strong indication that additional breakthroughs in efficiency may further reduce the computing demands of advanced AI presents encouraging possibilities for the future.

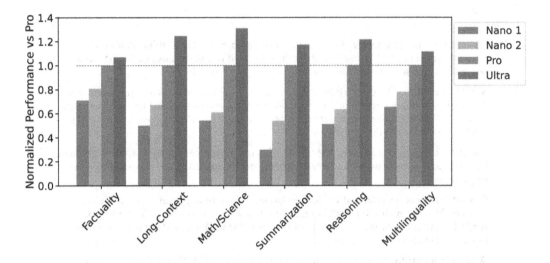

FIGURE 4.5: Relative performance of the Gemini Nano models compared to the larger Pro and Ultra models

DOMAIN-SPECIFIC MODELS

Since the development of LLMs, there has been pockets of interest in creating domain- or vertical-specific models that excel at multiple tasks within that domain. Intuitively, a model that is trained or fine-tuned with domain-specific data ought to be better than general-purpose models. In general, you can follow these two steps to create a domain-specific model:

1. Create a domain-specific tokenizer that can learn special vocabulary for your domain.

2. Use your new tokenizer to train or fine-tune a new model.

Why do we need to follow these steps? Training a new tokenizer is crucial when creating a domain-specific LLM, particularly in specialized fields like medicine and finance, due to the unique linguistic characteristics and terminology in these domains. A study highlighted the significant impact of tokenizer choice on LLM's downstream performance, training, and inference costs.

In medical and financial contexts, standard tokenizers might not efficiently capture the nuances of domain-specific language, leading to suboptimal model performance. For instance, in the medical field, where terminology is highly specialized and often involves complex compound words, a custom tokenizer can more effectively segment and understand these terms. Similarly, in finance, where specific jargon, numerical data, and unique compound words are common, a domain-specific tokenizer can accurately parse and interpret such language, enhancing the LLM's understanding and performance in these specific contexts.

Let's dive into an example within the financial field. Suppose you are using the standard OpenAI tokenizer, and you want to tokenize the following sentence in your training data:

```
Alphabet Inc Class A (GOOGL) is Alphabet's class A share, also known as common
stock. Alphabet' Class C shares are GOOG, which do not grant voting rights
```

The tokenizer (visualized using `https://platform.openai.com/tokenizer`) would give the output shown in Figure 4.6.

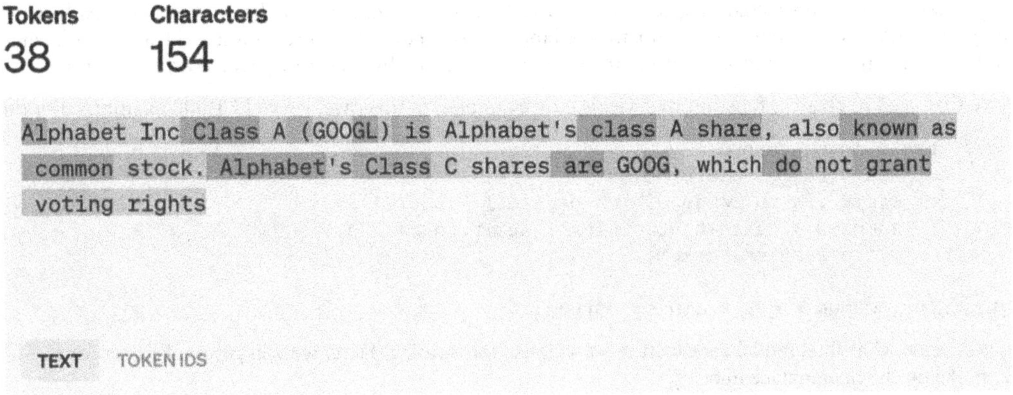

Tokens   Characters
38   **154**

Alphabet Inc Class A (GOOGL) is Alphabet's class A share, also known as
common stock. Alphabet's Class C shares are GOOG, which do not grant
voting rights

TEXT   TOKEN IDS

FIGURE 4.6: Output from a generic tokenizer on financial data

As you can see in Figure 4.6, the generic tiktoken tokenizer, which was trained with a large, generic corpora, splits the stock ticker symbols GOOG and GOOGL differently. The first token is common ("GO"), but the following tokens are different ("OG," "O," and "GL"). A trained tokenizer for the financial domain may see the slightly more frequent occurrence of GOOG and GOOGL in the data and decide to create a new token for "GOOG" (assuming a different token for "L" exists) to then refer to these symbols at a later point. Now, the performance impact of a tokenizer cannot be studied independently; we will need to do an end-to-end comparison of the same model using the generic tokenizer versus the domain-specific one. Now let's go into the details of the steps mentioned earlier.

Step 1 - Training Your Own Tokenizer

Now, let's look at how a new, domain-specific tokenizer can be trained. In this walk-through, we will continue exploring the stock example. We first need a dataset with relevant items; in this case, we will start with a stock tweets dataset from the Huggingface hub:

```
from datasets import load_dataset
raw_datasets = load_dataset("StephanAkkerman/stock-market-tweets-data","train")
```

This raw dataset contains close to a million stock-related tweets:

```
# Output of raw_datasets['train']

Dataset({
    features: ['id', 'created_at', 'text'],
    num_rows: 923673
})
```

What we are interested in is the raw "text" from each item in this dataset. Let's take a look at some examples:

➤ Pfizer Shares Acquired by Ipswich Investment Management $PFE https://t.co/gqXxIbbxIS

➤ Editor's Choice: Three Deals Needed ahead of Holiday Weekend @marcmakingsense $FXY $FXA $SPX $OIL $FXB $ACWI $FXE https://t.co/ozXzTbD8dM

➤ Treasury Secretary Mnuchin says US could be open for business in May from @CNBC $spx $ndx $biib $mrna $bntx $amzn $cost $wmt $gild https://t.co/eup9IRFyVZ

➤ Zacks: Brokerages Anticipate Fastenal $FAST Will Post Earnings of $0.34 Per Share https://t.co/mloI4GRLE7 #stocks

➤ RT @TDANetwork: 🎥 #TheWatchList panel assesses the big questions $AAPL will face over the next 6 months. 👏 📱

As you can see, these tweets include a special syntax for discussions about stocks: the $ symbol is usually followed by the stock ticker to refer to a company, the language is peculiar to stock trading, and special references are made to companies and analysts by using the @ symbol followed by their respective Twitter handles.

Now, we first need to create a function that yields new examples; in this case, we yield 1,000 examples at a time:

```python
def get_training_corpus():
    dataset = raw_datasets["train"]
    for start_idx in range(0, len(dataset), 1000):
        samples = dataset[start_idx : start_idx + 1000]
        yield samples["text"]

training_corpus = get_training_corpus()
```

Then, we decide what final model architecture we will use for training. Here, we will get a tokenizer for the GPT2 model on the huggingface hub:

```python
from transformers import AutoTokenizer
old_tokenizer = AutoTokenizer.from_pretrained("gpt2")
```

Lastly, we set the vocabulary size to 64000 (user defined) and then train our new tokenizer. That's it!

```python
new_tokenizer = old_tokenizer.train_new_from_iterator(training_corpus, 64000)
```

With close to a million examples, this training took about 2 minutes on a g5.4xlarge instance on AWS. It was definitely worth the wait. We can now compare the results between the old and the new tokenizer. Let's pick an input sentence for the comparison:

RT @TDANetwork: 🎥 #TheWatchList panel assesses the big questions $AAPL will face over the next 6 months. 🐻 📱

This is an interesting example as it contains references to TDA Network (the TD Ameritrade Network creates timely, relevant content by interpreting market news and conditions), hashtags (#), stock references ($AAPL), and emojis.

We can print the output tokens from each tokenizer using the following code:

```python
print(tokenizer.tokenize(example))
```

Now let's compare the tokens generated from the old and new tokenizers. As you can see in Figure 4.7, "A" captures the result of the old tokenizer, and "B" is for the new tokenizer. The center column, "A∩B," shows the tokens that are common to both tokenizers.

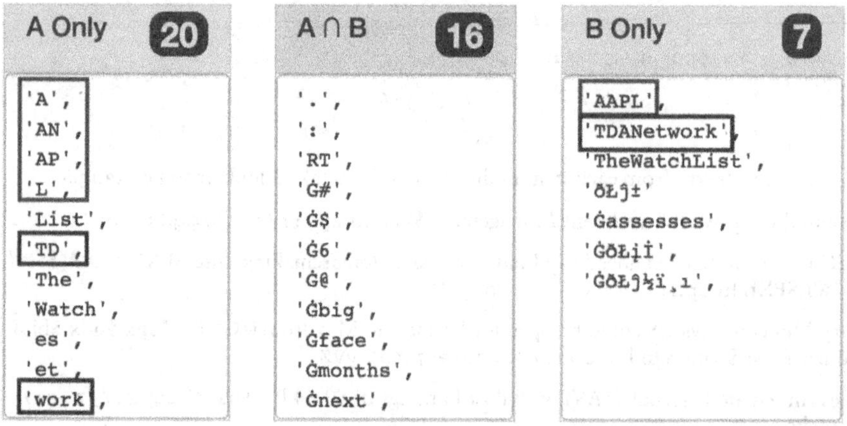

A Only 20	A ∩ B 16	B Only 7
'A',	'.',	'AAPL',
'AN',	':',	'TDANetwork',
'AP',	'RT',	'TheWatchList',
'L',	'Ġ#',	'ĠŁɟ±'
'List',	'Ġ$',	'Ġassesses',
'TD',	'Ġ6',	'ĠŏŁįİ',
'The',	'Ġ@',	'ĠŏŁɟĸİ,ı',
'Watch',	'Ġbig',	
'es',	'Ġface',	
'et',	'Ġmonths',	
'work',	'Ġnext',	

FIGURE 4.7: Comparing the outputs from the generic tokenizer, and a trained domain-specific tokenizer with stock tweets data

From Figure 4.7, you can observe a few points:

➤ A significant number of tokens are common between the two tokenizers.

➤ The new tokenizer has longer tokens, but a fewer number of tokens. This is an indication of specialization in this domain.

➤ The new tokenizer identifies special tokens like AAPL (red) and TDAnetwork (blue). The old tokenizer splits the stock symbol to A, AP, and L (also highlighted within boxes on the left).

In this section, we trained a domain-specific tokenizer trained on relevant corpora, which is essential for optimizing the performance of LLMs in specialized fields like medicine and finance, ensuring that the models are not only linguistically accurate but also contextually aware of the domain-specific nuances. Next, we can talk about training your own custom domain specific model.

Step 2 - Training Your Own Domain-Specific Model

Now that you have your own domain-specific tokenizer, there are two ways to train your own domain-specific model:

➤ Start from scratch and pretrain a model based on a well-known architecture and custom data.

➤ Start from a generic model and fine-tune it with custom data.

In Chapter 2, we talked in more detail about training, fine-tuning, and parameter efficient fine-tuning (PEFT). We also discussed at length why many organizations choose to fine-tune existing models. Let's once again visit the scaling laws, and assume your organization is interested in pretraining their own foundational model for finance. Leadership usually may justify this effort by claiming this foundation model will end up powering every future GenAI application, and fine-tuning this foundation model to downstream tasks within the company can be much more efficient, overall leading to higher ROI.

Another version of the scaling laws we visited earlier can help make this decision:

$$\tau \cdot T \cong 6 \cdot N \cdot D$$

Here, τ is the total compute that you have access to in your training cluster, measured in floating-point operations per second (FLOPS). FLOPS is a unit of measurement that calculates a computer's performance based on how many floating-point arithmetic calculations its processor can perform in one second. With deep learning applications, FLOPS also measures the performance of the entire compute cluster and not a single computer. T is the training time, and N and D are (similar to the earlier scaling law) the number of model parameters and number of tokens of training data, respectively.

Back to the case of the financial services company interested in training its own foundational model. Suppose the company decides to train this model with a cluster that is made up of the best-in-class NVIDIA GPU (an A100 or H100). Further assume the company is interested in training a 1 trillion parameter model and plans to create a dataset of 1 trillion tokens. The company would like to finish up this training within 100 days. When plugging in these values in the equation and using the average compute throughput for these GPUs, the company would need about 2225 GPUs of this class, assuming all goes well in training. Figure 4.8 shows different models placed on a scale of number of parameters and the optimal compute capacity needed.

For our fictitious financial-services company, this translates to using, for example, 278 P4de GPU instances on AWS, which would cost about $21.865 million! Not to mention the cost of preparing and curating the 1 trillion token dataset from the company's internal resources.

What may be a quicker, cheaper, but perhaps as rewarding of an endeavor is to train and fine-tune a smaller, existing model. As you have seen with the case studies in this chapter, smaller models, especially when they are trained with curated data, can yield surprisingly good results, sometimes surpassing the performance of models that are much larger in size.

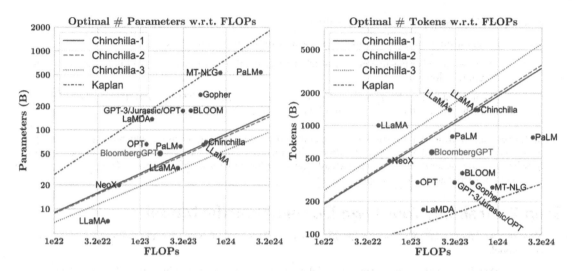

FIGURE 4.8: Compute capacity required to train different models. Adapted from the BloombergGPT paper at `https://arxiv.org/pdf/2303.17564.pdf`.

Today, several options exist for fine-tuning models once you have collected and curated your data. Data curation is no mean feat—this may in fact control how good your final model is. Once you have collected and organized your data, here are the many ways you can train your own model, based on where you want to do this:

Train a Model Locally with Your Own GPU Resources

First, load the dataset from local drives or a public dataset from the huggingface hub:

```
from datasets import load_dataset

dataset = load_dataset("curated_data")
```

We can now use our custom tokenizer from earlier to preprocess the text. This includes implementing a padding and truncation strategy to accommodate variable sequence lengths. For the efficient processing of a dataset in a single step, one should employ the huggingface Datasets map method. This method enables the application of a preprocessing function across the entire dataset.

```
from transformers import AutoTokenizer

tokenizer = AutoTokenizer.from_pretrained("new_tokenizer")

def tokenize_function(examples):
    return tokenizer(examples["text"], padding="max_length", truncation=True)

tokenized_datasets = dataset.map(tokenize_function, batched=True)
```

WAYS TO FINE-TUNE A MODEL

Typically, when we say "fine-tune a model," we are talking about causal language modeling. Causal Language Modeling (CLM) and Masked Language Modeling (MLM) are two distinct approaches used in natural language processing (NLP).

➤ **Causal Language Modeling:** CLM is a unidirectional approach where the model predicts the next token in a sequence based on the previous tokens. The model considers the context only to the left of the current position, making it suitable for tasks such as text generation. It doesn't see or use future tokens in its predictions. An example of a CLM model is GPT-2.

➤ **Masked Language Modeling:** In contrast, MLM is a bidirectional approach. A certain percentage of tokens in a sentence are masked, and the model is trained to predict these masked tokens based on the context from both the left and right sides of the mask. This approach allows the model to have a full understanding of the context within a sentence. MLM is particularly effective for tasks requiring deep contextual understanding. BERT is an example of an MLM model.

While CLM is more geared toward generative tasks, MLM excels in tasks requiring an understanding of context and relationships within a sentence. Both approaches have their unique advantages and are chosen based on the specific requirements of the NLP task at hand.

Now back to the task at hand. The huggingface library provides a very easy way to fine-tune an existing model. Recall that we used the GPT2 tokenizer. We will be fine-tuning the GPT2 model on huggingface next, starting with loading the model:

```
from transformers import AutoModelForCausalLM, TrainingArguments, Trainer

model = AutoModelForCausalLM.from_pretrained("gpt2")
```

Now that your model is loaded, you can create your training arguments, specify hyperparameters, and train your domain-specific model:

```
training_args = TrainingArguments(
    output_dir="my_awesome_domain_specific_model",
    evaluation_strategy="epoch",
    learning_rate=1e-5
)

trainer = Trainer(
    model=model,
    args=training_args,
    train_dataset=tokenized_dataset,
    data_collator=data_collator,
)

trainer.train()
```

This is great when you have a local GPU instance (or access to an on-prem cluster). But what do you do when the only computer you have access to is your laptop, with no access to GPUs? Let's explore the cloud training option next.

Train a model with remote GPU resources

Training the same model on the cloud is made very easy with tools like Amazon SageMaker. All we need to do is create a function with all the previous code and add a "remote" decorator:

```
#import sagemaker remote function decorator
from sagemaker.remote_function import remote

#import other libraries you need, like:

import torch
from transformers import AutoModelForCausalLM, BitsAndBytesConfig
import transformers
```

```
@remote(instance_type="ml.g5.12xlarge")
def train_fn(
        model_name,
        tokenized_dataset,
        per_device_train_batch_size=8,
        training_args):
```

Now when you call the `train_fn` function, Amazon SageMaker will bring up a dedicated g5.12xlarge GPU instance with four NVIDIA A10G GPUs to train your model. This lets you scale out your training to larger datasets or models.

Train a model with low- or no-code

Several tools emerged in 2023 for fine-tuning models with little or no code. One of the easiest ways to do this is with the huggingface Autotrain functionality. Autotrain creates a custom space on huggingface online that can help you fine-tune your own models using huggingface resources. It lets you select a stack and an instance type you want to base this training on, as shown in Figure 4.9.

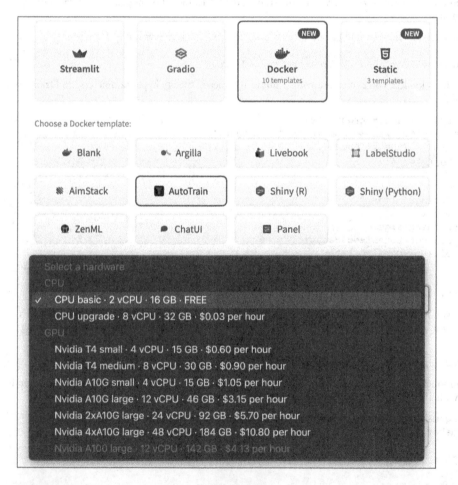

FIGURE 4.9: Setting up Autotrain on huggingface

Once the space is set up, you can create a project for fine-tuning the model by selecting the appropriate drop-down, as shown in Figure 4.10. More advanced use cases such as aligning your model using direct preference optimization (DPO), for example, are also shown.

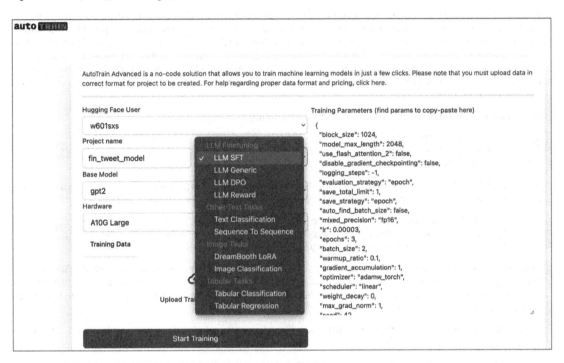

FIGURE 4.10: Creating a training job in Autotrain on huggingface

Other commercial services also provide great ways to easily fine-tune their proprietary base models with your data. OpenAI, one of the leading providers of foundational models, also provides a way to fine-tune models with your own data. Specifically focusing on smaller models, you can try fine-tuning the davinci and babbage models. Larger models like GPT3.5 Turbo can also be trained, while fine-tuning with GPT-4, their largest and most capable model, is an experimental feature at the time of this writing.

> **NOTE** *The OpenAI documentation on fine-tuning provides good guidance on when to do fine-tuning (https://platform.openai.com/docs/guides/fine-tuning/when-to-use-fine-tuning). Fine-tuning OpenAI's text generation models is beneficial for specific tasks but requires considerable time and effort. The guide advises to first try improving results through prompt engineering, prompt chaining (simplifying complex tasks into multiple prompts), and function calling for several reasons. Often, refining prompts can significantly enhance performance, making fine-tuning unnecessary. Prompt iteration is faster than fine-tuning, which involves dataset creation and training, as detailed in this section. If fine-tuning is needed, prior prompt engineering efforts are still valuable. Effective strategies for enhanced performance without fine-tuning are detailed in the OpenAI prompt engineering guide.*

Amazon Bedrock is a service on AWS that provides access to leading Amazon-built as well as external (e.g., Claude) models as you saw in previous chapters. As of November 2023, Bedrock also provides functionality to create custom models.

Amazon Bedrock allows users to fine-tune models to their specific needs through fine-tuning jobs or to extend model training via continued pre-training jobs. Begin by uploading your training and, if applicable, validation datasets to Amazon S3, supplying the S3 path to the job. While each model comes with preset hyperparameter values, these can be customized to influence the training process, with more details available in the console guide. After completing a model customization job, you can enable provisioned throughput for inference using API operations, as detailed in the "Run Inference Using Provisioned Throughput" section. For hands-on exploration, the text playground is available.

For continued pre-training jobs, you first create your training dataset as follows:

```
{"input": "<input text>"}
{"input": "<input text>"}
{"input": "<input text>"}
```

This is useful for domain adaptation. You may also have a task in mind within this domain (for example, sentiment analysis for financial tweets). For this, you prepare data for a fine-tuning job as follows:

```
{"prompt": "<prompt text>", "completion": "<expected generated text>"}
{"prompt": "<prompt text>", "completion": "<expected generated text>"}
{"prompt": "<prompt text>", "completion": "<expected generated text>"}
```

Once you create your dataset, you can upload this to Amazon S3, and then follow prompts on the Amazon Bedrock page, as shown in Figure 4.11. After pointing to your dataset and setting a few important hyperparameters like learning rate, batch size, and epochs, you can create your custom model by clicking Create Continued Pre-training Job or Fine-Tuning Job.

Similar functionality exists in other cloud providers like Microsoft and Google. For example, Vertex AI from Google supports three ways to fine-tune:

➤ **Supervised tuning:** Ideal for simple outputs in text models. Best for classification, sentiment analysis, entity extraction, simple content summarization, and domain-specific queries. The only option for code models.

➤ **Reinforcement learning from human feedback (RLHF) tuning:** Suitable for complex model outputs. Effective for question answering, complex content summarization, and creative content rewriting. Not supported for code models.

➤ **Tuning and distillation:** Optimal for reducing the size of large models without compromising performance. Results in a smaller, cost-effective model with lower latency.

Let's take a look at the basic supervised training. Once again, we follow three simple steps:

1. Prepare your data.

2. Upload to a cloud storage bucket.

3. Create a fine-tuning job.

As you can imagine, each cloud provider may have a slightly different data format requirement. For Vertex AI, the training data consists of pairs of input and output sentences and may look like this:

```
{"input_text": "question: How many copies of Gears of War 3 were sold?
context: Like its predecessors , the game received widespread critical
acclaim from critics . Critics praised its story , voice acting ,
graphics and visuals , and music , but criticized its lack of innovation .
Gears of War 3 sold over 3 million copies and was the second best
```

```
selling game in the U . S . ", "output_text": "over 3 million copies"}
{"input_text": "question:..", "output_text": "…"}

{"input_text": "question:..", "output_text": "…"}

{"input_text": "question:..", "output_text": "…"}

...
```

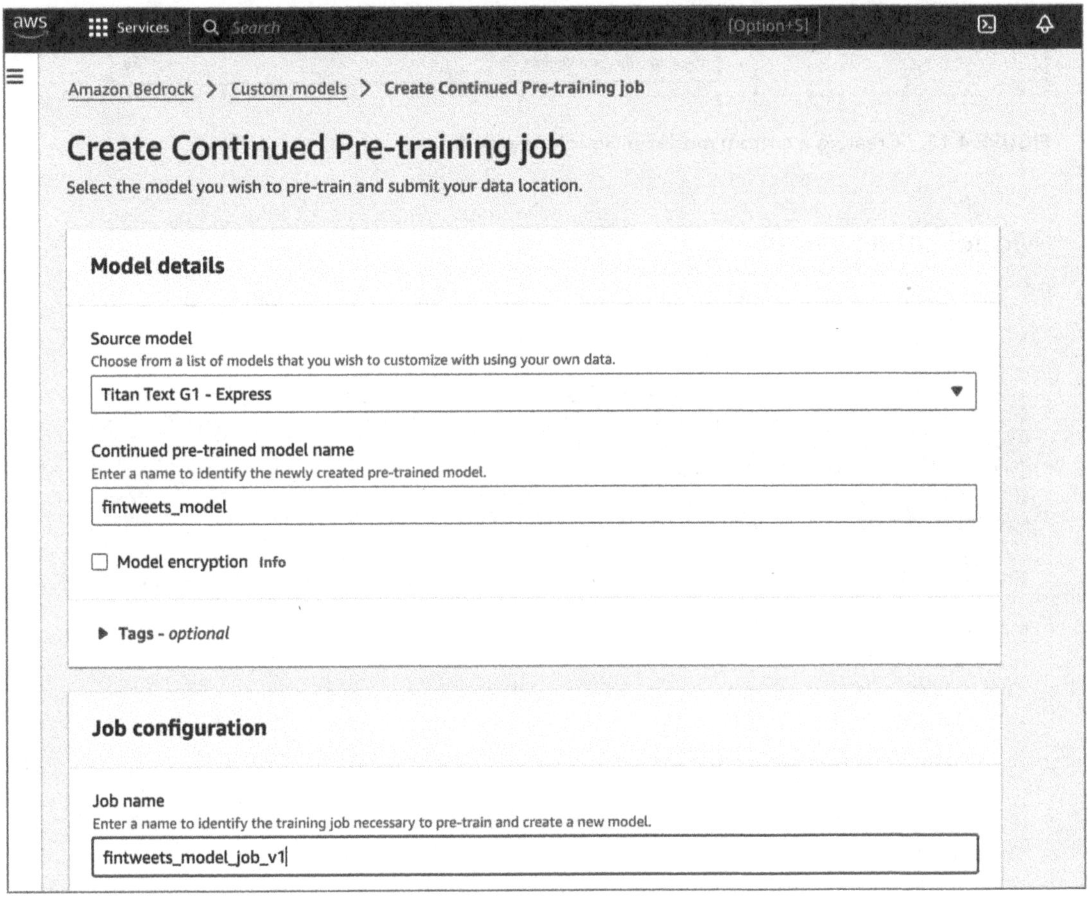

FIGURE 4.11: Creating a custom model in Amazon Bedrock

Once you have uploaded this training data to a storage bucket, you can then create a tuned model following the wizard in the Vertex AI console, as shown in Figure 4.12.

Similarly, Microsoft Azure Machine Learning also lets you easily create custom fine-tuned models. The steps broadly remain the same as what we saw earlier, going from preparing the data according to the format (check out the link in the "More References for Fine-Tuning " section) and then walking through a wizard for selecting and fine-tuning a custom model based on several available base models, as shown in Figure 4.13.

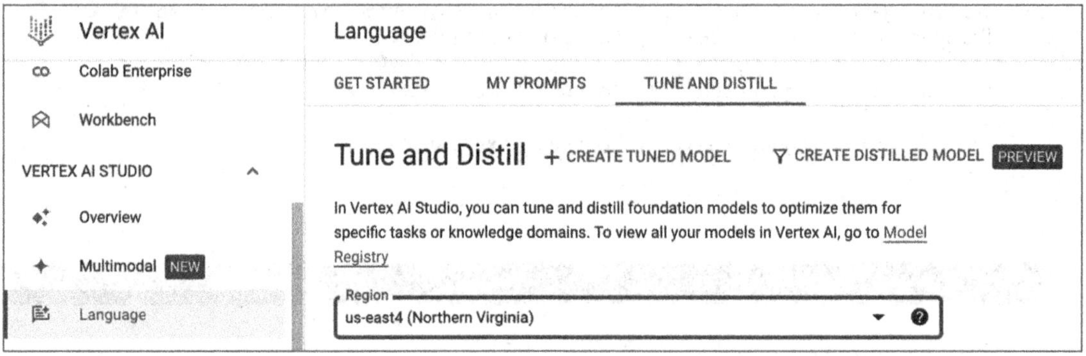

FIGURE 4.12: Creating a custom model in Google Vertex AI

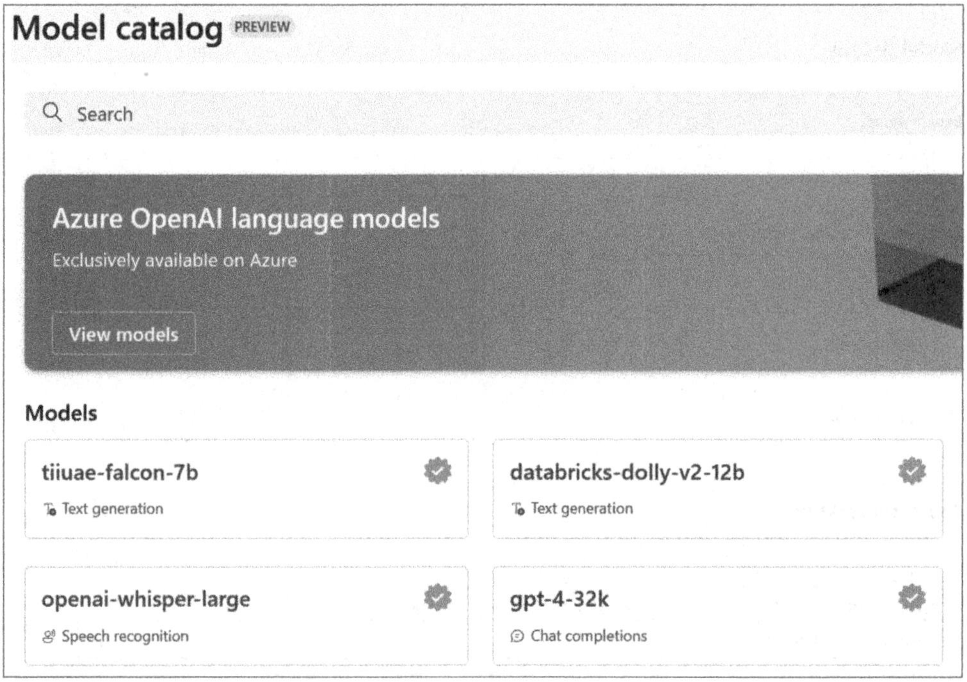

FIGURE 4.13: Creating a custom model in Microsoft Azure

More References for Fine-Tuning

Here are more references for fine-tuning:

➤ **Fine-tuning a pretrained model using huggingface libraries:** `https://huggingface.co/docs/transformers/training`

➤ **Loading datasets locally:** `https://huggingface.co/docs/datasets/loading`

➤ **CLM tutorial:** `https://huggingface.co/docs/transformers/tasks/language_modeling`

➤ **Training arguments:** `https://huggingface.co/docs/transformers/v4.36.1/en/main_classes/trainer#transformers.TrainingArguments`

➤ **Run local code as a remote training job:** `https://docs.aws.amazon.com/sagemaker/latest/dg/train-remote-decorator.html`

➤ **Huggingface Autotrain:** `https://huggingface.co/autotrain`

➤ **OpenAI fine-tuning:** `https://platform.openai.com/docs/guides/fine-tuning`

➤ **OpenAI prompt engineering guide:** `https://platform.openai.com/docs/guides/prompt-engineering`

➤ **Amazon Bedrock fine-tuning:** `https://docs.aws.amazon.com/bedrock/latest/userguide/custom-models.html`

➤ **Amazon Bedrock fine-tuning with no code on the console:** `https://docs.aws.amazon.com/bedrock/latest/userguide/model-customization-submit.html`

➤ **Fine-tuning foundation models on Vertex AI:** `https://cloud.google.com/vertex-ai/docs/generative-ai/models/tune-models`

Evaluating Domain-Specific Models vs. Generic Models

Domain-specific models are becoming increasingly popular as they can adapt better to the specific requirements of a domain, utilize resources more efficiently, and provide powerful language processing capabilities tailored to address particular challenges and tasks. They represent a significant advancement in the field of AI, offering more targeted and effective solutions compared to their general-purpose counterparts. What is important to note is that the evaluation of domain-specific models is as important as the custom fine-tuning.

Developing domain-specific models has traditionally been very challenging. Large enterprises have to create a strong horizontal data strategy to collect, curate, and use domain-specific data for model training and evaluation. In several domains, this data can be sensitive, protected, or both. This is especially true in the financial services and medical domain. Another major challenge when developing domain-specific models is the need for specialized expertise and knowledge, both in the domain itself and in AI modeling techniques. Experts in the field are required to accurately interpret the data, understand the nuances of the domain, and guide the model's training process to ensure it captures the necessary details and subtleties. Additionally, the complexity of certain domains can lead to difficulties in model validation and the need for robust, domain-specific metrics to assess model performance accurately.

As you read in this chapter, there are several easy ways to train your own domain- or task-specific model. Task-specific models themselves are useful only when you create one for a particular domain (think of predicting stock buy-sell-hold signals from financial tweets versus predicting buy-sell-hold signals from all tweets about all topics). There are three main ways of evaluating a domain-specific model:

➤ **Evaluate your trained model against a gold-standard, curated test dataset.** These datasets are created with significant effort with the help of a human workforce that is made up of subject-matter experts within the domain of choice. Every major cloud provider that lets you train a custom model as we discussed also lets you create and test your model with an evaluation dataset.

➤ **Evaluate your custom model that is task-specific, with a task-agnostic but domain-aligned larger foundation model.** Foundation models like GPT-4 can also be used to judge and more importantly score the outputs based on accuracy, usefulness, bias, toxicity, etc.

➤ **Use subject-matter experts to evaluate a select number of responses.** This is done in a way that the experts vote on which output they prefer without knowing which model generated each output (single blind).

Let's look at the first option. Take the BloombergGPT model we discussed earlier; it exemplifies the trend toward domain-specific large language models for large organizations with high-quality, curated internal data. Unlike general-purpose LLMs trained on diverse datasets to handle a wide range of tasks, domain-specific LLMs like BloombergGPT are tailored for particular sectors. BloombergGPT, in particular, is designed for the finance sector and is trained on a dataset specifically curated with financial data, making it highly specialized and efficient for finance-related tasks.

In the case of BloombergGPT, it's trained on a mix of domain-specific data from Bloomberg's extensive financial data sources and general-purpose datasets. This approach ensures that the model not only excels in finance-related tasks but also maintains a good performance on general LLM benchmarks.

The section on evaluation from the original BloombergGPT paper (https://arxiv.org/pdf/2303.17564 .pdf) provides a comprehensive evaluation of BloombergGPT's capabilities across two main domains: finance-specific and general-purpose tasks. The evaluation is structured to test the hypothesis that training Bloomberg-GPT on high-quality, finance-specific data enhances its performance on financial tasks. To this end, a variety of publicly available financial datasets encompassing different NLP tasks were utilized. Additionally, Bloomberg-GPT's proficiency in tasks pertinent to Bloomberg, such as sentiment analysis and named entity recognition, was assessed using high-quality, internal Bloomberg datasets.

In the realm of general-purpose tasks, the model's performance was benchmarked against existing standards with models of comparable sizes like GPT-NeoX, OPT, and BLOOM. The tasks were categorized into four groups: BIG-bench Hard, Knowledge Assessments, Reading Comprehension, and Linguistic Tasks. These categories were chosen to provide a broad spectrum assessment of BloombergGPT's general capabilities. The specific number of tasks in each category and their definitions are detailed in Table 5 of the paper. This structured approach allowed for a thorough examination of BloombergGPT's performance in both specialized and broad applications.

Figure 4.14 summarizes the performance of BloombergGPT on various finance-specific tasks. Except for one named entity recognition (NER) task where the GPT NeoX slightly outperforms this domain-specific model, BloombergGPT is shown to excel at multiple tasks that may be relevant to their business.

	BloombergGPT	GPT-NeoX	OPT$_{66B}$	BLOOM$_{176B}$
ConvFinQA	**43.41**	30.06	27.88	36.31
FiQA SA	**75.07**	50.59	51.60	53.12
FPB	**51.07**	44.64	48.67	50.25
Headline	**82.20**	73.22	79.41	76.51
NER	60.82	**60.98**	57.49	55.56
All Tasks *(avg)*	**62.51**	51.90	53.01	54.35
All Tasks *(WR)*	**0.93**	0.27	0.33	0.47

FIGURE 4.14: Evaluating domain-specific models: BloomberGPT results on financial domain tasks

Let's shift gears from the earlier financial services example into the medical domain. This time, we will manually judge the performance on some curated questions. Recall that this needs to happen at scale to be useful: a large group of domain experts need to collectively label this data (sometimes called *preference data*) to indicate which model outputs they prefer. Additionally, when multiple models are involved, a subset of the models can all be correct. However, the domain experts may prefer one model's output over all others. This feedback can be used to "align" the model using techniques like reinforcement learning with human feedback (RLHF) or direct preference optimization (DPO).

We will discuss two examples comparing the output of a domain-specific model in the medical domain (GPT MD) to the best-in-class general-purpose models like GPT-4. Each example has a prompt (input), followed by the output from the custom GPT MD model, GPT-4, and Google Bard. We then end with some general observations.

Example 1

Prompt:

> The most common cause of GERD (Gastroesophageal Reflux Disease) in adults is …

GPT MD:

> The most common cause of GERD (Gastroesophageal Reflux Disease) in adults is hiatal hernia (a small hole between the diaphragm and stomach). Hiatal hernias are often caused by poor posture or stress. Other possible causes include smoking, obesity, alcohol use disorder, chronic cough, asthma, pregnancy, diabetes, medications like proton pump inhibitors and histamine blockers, etc.

GPT-4:

> The most common cause of GERD (Gastroesophageal Reflux Disease) in adults is a weakened or dysfunctional lower esophageal sphincter (LES). The LES is a ring of muscle at the bottom of the esophagus that acts like a valve between the esophagus and the stomach. When it doesn't function properly, it allows stomach acid and contents to flow back (reflux) into the esophagus, which can lead to symptoms and complications of GERD. Factors that can contribute to this condition include obesity, pregnancy, certain medications, smoking, and certain foods and drinks.

GOOGLE BARD:

> While there are several contributing factors to GERD in adults, the most common cause is transient lower esophageal sphincter relaxations (TLESRs).
> TLESRs are brief moments where the lower esophageal sphincter (LES), the valve between your stomach and esophagus, relaxes unexpectedly. This allows stomach contents, including acid, to flow back up into the esophagus, causing the uncomfortable symptoms of GERD, such as heartburn, chest pain, and regurgitation.
>
> While the exact cause of TLESRs is still not fully understood, some factors that can contribute to their occurrence include:
>
> Dietary factors: Certain foods like fatty or spicy meals, chocolate, and caffeine can trigger TLESRs.
>
> Lifestyle habits: Smoking, alcohol consumption, and obesity can also increase the risk of TLESRs.
> Certain medications: Some medications, such as nitrates and calcium channel blockers, can weaken the LES and lead to TLESRs.
>
> Pregnancy: Hormonal changes during pregnancy can also relax the LES and contribute to GERD.
> It's important to note that while TLESRs are the most common cause of GERD, other factors like hiatal hernias (a condition where the upper part of the stomach bulges through the diaphragm) and delayed stomach emptying can also play a role in its development.
>
> If you're experiencing symptoms of GERD, it's important to talk to your doctor to get a diagnosis and discuss potential treatment options.
>
>
> I hope this information is helpful! Let me know if you have any other questions about GERD.

COMPARATIVE ANALYSIS:

GPT MD is notably specific, identifying a hiatal hernia as the most common cause of GERD. This detailed approach may provide a more useful perspective for those seeking precise medical explanations or for healthcare professionals looking for a clear diagnostic focus.

GPT-4 offers a broader explanation, concentrating on the dysfunction of the lower esophageal sphincter (LES) without narrowing it down to a specific condition like a hiatal hernia. This general approach may be more informative for individuals trying to understand the overall mechanism of GERD.

Google Bard introduces transient lower esophageal sphincter relaxations (TLESRs) as the primary cause, which differs from GPT MD's emphasis on hiatal hernias. This points to a disagreement between the models about what is considered the "most common" cause.

The disagreement between GPT MD and Google Bard could reflect variations in their training datasets or differences in how they prioritize medical literature.

All models agree on the multifactorial nature of GERD, citing lifestyle, dietary choices, and medications as contributing factors, but they differ in which factor they consider to be most prevalent.

Despite GPT MD and Google Bard both mentioning hiatal hernias, they place different degrees of emphasis on its role, which could potentially lead to varied clinical interpretations.

Finally, Google Bard uniquely provides action-oriented advice, encouraging readers to seek medical consultation, which could be particularly valuable for those experiencing GERD symptoms and seeking guidance on the next steps. Whether in the financial, medical, or other domains, it is a good idea to train your model to be honest about its capabilities and redirect the user to human help.

Example 2

Prompt:

```
What class of drug is each medication listed below:
1. atorvastatin
2. prednisolone
3. celecoxib
4. Prozac
Class of each drug above:
```

GPT MD:

```
1. HMG-CoA reductase inhibitor (statin)
2. Glucocorticoid steroid
3. COX 2 selective NSAID
4. Selective serotonin reuptake inhibitor (SSRI).
```

GPT 4:

```
The class of each medication listed is as follows:

1. Atorvastatin: Statin (cholesterol-lowering medication)
2. Prednisolone: Corticosteroid (anti-inflammatory)
3. Celecoxib: Nonsteroidal anti-inflammatory drug (NSAID), specifically a COX-2
inhibitor
4. Prozac (Fluoxetine): Selective serotonin reuptake inhibitor (SSRI)
(antidepressant)
```

Google Bard:

```
Here's the class of each medication listed:
1. atorvastatin: HMG-CoA reductase inhibitor (statin) - used for lowering
cholesterol.
```

```
2. prednisolone: Glucocorticoid steroid - used for reducing inflammation and
suppressing the immune system.
3. celecoxib: COX-2 inhibitor (nonsteroidal anti-inflammatory drug, NSAID) - used
for pain relief and inflammation.
4. Prozac (fluoxetine): Selective serotonin reuptake inhibitor (SSRI) - used for
treating depression, anxiety
disorders, and obsessive-compulsive disorder (OCD).
It's important to note that this information is for general knowledge only and
should not be used as a substitute for medical advice. Always consult your doctor
or pharmacist before taking any medication.
```

Comparative Analysis:

GPT MD provides a concise and medically precise classification for each medication. It uses terminology that is common within the medical field, which would be particularly useful for healthcare professionals or students.

GPT-4 gives a similar classification as GPT MD, but it also includes the general purpose of each medication class (e.g., cholesterol-lowering, anti-inflammatory), making the information more accessible to a general audience.

Google Bard offers the most detailed response by including not only the class but also the specific uses of each medication. It further adds a disclaimer about the information being general knowledge and not a substitute for medical advice, which can be an important reminder for the lay public.

All three models agree on the classifications of the medications, indicating a strong consensus on the subject matter.

The level of detail and context provided increases from GPT MD to GPT-4 to Google Bard, with Google Bard providing the most comprehensive information that could be useful for individuals seeking to understand the broader context of their medication's use.

There is no significant disagreement among the models regarding the drug classes; however, the way they communicate their utility varies, with Google Bard providing the most practical advice for end users.

Google Bard's advisory note suggests a level of caution for the reader, reinforcing the need for professional healthcare guidance, which could be especially beneficial for nonprofessionals interpreting this information.

Conclusion:

While all models provide correct classifications for the medications, they cater to different audience needs: GPT MD for precision, GPT-4 for clarity with some context, and Google Bard for detailed explanations along with practical guidance.

These examples should show you how close subjective evaluations can be. Beyond scoring a couple of points in benchmark evaluations, it is important to involve subject-matter experts in evaluating domain-specific models and also involve the same experts in the loop before deploying these models in production for use in GenAI applications.

As the integration of LLMs into various industries deepens, you can expect to see an increase in collaborative efforts between LLM experts and domain professionals, leading to models that are not only more precise but also more aligned with the practical considerations of each field. Another key aspect will be the focus on making these models more interpretable and transparent, which is critical for trust and reliability, especially in sensitive domains such as healthcare and finance. Furthermore, the development of more efficient training methods will enable the creation of powerful models even with limited domain-specific data. Lastly, the application of federated learning and privacy-preserving techniques to LLMs will soon play a significant role in the development of domain-specific models, allowing for the utilization of sensitive data without compromising privacy. Overall, the future of domain-specific models is poised to be a blend of technological innovation, interdisciplinary collaboration, and a focus on ethical AI practices.

THE POWER OF PROMPTING WITH GENERAL-PURPOSE MODELS

In the previous section, you saw how domain-specific models can be smaller and, therefore, more efficient to train and deploy but as capable as much larger domain-agnostic models. Recent research is once again reversing this intuition and proving the domain-agnostic models still have some ways to outperform even domain-specific models.

Recently, the Medprompt paper by Microsoft (`https://arxiv.org/pdf/2311.16452.pdf`) studied how GPT-4, with the right prompting strategies, can outperform domain-specific models fine-tuned on medical. Figure 4.15 shows the final evaluation of the prompt against specialized models.

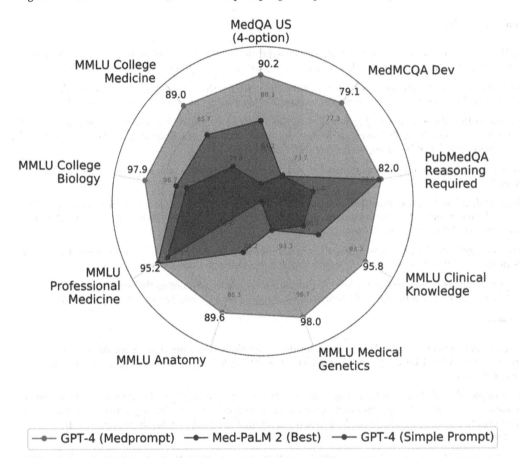

FIGURE 4.15:   Evaluating Medprompt with GPT-4 against Med Palm2

In this study, researchers developed a cost-effective and universally applicable prompting method for GPT-4, named Medprompt, specifically targeting medical problem-solving scenarios. This method activates the inherent capabilities of GPT-4 to function at a specialist level without the need for complex prompt engineering. Medprompt has shown significant improvements over both standard GPT-4 prompting techniques and advanced models like Med-PaLM 2 across various medical question-answering datasets. A notable accomplishment of Medprompt is its performance on the MedQA dataset, based on the USMLE exam, where it achieved a nine-point absolute increase in accuracy, surpassing the 90% mark for the first time in this benchmark. This advancement sets a new precedent in AI-assisted medical diagnostics and problem-solving.

During the inference phase, the researchers re-embed each test question using the same embedding model applied in the preprocessing stage. They then employ a k-nearest neighbors (kNN) algorithm to identify similar instances from the preprocessed data pool. These instances, along with their GPT-4 generated reasoning chains, are formatted to serve as contextual input for GPT-4. The test question and its possible answers are then added to this context, forming the final prompt for the model. GPT-4, following the format of a few previously given examples, generates a reasoning chain and proposes an answer. To enhance the robustness of their approach, the researchers introduced an ensembling process. This process involves repeating the aforementioned steps multiple times, with a focus on increasing diversity, by randomly rearranging the answer choices for each test question. The final predicted answer is determined by selecting the most frequently occurring answer from these iterations, as outlined in their methodology illustrated in Figure 4.16.

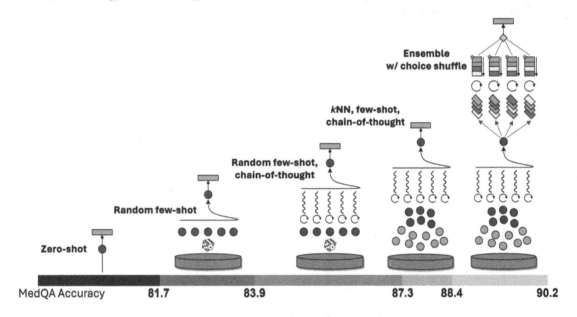

FIGURE 4.16: Increasing accuracy using multiple strategies of Medprompt with GPT-4

GPT-4, without any specialized prompt crafting, exceeds the passing score on USMLE by more than 20 points and outperforms earlier general-purpose models (GPT-3.5) as well as models specifically fine-tuned on medical knowledge (Med-PaLM, a prompt-tuned version of Flan-PaLM 540B).

An important aspect of this study is that intelligent prompting strategies were used to completely eliminate the cost of fine-tuning. The outcomes from Medprompt were achieved using a configuration that incorporates five k-nearest neighbors (kNN) selected exemplars, combined with five parallel API calls in the choice-shuffle ensemble method. This experimental setup was selected as it offers an optimal balance, effectively minimizing the cost associated with inference while simultaneously maximizing accuracy. Different setups can also provide changes in the relative cost when trading accuracy and inference latency.

We are currently witnessing two large, opposing views. One argues that domain-specific models will ultimately be more useful, while the other argues that larger and larger models will lead to artificial general intelligence (AGI), which will obviate the need for domain or task-specific models. It is difficult to assess which view will reign supreme in the long term, but in the shorter term, you can expect that higher-quality, domain-specific data will lead to higher-quality and sometimes smaller models with better capabilities within that task or domain than general-purpose LLMs.

SUMMARY

In this chapter, we explored several smaller models that match and sometimes surpass the performance of some published larger models. The success of models such as Mistral and Orca 2 has significant implications for the future of language model development. It demonstrates the potential of smaller models in scenarios where a balance between efficiency and capability is crucial. The strategic use of tailored synthetic data and diverse reasoning techniques in Orca 2's training process has paved the way for achieving performance levels that rival or surpass those of larger models, especially in zero-shot reasoning tasks. Further, we studied how domain-specific models can surpass the performance of much larger general-purpose foundation models. Lastly, we saw how prompt engineering still is not dead! General-purpose models when prompted well with dynamic few shots can also perform domain-specific models.

5

Infrastructure and Deployment Tuning Strategies

WHAT'S IN THIS CHAPTER?

➤ Introduction to Tuning Strategies

➤ Hardware Utilization and Batch Tuning

➤ Inference Acceleration Tools

➤ Monitoring and Observability

INTRODUCTION TO TUNING STRATEGIES

The development and optimization of neural network models require not only algorithmic expertise but also an understanding of the underlying hardware and deployment infrastructure. The growth of computational resources and the advent of parallel processing have catalyzed advancements in deep learning, but they also present new challenges in the efficient utilization of these resources. In this chapter, we delve into strategies for infrastructure and deployment tuning, focusing on maximizing hardware utilization, accelerating inference, and employing monitoring and optimization to ensure sustained performance.

We first return to the basics and explain why it is so difficult to tune hardware utilization for LLMs. Then, we address the intricacies of training and inference, highlighting the need for strategic batch processing during training to fully exploit computational power while preserving model generalization. We also examine the critical role of inference acceleration in deployment, where the emphasis is on achieving cost-effective and high-performance models suitable for diverse application requirements. Integrating these strategies is essential for the successful deployment of deep learning models, ensuring they are both effective and efficient across various platforms and in real-world scenarios.

HARDWARE UTILIZATION AND BATCH TUNING

As you already know, the heart of LLMs like GPT and BERT is the transformer architecture, which has revolutionized the way we understand and generate human language. The transformer uses a mechanism called *self-attention,* allowing each word in a sentence to interact with all others, effectively understanding the context and the relationships between words. Each token in the input sequence is represented by a vector, which undergoes a series of transformations through what we call the *attention mechanism.* This mechanism computes three vectors for each token: query (Q), key (K), and value (V). In the context of LLMs, the queries correspond to the current token being processed, while the keys and values are derived from all previous tokens. When looking at a single layer, the self-attention calculation looks like Figure 5.1.

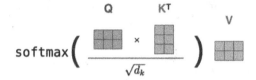

FIGURE 5.1: Self-attention calculation visualized (Alammar, J (2018) / Jay Alammar / CC BY 4.0.)

This represents a single self-attention head (of multiple heads) of a single layer in an encoder or decoder architecture (remember, current LLMs are generally decoder-only architectures). This is shown in Figure 5.2, along with the rest of the transformer architecture for LLMs, which contains multiple such layers.

Now, a transformer-based generative model operates autoregressively, predicting each token based on the sequence of previously generated tokens. As it generates text one token at a time, the model iteratively attends to all past tokens to inform the next token's generation. Each transformer layer stack featuring the self-attention layer references information from all previous tokens to generate the subsequent one. For instance, during the i-th iteration, the current token (t_i) is attended to by all preceding tokens (t_0 to t_{i-1}) within the self-attention layer.

What does this attention look like? Let's take an example sentence that is being generated by an LLM:

```
sentence = "At the store, Ada bought some algorithmic muffins, chips and electrons"
```

For this visualization, there are some useful libraries like bertviz (https://pypi.org/project/bertviz). Let's look at GPT-2 as an example model (similar visualizations can be made for other models). In the next code section, we initialize the tokenizer and model:

```
from bertviz.transformers_neuron_view import GPT2Model, GPT2Tokenizer
from bertviz.neuron_view import show
model_version = 'gpt2'
model = GPT2Model.from_pretrained(model_version)
tokenizer = GPT2Tokenizer.from_pretrained(model_version)
```

Finally, use the show function to interactively visualize the attention. When hovering over the word *chips,* Figure 5.3 shows a visualization of the K and Q parameters of a single head in a single layer (blue values are more negative, and orange values are more positive).

```
show(model, model_version, tokenizer, sentence)
```

Figure 5.3 shows the K and Q tensors, elementwise multiplication (QxK), and the tokens picked based on the softmax of these scores. As we can see in this example, the token "chips" attend to "algorith" and "muff" (can you guess why?). The Q, K, and V tensors, as you saw in Chapter 2, are a result of multiplying learnable weights Wq, Wk, and Wv with the input to each layer.

The transformer architecture, with its reliance on the autoregressive generation and self-attention mechanisms, presents unique challenges in terms of hardware utilization and model tuning. First, the process of generating text token-by-token, where each token's generation depends on all previous tokens, demands significant computational resources. This is because, in each step, the model must compute and store the relationships (attention scores) between the current token and all preceding tokens. As the sequence length increases, the computational complexity grows quadratically, leading to substantial memory requirements. In terms of hardware utilization, this means that transformer models, especially larger ones, require high-end GPUs or TPUs with substantial memory capacity to handle these computations efficiently. The quadratic scaling of memory requirements with sequence length also limits the maximum sequence length that can be processed in a single pass, which can be a bottleneck for tasks requiring long context windows. Additionally, the self-attention mechanism's global nature makes parallel processing challenging. While certain operations within a transformer can be parallelized, the sequential dependency of token generation means that each token can be processed only after all its predecessors have been generated. This inherent sequentiality limits the extent to which parallelization can speed up the training and inference processes. Next, let's dive deeper into the memory requirements of these kinds of models.

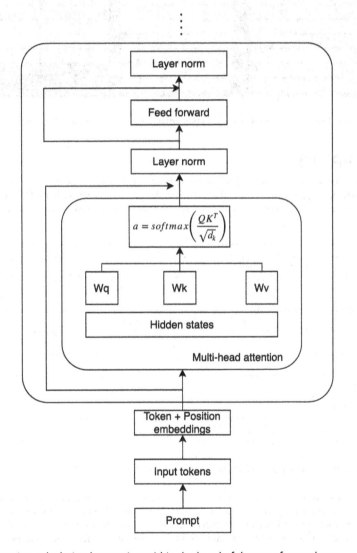

FIGURE 5.2: Self-attention calculation happening within the head of the transformer layer

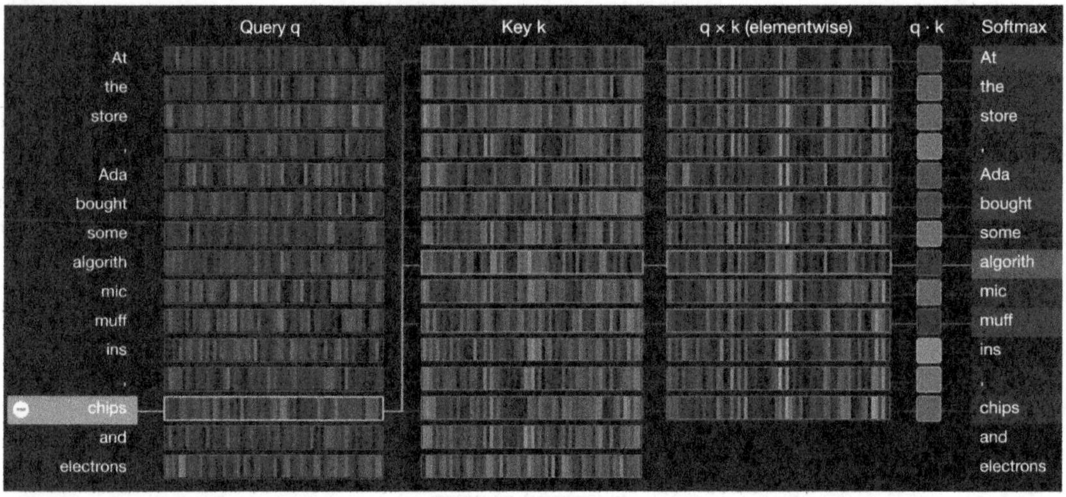

FIGURE 5.3: Self-attention using bertviz neuron view within a head of the transformer layer

Memory Occupancy

Each learnable parameter occupies some GPU memory; how much memory depends on the type of the tensor (float32, float16, int8), the framework used, the GPU, etc. Assume you start with a GPU with no tensors loaded. The nvidia-smi command on the terminal will show you that you are starting with 0 MB, as shown in Figure 5.4.

```
+-----------------------------------------------------------------------------+
| NVIDIA-SMI 470.57.02    Driver Version: 470.57.02    CUDA Version: 11.8     |
|-------------------------------+----------------------+----------------------+
| GPU  Name        Persistence-M| Bus-Id        Disp.A | Volatile Uncorr. ECC |
| Fan  Temp  Perf  Pwr:Usage/Cap|         Memory-Usage | GPU-Util  Compute M. |
|                               |                      |               MIG M. |
|===============================+======================+======================|
|   0  Tesla T4            Off  | 00000000:00:1E.0 Off |                    0 |
| N/A   26C    P0    25W /  70W |      0MiB / 15109MiB |      0%      Default |
|                               |                      |                  N/A |
+-------------------------------+----------------------+----------------------+

+-----------------------------------------------------------------------------+
| Processes:                                                                  |
|  GPU   GI   CI        PID   Type   Process name                  GPU Memory |
|        ID   ID                                                   Usage      |
|=============================================================================|
|  No running processes found                                                 |
+-----------------------------------------------------------------------------+
```

FIGURE 5.4:   0 MB GPU memory utilization at the beginning

Each float32 parameter occupies, by definition, 4 bytes in memory. However, depending on the GPU used, the framework, any overhead memory allocation, the size of a single size 1 tensor, or the entire weight of an LLM can be difficult to predict exactly but can be estimated. When we create a size-1 tensor in PyTorch as follows, Figure 5.5 shows a higher-than-expected size allocated in memory due to the aforementioned reasons.

```
import torch
torch.ones((1, 1)).to("cuda")
```

```
+----------------------------------------------------------------------+
| NVIDIA-SMI 470.57.02    Driver Version: 470.57.02    CUDA Version: 11.8 |
|-------------------------------+----------------------+-----------------|
| GPU  Name        Persistence-M| Bus-Id        Disp.A | Volatile Uncorr. ECC |
| Fan  Temp  Perf  Pwr:Usage/Cap|          Memory-Usage | GPU-Util  Compute M. |
|                               |                      |               MIG M. |
|===============================+======================+=================|
|   0  Tesla T4           Off   | 00000000:00:1E.0 Off |                    0 |
| N/A  27C    P0    25W /  70W  |    119MiB / 15109MiB |      0%      Default |
|                               |                      |                  N/A |
+-------------------------------+----------------------+-----------------+

+----------------------------------------------------------------------+
| Processes:                                                           |
|  GPU   GI   CI        PID   Type   Process name            GPU Memory |
|        ID   ID                                             Usage      |
|======================================================================|
+----------------------------------------------------------------------+
```

FIGURE 5.5: 119 MB GPU memory utilization after loading a size 1 tensor with PyTorch

When initializing a model for inference, the number of parameters times 4 bytes per parameter gives us a lower bound of the memory on GPU, when the model is loaded in float32 (full float size). For example, GPT-2, a 137 million parameter model, will occupy a little more than 137e6 times 4 bytes, or over 548 MB, as shown in Figure 5.6.

```
# Load model directly
from transformers import AutoTokenizer, AutoModelForCausalLM
tokenizer = AutoTokenizer.from_pretrained("gpt2")
model = AutoModelForCausalLM.from_pretrained("gpt2")
```

```
+----------------------------------------------------------------------+
| NVIDIA-SMI 470.57.02    Driver Version: 470.57.02    CUDA Version: 11.8 |
|-------------------------------+----------------------+-----------------|
| GPU  Name        Persistence-M| Bus-Id        Disp.A | Volatile Uncorr. ECC |
| Fan  Temp  Perf  Pwr:Usage/Cap|          Memory-Usage | GPU-Util  Compute M. |
|                               |                      |               MIG M. |
|===============================+======================+=================|
|   0  Tesla T4           Off   | 00000000:00:1E.0 Off |                    0 |
| N/A  27C    P0    25W /  70W  |    651MiB / 15109MiB |      0%      Default |
|                               |                      |                  N/A |
+-------------------------------+----------------------+-----------------+

+----------------------------------------------------------------------+
| Processes:                                                           |
|  GPU   GI   CI        PID   Type   Process name            GPU Memory |
|        ID   ID                                             Usage      |
|======================================================================|
+----------------------------------------------------------------------+
```

FIGURE 5.6: 651 MB GPU after initializing a GPTJ model with 137M parameters

Similarly, when loading increasingly larger models, we should expect even larger memory consumption. For example, when loading the 1.3 billion parameter OPT model (10x larger than the OPT model) from Facebook on huggingface with the following transformer code, Figure 5.7 shows the result of running the nvidia-smi command:

```
# Load model directly
from transformers import AutoTokenizer, AutoModelForCausalLM
tokenizer = AutoTokenizer.from_pretrained("facebook/opt-1.3b")
model = AutoModelForCausalLM.from_pretrained("facebook/opt-1.3b")
```

```
+-------------------------------------------------------------------------+
| NVIDIA-SMI 470.57.02     Driver Version: 470.57.02    CUDA Version: 11.8 |
|-------------------------------+----------------------+------------------|
| GPU  Name         Persistence-M| Bus-Id        Disp.A | Volatile Uncorr. ECC |
| Fan  Temp   Perf  Pwr:Usage/Cap|           Memory-Usage | GPU-Util  Compute M. |
|                                |                      |              MIG M. |
|===============================+======================+==================|
|    0  Tesla T4            Off | 00000000:00:1E.0 Off |                   0 |
| N/A   26C    P0    25W /  70W |  5689MiB / 15109MiB |      0%      Default |
|                                |                      |                 N/A |
+-------------------------------+----------------------+------------------+

+-------------------------------------------------------------------------+
| Processes:                                                              |
|  GPU   GI   CI        PID   Type   Process name              GPU Memory |
|        ID   ID                                               Usage      |
|=========================================================================|
```

FIGURE 5.7: 5689 MB GPU after initializing an OPT model with 1.3 billion parameters

As we keep increasing the size of the model, we will quickly exceed the available memory on a single GPU, as shown in Table 5.1.

TABLE 5.1: Experiment recording memory required for increasing sizes of models on Huggingface

MODEL	NUMBER OF PARAMETERS	SIZE IN GPU MEMORY (GB)	ESTIMATED ACTUAL SIZE IN MEMORY (GB)	CUDA OOM
GPT-2	137 million	0.51 GB	0.64 GB	No
facebook/opt-1.3b	1.3 billion	4.84 GB	5.56 GB	No
5 Microsoft/phi-2	2 billion	7.45 GB	8.94 GB	No
meta-llama/Llama-2-7b-hf	7 billion	26.08 GB	31.29 GB	Yes
meta-llama/Llama-2-13b-hf	13 billion	48.43 GB	58.11 GB	Yes
tiiuae/falcon-40b	40 billion	149.01 GB	178.81 GB	Yes
bigscience/bloom	176 billion	655.65 GB	786.78 GB	Yes

Table 5.1 describes only a snapshot of GPU memory requirements when the model is loaded for inference or predictions. In training, additional memory is required to store gradients, optimizer states, tensor caches, and data batches, which can result in a requirement of four to six times that of inference.

Strategies to Fit Larger Models in Memory

As you saw earlier, commonly used models such as the 7 billion parameter Llama model cannot fit in memory. As mentioned in the earlier chapters, when dealing with the constraints of GPU memory for both training and inference of large models, dynamic memory management becomes critical. Strategies such as mixed precision and model parallelism, where the model's parameters are distributed across multiple GPUs, are common to both phases.

To accommodate increasingly larger models within the constraints of GPU memory for training, several strategies can be employed. Model parallelism is one approach, where the model is split across multiple GPUs, allowing each GPU to store and process a fraction of the model's parameters. Another method is to use mixed precision training, which involves representing numbers using both 16-bit (half-precision) and 32-bit (full-precision) floating points, thereby reducing the memory footprint. Additionally, techniques such as gradient checkpointing, where intermediate activations are not stored during the forward pass but are recomputed during the backward pass, can save memory at the cost of additional computation. Lastly, offloading parts of the model or activations to CPU memory when not in active use can also be a viable solution, though it may affect computational speed. These strategies, individually or in combination, can enable the use of larger LLMs within existing hardware limitations.

For inference, particularly with large models, a similar approach is adopted with added methods. Huggingface's Accelerate library facilitates this by initially loading an empty model structure, significantly reducing memory usage. The weights are then dynamically loaded and dispatched across available devices. This dynamic computation allows for layer-by-layer processing, where memory-intensive operations are offloaded between the CPU and GPU as needed. Alongside these, prefetching and caching strategies are applied to minimize data transfer overheads and optimize the use of GPU memory, allowing even the largest models to be accommodated within the available hardware resources. These strategies ensure efficient utilization of memory, maintaining the delicate balance between performance and resource constraints.

Several advanced techniques are emerging for inference over LLMs using GPUs, including post-training quantization techniques that were dealt with in earlier chapters. For inference, dynamic scheduling enables running larger models by managing tensor allocation and movement between the GPU and CPU, often using pinned CPU memory as a temporary store to facilitate this exchange. Similarly, mixed precision representation, which reduces memory footprint by using both 16-bit and 32-bit floating points, is effective in both training and inference. Techniques like offloading, prefetching, and caching tensors on GPU DRAM are specialized for inference to minimize the need for continuous data transfer, optimizing the limited GPU memory for larger neural network execution. These methods, while adding some overhead, allow for the running of models that would otherwise exceed GPU capacity, thus enabling more complex model deployments on constrained hardware.

While the advanced techniques for running large language models (LLMs) on GPUs mentioned earlier—such as post-training quantization, dynamic scheduling, mixed precision representation, and specialized inference strategies like offloading, prefetching, and caching—offer significant advantages, they also introduce trade-offs between speed, computational efficiency, and model complexity in real-world scenarios. Post-training quantization, although reducing model size and accelerating inference, can potentially lead to a loss in accuracy. Dynamic scheduling, which allows for running larger models, adds overhead because of the management of tensor allocation and movement, potentially impacting the speed of model execution. Mixed precision representation strikes a balance between computational demand and precision, but the use of lower precision (e.g., 16-bit floats) can sometimes affect the model's performance and accuracy.

Hence, it is important to carefully evaluate and choose the right combination of these techniques based on the specific requirements and constraints of each use case. This involves a nuanced understanding of the trade-offs between model size, speed, and accuracy. For instance, in applications where real-time response is critical, prioritizing speed and computational efficiency might be more important, even if it means compromising slightly on model accuracy or complexity. Conversely, in scenarios where the accuracy and depth of model responses are paramount, such as in medical diagnostics or complex data analysis, it might be necessary to allocate more resources toward maintaining high precision, even if this results in slower inference times or the need for more powerful hardware.

Furthermore, continuous monitoring and optimization of these models in real-world applications are crucial. This might include regular updates to the model to accommodate new data or changes in the domain, as well as adjustments to the balance of precision and efficiency as hardware capabilities evolve. The goal is to maintain an optimal balance that maximizes the utility and performance of LLMs while minimizing costs and resource consumption. This process often involves iterative testing and refinement to ensure that the models not only maintain high standards of accuracy and efficiency but also remain aligned with the evolving needs and expectations of users and stakeholders in various domains.

KV Caching

The key and value vectors we covered earlier in this chapter are usually stored in a cache during inference to be used for generating predictions for subsequent tokens. A key-value cache (or KV cache) is needed in transformer models to efficiently access the historical context of a sequence during the prediction phase. When generating new output, the model uses the KV cache to draw upon previously computed key and value pairs, which represent prior tokens and their associated information. This enables the model to maintain an understanding of the sequence's context without recomputing the attention for past tokens with each new token generated, thus saving computational resources and time. The KV cache is critical for producing outputs that are contextually coherent and accurate.

As the sequence grows longer, so does the KV cache, requiring more GPU memory. Without this cache, the model would have to store hidden states for all previous tokens and perform matrix multiplication with the weight matrix Wq, Wk, and Wv at every layer, which would be computationally equivalent to the self-attention computations for the current token. For example, GPT-NeoX, a model with 20 billion parameters, features 44 layers and a hidden dimension of 6144, resulting in a requirement of approximately 1 MB per token for the KV cache.

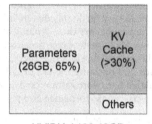

NVIDIA A100 40GB

FIGURE 5.8: GPU memory space occupied by the model weights compared to the KV cache. (Kwon et al., (2023) / Association for Computing Machinery / CC BY 4.0.)

Figure 5.8 shows a rough sketch of how much GPU memory the actual model occupies, how much the KV cache occupies, and what the typical overhead looks like. For a large model with 13 billion parameters running on a Nvidia A100 GPU with 40GB of RAM, most of the memory goes to the model's fixed weights. The rest is used for the changing parts of the requests, like the KV cache. This part of the memory keeps track of what has been done before in the sequence to help come up with the next part of the sequence.

As the model weights are fixed and the activations require minimal GPU memory, the management of the KV cache plays a pivotal role in determining the upper limit of the batch size, which improves overall performance of any LLM application. This substantial memory requirement underscores the need for efficient memory management strategies to handle the KV cache during the inference of LLMs, where every byte saved can significantly impact overall performance and scalability. With this basic understanding of memory requirements for loading a model and KV caches, we will go through some recently published techniques for LLM memory management that enables higher throughput generation.

> **NOTE** *Given the current trends, GPU computation speed grows much faster than the memory capacity. For example, from Nvidia A100 to the newer H100s, the compute capacity in FLOPS increased by more than 2x, but the GPU memory stays at a maximum of 80GB. Therefore, memory will become an increasingly significant bottleneck for LLM training and serving.*
>
> *In earlier chapters, we saw how increasingly larger models are being created alongside new techniques that create smaller and more capable models for certain tasks. These models occupy a fixed real-estate in the GPU, but the KV cache size grows quickly with the number of requests. As an example, for the 13 billion parameter OPT model, the KV cache of a single token demands 800 KB of space (two key and value vectors × 5120 (hidden state size) × 40 (number of layers) × 2 (bytes per FP16). Since OPT can generate sequences up to 2,048 tokens, the memory required to store the KV cache of one request can be as much as 1.6 GB. Concurrent GPUs have memory capacities in the tens of gigabytes. Even if all available memory was allocated to KV cache, only a few tens of requests could be accommodated. Moreover, inefficient memory management can further decrease the batch size, thereby reducing the throughput of your LLM stack.*

PagedAttention

In the previous section, we talked at length about the importance of managing the KV cache in LLM systems. Existing methods for serving large language models often struggle with efficiently managing the key-value cache memory. This memory, which stores the states of the requests, is dynamic, growing and shrinking as new tokens are generated. Inefficient management leads to memory fragmentation and redundant duplication, limiting batch sizes and throughput. Traditional systems store the KV cache in contiguous memory space, leading to internal and external memory fragmentation. Furthermore, these systems miss opportunities for memory sharing, especially in scenarios using advanced decoding algorithms like parallel sampling and beam search.

To address these challenges, PagedAttention was introduced (see https://arxiv.org/pdf/2309.06180 .pdf), drawing inspiration from virtual memory and paging techniques in operating systems. PagedAttention divides the KV cache into blocks, each containing the attention keys and values of a fixed number of tokens. These blocks are not necessarily stored contiguously, allowing for more flexible management akin to OS's virtual memory: blocks can be thought of as pages, tokens as bytes, and requests as processes. This approach alleviates internal fragmentation through smaller blocks and eliminates external fragmentation, as all blocks are uniform in size. It also enables memory sharing at the granularity of a block, both within and across requests. The authors implement PagedAttention in a package called vLLM, an LLM serving system that achieves near-zero waste in KV cache memory and flexible sharing of KV cache within and across requests to further reduce memory usage.

> **NOTE** *The term* paged *in PagedAttention derives from this approach's similarity to paging in operating systems, where memory is divided into blocks (pages) that can be stored non-contiguously and managed dynamically. This analogy extends to the handling of memory allocation, fragmentation, and sharing.*

How Does PagedAttention Work?

To illustrate how vLLM implements PagedAttention and manages memory in the decoding of a single input sequence, consider the following example: Similar to the way operating systems manage virtual memory, vLLM initially does not reserve memory for the entire potential length of the generated sequence. Instead, it only reserves necessary KV blocks for the KV cache produced during the computation of the prompt. For instance, if the prompt consists of seven tokens, vLLM maps the first two logical KV blocks (0 and 1) to two physical KV blocks (7 and 1, for example), as shown in in Figure 5.9. In the prefill stage, vLLM generates the KV cache for the prompt and the initial output token using a standard self-attention algorithm. It then stores the KV cache of the first four tokens in logical block 0 and the subsequent three tokens in logical block 1, keeping a slot reserved for later phases of autoregressive generation.

In the first step of autoregressive decoding, vLLM creates a new token using the PagedAttention algorithm, focusing on physical blocks 7 and 1. As there is an available slot in the last logical block, the newly generated KV cache is stored there, and the record in the block table is updated to reflect this. When the last logical block becomes full during the second decoding step, vLLM transfers the newly generated KV cache to a new logical block. This involves allocating a new physical block (physical block 3) and recording this assignment in the block table.

Throughout each decoding iteration, vLLM selects a set of candidate sequences for batching and assigns physical blocks to the newly required logical blocks. It then merges all input tokens from the current iteration for processing.

Comparisons, Limitations, and Cost Considerations

In comparisons with other methods, PagedAttention has shown substantial improvements in LLM serving throughput by two to four times without affecting model accuracy. The performance gains are more pronounced with longer sequences, larger models, and more complex decoding algorithms. This is primarily due to the near-zero waste in KV cache memory and the flexible sharing of KV cache, enabled by the paged memory management approach.

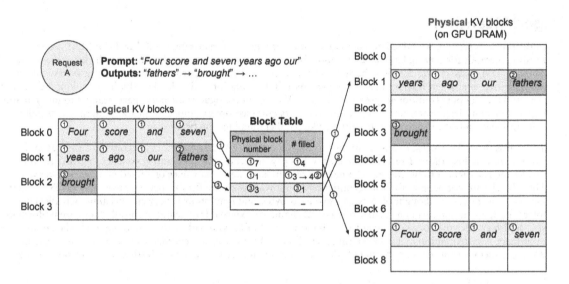

FIGURE 5.9: Schematic showing how PagedAttention works in vLLM. This can be extended beyond the case where only a single request is being served unlike what is shown in the picture.

As shown in the paper introducing PagedAttention (https://arxiv.org/abs/2309.06180), the concept of virtual memory and paging proves to be highly effective in managing the KV cache for LLM serving. This effectiveness stems from the dynamic nature of memory allocation required in LLM serving, as the length of the output is not predetermined, and the overall performance is largely constrained by the GPU's memory capacity. However, this approach is not universally applicable to all types of GPU workloads. For instance, during deep neural network (DNN) training, the shapes of tensors are usually fixed, allowing for memory allocation to be optimized in advance. Similarly, when serving DNNs other than LLMs, an increase in memory efficiency might not lead to any significant performance gains, as these tasks are predominantly compute-bound rather than memory-bound. In such cases, applying the techniques used in vLLM could potentially hinder performance because of the additional complications arising from memory indirection and the use of noncontiguous block memory.

However, the paper also identifies certain limitations of PagedAttention. One such shortcoming is the added overhead due to noncontiguous memory access and the need for extra memory management mechanisms. This overhead can impact the latency of individual requests, particularly when dealing with very large models or highly complex decoding tasks. Additionally, while PagedAttention significantly improves memory efficiency, it may introduce complexity in implementation, especially when integrated into existing systems or adapted for other types of neural network models beyond LLMs. Despite these limitations, PagedAttention represents a significant advancement in efficient memory management for LLM serving, offering a scalable solution to meet the growing demand for these models in various applications.

The impact of PagedAttention on cost is multifaceted, primarily focusing on improving memory efficiency and throughput in LLM serving systems. A key aspect of PagedAttention is its ability to enable memory sharing, allowing different sequences to share the same physical block. This sharing capability can reduce memory usage by up to 55%, leading to an overall throughput improvement of up to 2.2x. This enhancement in memory efficiency and throughput translates into direct cost savings for platforms utilizing LLMs, as it allows for more efficient use of computing resources, potentially reducing the need for additional hardware investments to handle large-scale LLM operations.

AlphaServe

As you saw in Table 5.1, larger models demand exceedingly larger amounts of GPU memory for serving purposes. In the AlphaServe paper (see `https://arxiv.org/pdf/2302.11665.pdf`), the authors estimate that for hosting GPT-3, we would require at least 325 GB of GPU memory (somewhere between the Flacon 40B and Bloom models in Table 5.1). Since many GenAI applications with LLMs at their core have spiky workloads, the naïve serving framework needs to allocate enough capacity for the peak expected loaded in order to always satisfy the service level objective (SLO) of required minimum latency. In today's GenAI applications, it is becoming common practice to serve not one but several versions of models for different use cases and tasks.

The AlphaServe paper identifies that although ModelParallel settings have been well studied in the training world, its advantages in serving, especially in latency-constrained settings, are not explored. However, it is certainly not simple deciding how to split and place multiple models across multiple GPUs. To this end, AlphaServe automatically and efficiently explores the trade-offs among different parallelization and placement strategies for model serving.

The AlphaServe system can dynamically adapt to optimize the serving of large models by reducing latency and accommodating traffic spikes. It leverages a complex algorithm that considers the trade-offs between various parallelization strategies and efficiently assigns models to different GPUs within a cluster. This approach is shown to improve the serving rates significantly while maintaining latency constraints for the vast majority of requests.

How Does AlphaServe Work?

AlphaServe enhances the efficiency of models serving in deep learning by leveraging model parallelism for both large and small models that traditionally would fit on a single device. It introduces an automatic parallelization method tailored for inference, which involves a dynamic programming approach that minimizes latency and optimizes resource utilization. The system's architecture consists of a centralized controller that directs requests to device groups, each running a shared model-parallel runtime. Let's explore why this is useful in Figure 5.10.

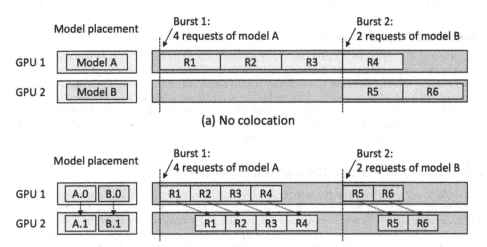

FIGURE 5.10: Collocation of multiple models can lead to better performance (lower latency) overall.

This diagram explores two strategies for deploying two models across two GPUs, highlighting their behavior under bursty workloads. The left panels depict the physical placement, while the right panel illustrates corresponding request timelines. In scenario 1, both models reside entirely on separate GPUs. When Burst 1 arrives, all four Model A requests queue behind the ongoing Model B inference, potentially leading to increased latencies. Conversely, scenario 2 leverages model parallelism, splitting Model A across both GPUs. This allows simultaneous processing of Burst 1 tasks, significantly reducing average completion times under such peak loads. Therefore, for systems expecting bursty traffic, model parallelism emerges as a key strategy for optimized performance, enabling efficient utilization of available GPU resources.

The placement algorithm is a key component of AlphaServe, tasked with distributing models across the cluster to maximize SLO attainment. It employs a two-level approach where a greedy algorithm guided by simulation selects models for each group, while a more comprehensive enumeration-based method determines the overall optimal placement within the cluster.

At runtime, AlphaServe follows a simple scheduling policy where a centralized controller handles request dispatching. The requests are assigned to the group with the shortest queue, adhering to a first-come, first-served principle. This ensures that requests are served within the set SLOs by leveraging the predictability of DNN execution times. The system's design also accommodates dynamic batching, which increases GPU utilization and further enhances throughput without compromising the tight latency requirements imposed by the SLOs.

Impact of Batching

In the context of other serving systems, batching has been a prevalent method to enhance GPU utilization and throughput. However, when it comes to large models, the advantages of batching are notably constrained. This is because even a minimal batch size is sufficient to fully engage the GPU's capacity, leaving little room for performance gains from processing additional requests simultaneously. Moreover, as batch size increases, so does execution latency, making batching impractical under stringent SLO conditions. In the case of AlphaServe, standard batching mechanisms have been implemented to validate their independence from model parallelism's benefits. This was tested with smaller models where even modest batch sizes could maximize GPU usage, proving that further increases in batch size do not translate into performance benefits. Comparison of AlphaServe's performance with and without batching under different SLO scales revealed that when SLOs are stringent, batching fails to offer any advantage and may even hinder SLO compliance.

Cost and Performance Considerations

While AlpaServe may initially appear to increase costs because of the use of multiple GPUs, it actually offers a cost-effective solution for deep learning model serving. By optimizing model parallelism and placement strategies, AlpaServe enables efficient resource utilization, which can lead to significant cost savings. For instance, it can reduce the number of devices needed by up to 2.3 times, handle rates 10 times higher, and manage six times more burstiness, while still meeting the latency SLOs for more than 99% of requests. These efficiencies may balance out the higher costs associated with larger multi-GPU instances, making AlpaServe a potentially cost-effective option for organizations looking to serve large models more efficiently.

S3: Scheduling Sequences with Speculation

In the preceding discussions, we delved into the intricacies of KV cache management in LLMs and identified memory capacity as a significant bottleneck, often leading to suboptimal GPU utilization. The traditional approach in LLM serving frameworks reserves memory for the maximum sequence length of the KV cache, resulting in inefficiencies due to the inability to predict the output sequence length in advance. As discussed in the "PagedAttention" section, one way to manage this is by dynamically partitioning the KV cache into manageable blocks, enabling more flexible and efficient memory usage without having to reserve excessive amounts of contiguous space. In a paper titled "S3: Increasing GPU Utilization during Generative Inference for Higher Throughput," S3 has been proposed as an alternative way to manage this, by predicting the output sequence length to allocate memory more accurately and scheduling generation queries based on these predictions, which enhances device resource utilization and throughput while handling mispredictions effectively.

In response to this challenge, S3 has been proposed; this system is designed to predict (or "speculate") the output sequence length, thereby enhancing device resource utilization and overall throughput. S3's predictive mechanism and dynamic scheduling promise to mitigate the memory allocation overhead prevalent in existing LLM serving frameworks, aiming for a more efficient use of the available computational resources. This introduction sets the stage for a detailed examination of how S3 operates and its potential to revolutionize the serving of generative models.

> **NOTE** *Note that the S3 discussed here is different from Amazon's Simple Storage Service (also known as Amazon S3), which is a scalable object storage service.*

How Does S3 Work?

The S3 system, as detailed in the aforementioned paper, is designed to maximize GPU utilization and throughput for generative models by intelligently managing memory. It consists of these three main components:

➤ **Output sequence length predictor:** The output sequence length predictor in S3 was created by fine-tuning a Distilbert model, a smaller and faster variant of the BERT model, for sequence classification. This fine-tuning process involved using datasets like Alpaca, which contain question-and-answer pairs. The questions served as inputs, and the lengths of the answers were the targets for training the model to predict output sequence lengths.

In terms of its predictive accuracy, the model demonstrated high effectiveness. It was able to correctly predict the length bucket of the output sequence with a remarkable accuracy of 98.61%. Even when predictions were incorrect, the average distance between the predicted and actual buckets was only about 1.03, indicating that most errors were close to the correct value.

This high level of accuracy is significant for the system's efficiency, as accurate length predictions directly influence the effective allocation of GPU memory resources in the S3 framework.

➤ **Length-aware sequence scheduler:** This scheduler is responsible for batching and scheduling sequences based on the length predictions. It uses an algorithm akin to the "decreasing first fit" approach in bin packing. The scheduler sorts the sequences by their predicted length and batches them in a way that maximizes GPU utilization without exceeding memory limits. It also incorporates ORCA's iteration-level scheduling technique, allowing for higher flexibility and reduced waiting time.

➤ **Supervisor:** The supervisor oversees GPU utilization and handles mispredictions. It monitors sequence generation, preempting sequences that exceed their allocated memory and reallocating resources as needed. Additionally, it continuously retrains the predictor based on its mistakes, ensuring the system adapts and improves over time.

Putting these components together, S3 efficiently handles sequence-generation requests. Requests arrive at a pool, where the predictor estimates their output lengths. The scheduler then batches these requests, optimizing GPU memory use. The GPU generates the texts for these batches while the supervisor monitors and adjusts resource allocation, ensuring optimal operation even in the face of prediction errors. This holistic approach allows S3 to enhance throughput significantly while managing memory resources more effectively than traditional methods.

Performance and Cost

In the offline scenario described in the paper, S3's maximum throughput for various models was assessed using the maximum batch size for each configuration. This analysis revealed that S3's throughput surpasses ORCA's (see www.usenix.org/system/files/osdi22-yu.pdf) by a factor ranging from 1.13x to 6.49x, and it approaches Oracle's performance with a difference of 9.34% to 40.52%. Figure 5.11 reproduces the results from the S3 paper.

The disparity in performance observed becomes more pronounced with larger models due to the limitations in batch size imposed by the high bandwidth memory (HBM) usage for model weights. The unique architecture of transformers contributes to these results, where feed-forward layers benefit more from batching compared to self-attention layers. In an online scenario with a latency SLO constraint based on average English reading speed, S3's throughput was evaluated under these time constraints, demonstrating its effectiveness in managing latency while maintaining high throughput in a real-world system.

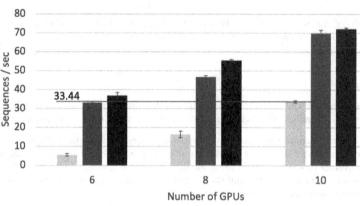

FIGURE 5.11: Results comparing the performance of S3 to another system ORCA, and an ideal Oracle with prior knowledge of response length

S3 was tested on various configurations using different numbers of GPUs to evaluate its performance. For GPT-3, the system was set up in a pipeline parallel manner with configurations of 6, 8, and 10 GPUs. In these setups, 16 and 12 transformer layers were allocated per GPU for the 6 and 8 GPU configurations, respectively. The 10 GPU configuration involved distributing 10 layers to 9 of the GPUs and 6 layers to the remaining one. S3's design allows for the concurrent processing of batches across all GPUs, effectively minimizing idle time. Surprisingly, S3 achieved comparable throughput with 6 GPUs to ORCA's performance with 10 GPUs, despite the former having a significantly larger batch size. This similarity in throughput can be attributed to the pipeline execution strategy and the sequential nature of self-attention layers in transformer-based models. The increased latency in larger batch sizes, however, neutralizes some of the throughput benefits, leading to nearly identical performance between the two systems, even when S3 used a larger batch size.

The cost advantages of using S3, especially in configurations with fewer GPUs, are noteworthy. By achieving similar throughput levels with fewer GPUs compared to systems like ORCA, S3 demonstrates a more efficient utilization of resources. This efficiency translates into direct cost savings for organizations, as fewer GPUs mean lower hardware acquisition and maintenance costs, as well as reduced energy consumption. The ability of S3 to optimize memory allocation and manage batch sizes effectively allows for significant savings, particularly in large-scale deployments where the costs associated with additional GPUs can be substantial. This makes S3 not only a performance-efficient choice but also a cost-effective one for handling large language models.

Streaming LLMs with Attention Sinks

It is technically very challenging for a model to "extrapolate" or generate tokens beyond the maximum number of tokens it has been trained for. For example, a Llama 7B model with a 4K context can generate only up to a maximum of 4,000 tokens. For most use cases, this is sufficient. Other, more recent open source and commercial models are being created with larger and larger context lengths, like the Claude model with more than 100,000 tokens. While it is rare for applications to need this long of a context length, the fact remains that the context length itself is an upper-bound parameter that remains fixed.

Let's revisit our discussion on the KV cache. As we know by now, different strategies of managing the KV cache have their unique set of challenges and benefits. Dense Attention, for instance, exhibits a quadratic time complexity ($O(T^2)$) and an increasing cache size, leading to a decline in performance when the text length surpasses the pre-training text length. In contrast, Window Attention focuses on caching the most recent L tokens' KV states. This approach is efficient during inference, but its performance deteriorates rapidly once the initial tokens' keys and values are used.

Fixed to Sliding Window Attention

Rather than having a fixed size window, we can implement a sliding window with the most recent tokens. As the model processes a text, the sliding window fills with the KV states of tokens, maintaining a balance between efficiency and memory management. This fixed-size window ensures that only a certain number of the most recent tokens are held in the KV cache, optimizing memory usage and processing times. As new tokens are added, older ones are evicted to make room.

This mechanism is efficient up to the maximum capacity of the window. When the sequence length surpasses this capacity, the performance of the model starts to decline. This decline is due to the loss of earlier context, as the KV states of older tokens are evicted. This loss is particularly problematic in scenarios where understanding the entire text is vital, as the model may lose important contextual information from the beginning of the text. Window Attention is more suited for texts that fit within the window's capacity, where it can efficiently manage memory and processing speed. However, its limitations become significant with longer texts. In such cases, the inability to retain context from the text's beginning can impact the model's performance and accuracy. So with this method, the model's effectiveness collapses once the sequence length surpasses the cache size.

To understand why window attention fails, it's important to note a peculiar aspect of autoregressive LLMs. A significant amount of attention score is often allocated to the initial tokens, regardless of their relevance to the task at hand. These tokens, termed *attention sinks*, attract significant attention scores despite their lack of semantic significance. This phenomenon arises due to the Softmax operation in the LLMs, which necessitates attention scores to sum up to one across all contextual tokens. Consequently, even when the current query lacks a strong match in many previous tokens, the model is compelled to allocate attention values to these initial tokens, which are more visible to subsequent tokens due to the autoregressive nature of the language modeling. This understanding is pivotal in refining strategies for LLM deployment in scenarios demanding infinite input lengths, guiding future advancements in the field.

Extending the Context Length

Length extrapolation in language models is an area of research that seeks to enable models trained on shorter texts to adeptly handle longer ones during testing phases or actual deployment. This capability is especially pertinent for applications that involve streaming text, where data flows continuously and unpredictably in length. Efforts have been directed toward developing relative position encoding methods for transformer-based models, which are fundamental in allowing these models to function effectively beyond their initial training constraints. Initiatives like Rotary Position Embeddings (RoPE) embody this research direction by integrating relative position information into the queries and keys of each attention layer, aiming to maintain contextual awareness over extended sequences. You can read more about RoPE at https://arxiv.org/abs/2104.09864.

However, the promise of techniques like RoPE has been met with challenges; subsequent research has shed light on their underperformance with text lengths that exceed the training window of the models. Another methodology, ALiBi (https://arxiv.org/abs/2108.12409), attempts to address this by biasing the attention scores based on the relative distances between tokens, aiming to inject a sense of position without explicit positional encodings. While this has led to some improvements in the model's ability to extrapolate to longer text lengths, tests on MPT models have revealed a breakdown in performance when confronted with texts much longer than the training length. The quest for a model that can seamlessly handle infinite length extrapolation remains unfulfilled, leaving a gap in the current capabilities of LLMs for streaming applications, where the volume of data can be vast and unending.

Working with Infinite Length Context

Streaming incoming or outgoing text can be considered as having infinite context length. As the LLM processes and outputs text, new input text is being sent to it for processing. Building on the concept of infinite context length in streaming text, StreamingLLM (https://arxiv.org/pdf/2309.17453.pdf) presents a novel solution. This framework accommodates the processing of continuous text streams by exploiting the properties of attention sinks. Attention sinks, as earlier established, are tokens that attract a disproportionately high amount of attention. By selectively preserving the KV states of just a few of these attention sinks, specifically the initial four tokens, StreamingLLM ensures that the distribution of attention scores remains close to what is expected during normal model operation.

StreamingLLM integrates these preserved attention sinks with a sliding window's KV cache, creating a stable anchor for attention computation. This innovation circumvents the need for the model to retain an extensive history of KV states, thereby sidestepping the issues related to the growing memory demands and computational complexity associated with processing long text sequences.

How Does StreamingLLM Work?

The authors of the StreamingLLM paper suggest a simple yet effective method to facilitate streaming in pre-trained LLMs without the necessity for model fine-tuning. This method involves the reintegration of the KV states of a select number of starting tokens (in their case, four) into the attention calculation, alongside the tokens from the current sliding window.

Conceptually, the KV cache in StreamingLLM is bifurcated into two distinct components, as depicted in Figure 5.12. The first components are the attention sinks, consisting of four initial tokens that provide stability to the attention computations; the second is the rolling KV cache, which is responsible for holding the most recent tokens that are pivotal for current language modeling tasks. The design of StreamingLLM is not only flexible but also readily adaptable to any autoregressive language model that utilizes relative positional encoding methods, including those like RoPE and ALiBi, thus enhancing their capacity to handle the streaming of text.

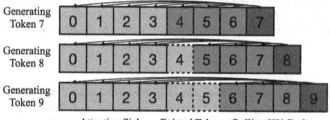

FIGURE 5.12: KV cache in a streaming context with StreamingLLM

The design of StreamingLLM takes an innovative approach to positional information, focusing on the relative positions within the cache rather than referencing the positions from the original text, a strategy pivotal to the model's performance. For example, when the model's current cache, as illustrated in Figure 5.12, contains the sequence of tokens [0, 1, 2, 3, 6, 7, 8] while decoding the ninth token, StreamingLLM assigns positions [0, 1, 2, 3, 4, 5, 6, 7] that correspond to their order in the cache, not their absolute positions [0, 1, 2, 3, 6, 7, 8, 9] in the original text. This relative positioning within the cache is essential for the model to maintain coherence and context during the streaming of text data.

In terms of integrating with specific encoding methods like RoPE, StreamingLLM adopts a procedure where the keys of tokens are cached before the rotary transformation is applied. During each phase of decoding, the position transformation is then applied to the keys within the rolling cache. The interaction with ALiBi is somewhat more straightforward, where a contiguous linear bias, as opposed to a "jumping" bias, is applied to the attention scores. This technique of assigning positional embeddings within the cache is fundamental to StreamingLLM's operation, ensuring that the model not only functions efficiently but also retains its effectiveness beyond the attention window size for which it was originally trained. This capability is particularly critical for allowing pretrained LLMs to adapt to the demands of streaming applications, where they must process text sequences that are potentially infinite in length.

Performance and Results

To test the performance of StreamingLLM, the authors use a continuous stream of concatenated question-answer pairs from the ARC-[Challenge, Easy] datasets that were fed into the Llama 2 (7, 13, 70B) Chat models. The accuracy of the models was then assessed at each answer position using an exact match criterion. The results, as presented in Table 5 of the original paper were revealing. Dense attention mechanisms, while powerful, led to out-of-memory (OOM) errors, rendering them impractical for streaming applications. The window attention method, though efficient in terms of memory and processing, suffered from low accuracy. This drop in performance was particularly pronounced when the input length went beyond the model's cache size, resulting in random outputs.

In stark contrast, StreamingLLM demonstrated its superiority by not only efficiently handling the streaming data format but also by maintaining accuracy that aligns with the one-shot, sample-by-sample baseline. This indicates that StreamingLLM not only solves the memory issues associated with dense attention but also overcomes the accuracy limitations of window attention methods in a streaming setting. The model's ability to manage the continuous flow of data without sacrificing performance or encountering memory limitations is a significant advancement, suggesting that StreamingLLM could be a robust solution for real-world applications that require LLMs to process extensive and unending streams of text.

The practical advantages of this approach are significant: models such as Llama 2 (7, 13, and 70B), MPT (7 and 30B), Falcon (7 and 40B), and Pythia (2.9, 6.9, and 12B), which were previously constrained by finite attention windows, can now reliably process texts up to 4 million tokens in length, and potentially even more. This is a substantial leap in capability when compared to the previously viable approach of a sliding window with recomputation, which StreamingLLM outpaces by achieving up to a 22.2× speedup.

Cost Considerations

The implementation of StreamingLLM alongside other context length extension techniques such as RoPE and ALiBi represents a paradigm shift in the deployment of LLMs for streaming applications. However, this technological leap comes with considerations regarding computational efficiency and economic cost. StreamingLLM, by allowing LLMs to handle extended or even potentially infinite sequences, circumvents the need for intensive model retraining or fine-tuning for different context lengths. This is a marked advantage over dense attention mechanisms that not only incur substantial memory overheads, leading to OOM errors, but also necessitate greater computational resources that can inflate costs significantly.

The integration of StreamingLLM with methods like RoPE and ALiBi introduces a nuanced understanding of relative positional encoding, which is inherently more memory-efficient than traditional absolute positional encodings. This efficiency reduces the frequency and magnitude of memory-related bottlenecks, consequently lowering the computational load and associated costs. Furthermore, the reduction in the need for re-computation, as demonstrated by StreamingLLM's performance relative to sliding window techniques, translates into a direct reduction in the cost of processing each token within a stream.

However, it is important to note that while StreamingLLM minimizes memory and computation requirements, the initial setup and integration with existing systems could entail development costs. Organizations would need to consider the trade-off between these initial setup costs against the long-term savings in computational resources. Additionally, the financial implications of the reduced latency and increased throughput provided by StreamingLLM could be substantial, potentially resulting in enhanced user experiences and new capabilities for real-time applications, which in turn could lead to increased revenues.

In conclusion, while StreamingLLM and related context length extension techniques present an up-front investment, their impact on reducing computational costs and improving efficiency holds promise for a more cost-effective and scalable application of LLMs in various domains, especially those requiring the processing of large-scale or streaming data. Specifically, this advancement realizes the potential for streaming use of LLMs, opening up new avenues for their application in real-time scenarios where text data is continuously generated or received, such as live translations, real-time content moderation, and interactive dialogue systems.

Batch Size Tuning

As we transition into the nuances of batch tuning within the realm of LLMs, it's essential to recognize how this process interlinks with the previously optimized methods for utilizing KV caching and extending context length. With these advancements in place—such as the implementation of StreamingLLM, PagedAttention, and efficient scheduling systems—we lay the groundwork for refining another critical parameter: the batch size. The optimization of batch size is pivotal in harnessing the full potential of LLMs, as it directly influences the model's throughput, latency, and resource consumption.

By maximizing batch size, we aim to increase the computational efficiency of LLMs, allowing them to process larger amounts of data in parallel without compromising the gains achieved through improved KV cache strategies and extended context lengths. This balancing act is not trivial; it requires a careful evaluation of the trade-offs between speed and accuracy, memory usage, and processing capabilities of the underlying hardware. Let's take a look at the resource utilization of two different models in Figure 5.13.

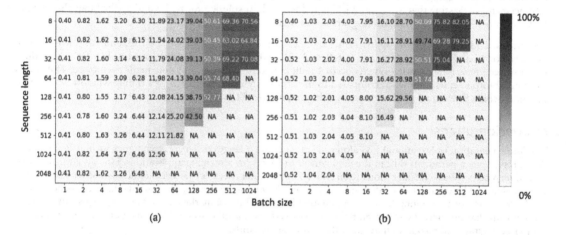

(a)

Sequence length \ Batch size	1	2	4	8	16	32	64	128	256	512	1024
8	0.40	0.82	1.62	3.20	6.30	11.89	23.17	39.04	50.61	69.36	70.56
16	0.41	0.82	1.62	3.18	6.15	11.54	24.02	39.03	50.45	63.02	64.84
32	0.41	0.82	1.60	3.14	6.12	11.79	24.08	39.13	50.39	69.22	70.08
64	0.41	0.81	1.59	3.09	6.28	11.98	24.13	39.04	55.74	68.40	NA
128	0.41	0.80	1.55	3.17	6.43	12.08	24.15	38.75	52.77	NA	NA
256	0.41	0.78	1.60	3.24	6.44	12.14	25.20	42.50	NA	NA	NA
512	0.41	0.80	1.63	3.26	6.44	12.11	21.82	NA	NA	NA	NA
1024	0.41	0.82	1.64	3.27	6.46	12.56	NA	NA	NA	NA	NA
2048	0.41	0.82	1.62	3.26	6.48	NA	NA	NA	NA	NA	NA

(b)

Sequence length \ Batch size	1	2	4	8	16	32	64	128	256	512	1024
8	0.40	1.03	2.03	4.03	7.95	16.10	28.70	50.09	75.82	82.05	NA
16	0.52	1.03	2.03	4.02	7.91	16.11	28.91	49.74	69.28	79.25	NA
32	0.52	1.02	2.02	4.00	7.91	16.27	28.92	50.51	75.04	NA	NA
64	0.52	1.03	2.01	4.00	7.98	16.46	28.98	51.74	NA	NA	NA
128	0.52	1.02	2.01	4.05	8.00	15.62	29.56	NA	NA	NA	NA
256	0.51	1.02	2.03	4.04	8.10	16.49	NA	NA	NA	NA	NA
512	0.51	1.03	2.04	4.05	8.10	NA	NA	NA	NA	NA	NA
1024	0.52	1.03	2.04	4.05	NA	NA	NA	NA	NA	NA	NA
2048	0.52	1.04	2.04	NA	NA	NA	NA	NA	NA	NA	NA

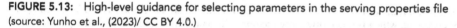

Batch size

FIGURE 5.13: High-level guidance for selecting parameters in the serving properties file (source: Yunho et al., (2023)/ CC BY 4.0.)

Figure 5.13(a) illustrates how GPU utilization varies with batch sizes and sequence lengths, highlighting that larger batch sizes lead to better utilization until a "memory cliff" occurs, resulting in an out-of-memory error. For instance, with a sequence length of 1024, the highest batch size without hitting this cliff is 8, capping utilization at 12.19%. Figure 5.13(b) reveals a similar pattern of underutilization for the larger GPT-NEOX model, which hits the memory cliff even with smaller batches and shorter sequences due to its higher memory demand. The HF-Transformers need to anticipate the output sequence length to mitigate this issue. While larger batch sizes can improve throughput by allowing the GPU to manage model weights and engage idle compute resources efficiently, the challenge remains to avoid the memory cliff and fully leverage the available GPU resources. This could be addressed by precisely knowing the sequence length to be generated, allowing for exact memory allocation and eliminating the need for repeated memory reservations.

The process of batch size tuning can be approached manually, which offers precise control but can be time-consuming and may not always yield optimal results because of the complex interplay of factors affecting LLM performance. Alternatively, automatic exploration methods can be deployed, leveraging algorithms to dynamically adjust batch sizes in response to varying data streams and computational loads. This automatic tuning is based on real-time metrics, adjusting the batch size to maintain a balance between resource utilization and the quality of output from the LLM.

In this section, we will delve into both strategies for batch size tuning, dissecting their advantages, limitations, and the circumstances under which each might be preferable. The objective is to equip the LLMs with the capability to process data streams efficiently, maintaining a high standard of performance while optimizing the cost-effectiveness of their operation.

Frameworks for Deployment Configuration Testing

Several frameworks exist today for you to test various configurations. As you can tell from the discussion so far, deployment configurations can be complex. One of the most important choices you have to make is choosing the right tools and frameworks to optimize the inference performance of LLMs effectively.

Nvidia's FasterTransformer library allocates memory for the longest possible sequence for each input, ensuring enough space for sequences that might reach the maximum length. Although this method avoids unnecessary memory operations by adding to the allocated space as needed, it can be wasteful. For instance, even if a sequence has only 50 tokens, FasterTransformer sets aside space for 2,048 tokens when dealing with models like GPT-NEOX, which have a maximum sequence length of 2,048 tokens. Consequently, on an 80GB A100 GPU, the library can handle a batch size smaller than 20 for a model size of 40GB, consuming 2.2 GB for each sequence. This conservative memory reservation leads to underutilization of the GPU's substantial computational capabilities. Nonetheless, the trade-off is accepted to guarantee full sequence generation, aiming to improve the user experience.

TensorRT-LLM, provided by Nvidia, is a compelling choice. It offers an easy-to-use Python API to define LLMs and build TensorRT engines that contain state-of-the-art optimizations, particularly for inference on Nvidia GPUs (`https://github.com/Nvidia/TensorRT-LLM/tree/main`). This library is not only the optimization backbone for LLM inference in Nvidia's NeMo (`www.nvidia.com/en-us/ai-data-science/genera-tive-ai/nemo-framework/`) but also accelerates inference performance substantially, with enhancements delivering up to a 6.7x speedup on models like Llama 2 70B LLM.

Furthermore, TensorRT-LLM wraps Nvidia's deep learning compiler, which includes optimized kernels from FasterTransformer, pre- and post-processing, and even multi-GPU and multinode communication. This is especially beneficial for running huge models like Falcon-180B on a single GPU, showcasing the capability to scale up operations while remaining efficient. Additionally, it has been shown that on RTX-powered Windows PCs, LLMs can operate up to four times faster, which is significant for sophisticated LLM uses such as writing and coding assistants.

DeepSpeed by Microsoft provides another comprehensive solution for serving transformer-based models. DeepSpeed-Inference supports model parallelism, allowing large models to fit into GPU memory and smaller models to benefit from reduced latency during inference. It provides a seamless inference mode for models trained with frameworks like DeepSpeed, Megatron, and Huggingface, meaning there's no need for any significant changes on the modeling side. DeepSpeed also handles model partitioning, kernel injection, and inter-GPU communication automatically, simplifying the deployment process.

Furthermore, DeepSpeed offers the init_inference API, which allows users to load models for inference, specifying model parallelism degree and data types. It supports different data types such as fp32, fp16, and int8, optimizing the inference according to the chosen datatype. DeepSpeed's quantization approach, MoQ, helps to reduce the model size and the cost of inference at production by quantizing the models. Additionally, DeepSpeed can run models with a different model parallelism degree than they were trained with, providing flexibility and optimization opportunities.

In the context of batch size tuning, these frameworks allow for experimentation with various batch sizes to find the sweet spot between computational efficiency and model performance. By optimizing the batch size, we can ensure that the models are neither overwhelmed with data nor underutilized, which can lead to cost savings and enhanced performance. Both manual and automatic exploration can be employed to maximize the batch size, leveraging the advanced capabilities of TensorRT-LLM and DeepSpeed to ensure optimal model execution.

For readers interested in a deeper look into these frameworks, I suggest the following blogs covering DeepSpeed, TensorRT, and FasterTransformer:

➤ https://aws.amazon.com/blogs/machine-learning/deploy-large-models-at-high-performance-using-fastertransformer-on-amazon-sagemaker

➤ https://developer.nvidia.com/blog/nvidia-tensorrt-llm-supercharges-large-language-model-inference-on-nvidia-h100-gpus

➤ www.microsoft.com/en-us/research/blog/deepspeed-zero-a-leap-in-speed-for-llm-and-chat-model-training-with-4x-less-communication

Cloud-Native Inference Frameworks

Cloud-native options use the open-source tooling mentioned earlier like TensorRT and DeepSpeed and greatly simplify the experience of deploying the model. For example, with Amazon SageMaker, deploying a model is as simple as creating a serving properties file using a single API to create a persistent endpoint. Typically, these API endpoints containerize a particular framework and manage the hosting of your model.

Amazon SageMaker announced (November 2023) the release of version 0.25.0 of its large model inference (LMI) deep learning containers (DLCs), incorporating support for Nvidia's TensorRT-LLM Library. This integration facilitates optimized utilization of LLMs within SageMaker, offering significant improvements in cost-effectiveness. The LMI TensorRT-LLM DLC is reported to reduce latency by 33% and increase throughput by 60% for models such as Llama 2 70B, Falcon 40B, and CodeLlama 34B, compared to the previous iterations.

The challenge of fitting LLMs onto single accelerators or GPU instances has been a barrier to achieving both low-latency inference and scalability. To address this, SageMaker's LMI DLCs have been designed to maximize resource utilization and enhance performance. The newest DLCs support continuous batching for inference requests and efficient collective operations for better latency management. They also include Paged Attention V2 for longer sequence lengths and the updated TensorRT-LLM library to optimize GPU performance. Simplifying the optimization process, these LMI DLCs require minimal coding, only needing the model ID and any optional parameters to compile with TensorRT-LLM. The compilation and creation of an optimized model repository are automated within the DLC. Moreover, the latest DLCs incorporate advanced quantization techniques like GPTQ, AWQ, and SmoothQuant. Through these LMI DLCs on SageMaker, users can hasten the deployment of generative AI applications and fine-tune LLMs for preferred hardware, ensuring top-tier price-performance metrics.

Other cloud services like Azure and GCP also provide similar functionality to deploy your own API endpoints with LLMs. For example, deploying your own endpoint with Azure's OpenAI can be done with an OpenAI base model or a model of your choice. However, this option does not give you as much control over the stack used to deploy the model (or, from the previous discussion, serving parameters). To read more about how to deploy an LLM with Azure OpenAI, start at https://learn.microsoft.com/en-us/training/modules/large-language-model-deployment/4-deploy-model.

Consider reading more about the Azure ML platform and how you can pick popular models from a catalog for deployment from these links:

➤ https://techcommunity.microsoft.com/t5/ai-machine-learning-blog/welcoming-mistral-phi-jais-code-llama-nvidia-nemotron-and-more/ba-p/3982699

➤ https://techcommunity.microsoft.com/t5/ai-machine-learning-blog/model-benchmarks-in-azure-ai-studio/ba-p/3982282

Deep Dive into Serving Stack Choices

Most inference containers for LLMs use popular open-source libraries like DeepSpeed and TensorRT for high-throughput, low-latency inferencing. As mentioned earlier, services like SageMaker simplify the action of deploying these models to an endpoint using a simple serving properties file. But what do these files look like? What choices can you make? Let's take a look at a sample serving properties file to dig deeper.

Assume you want to deploy the Llama2 7B model from Huggingface (`https://huggingface.co/The-Bloke/Llama-2-13B-fp16`). The most basic serving properties file would look like this:

```
engine = Python
option.entryPoint = djl_python.huggingface
option.model_id = TheBloke/Llama-2-13B-fp16
option.dtype=fp16
```

What this humble four-line serving properties file says is to deploy the previous Llama2 model using the Python engine (rather than the MPI engine that will be covered later). Remember that the action of actually deploying the model has not been done yet; we are still defining the serving configuration. In many LLM cases, the default model loading timeout (or the amount of time for the serving stack to wait for before declaring that the model has not been loaded) is too small. To extend this, we can add a timeout line:

```
engine = Python
option.entryPoint = djl_python.huggingface
option.model_loading_timeout = 900
option.model_id = TheBloke/Llama-2-13B-fp16
```

Great! Now the model serving stack is instructed to wait for 900 seconds to load the Llama 2 model. This works for an instance with a single GPU. If your model fits in one GPU, it may be natural to consider single GPU instances like the G5.4x or G5.8x instances on AWS, for example. Even for models that fit entirely on one GPU as we have seen, balancing the real estate that is shared between the model, the KV cache, and the incoming batches of text is important. When models need to be split up (model parallel) to fit into a single instance with multiple GPUs, we can use the tensor parallel degree option, as shown here:

```
engine = Python
option.entryPoint = djl_python.huggingface
option.tensor_parallel_degree = 2
option.model_loading_timeout = 900
option.model_id = TheBloke/Llama-2-13B-fp16
```

Changing the tensor parallel degree in this code snippet for the serving parameters file will have a significant impact on model latency. Particularly in this setting, the model is not streaming text output to the calling entity. The entire text, which depends on the input tokens, needs to be generated before returning a payload with the output tokens to the caller. When expecting a large number of output tokens, you can obviously expect the response to take much longer. Next, we will look at batching options.

Batching Options

We have covered more than three types of batching in the chapters so far:

➤ Dynamic batching

➤ Continuous batching

➤ PagedAttention batching

The choice of which type of batching to use depends on the batch size, model of choice, and benchmarking since the impact of this choice is also influenced by other choices in the serving parameter file. We will dive deeper into how to automate this choice along with benchmarking. Before we cover choosing the right parameters, not just for batching options but for all options, let's first look at what the serving parameters file looks like for dynamic batching. Dynamic batching aggregates the received requests within a specified time frame, batches them together, and sends the batch for inference. Once the inference is processed by the LLM, the results of the batch are sent back to the calling entity. To implement this, we simply add a desired `batch_size` and a `max_batch_delay` as shown here:

```
engine = Python
option.entryPoint = djl_python.huggingface
option.tensor_parallel_degree = 2
batch_size = 64
max_batch_delay = 1000
option.model_loading_timeout = 900
option.model_id = TheBloke/Llama-2-13B-fp16
```

With continuous batching, we use iteration-level scheduling, which sets the batch size dynamically with each iteration rather than static batching. This means that as soon as one sequence in a batch is finished, it's replaced immediately with a new one. This approach keeps the GPU working at a higher capacity, as there's no downtime waiting for the entire batch to finish. To use dynamic batching, we change the engine to MPI and set a few other parameters for rolling batch as follows:

```
engine = MPI
option.entryPoint = djl_python.huggingface
option.rolling_batch = auto
option.max_rolling_batch_size = 64
option.paged_attention = false
option.max_rolling_batch_prefill_tokens = 16080
option.tensor_parallel_degree = 2
option.model_loading_timeout = 900
option.model_id = TheBloke/Llama-2-13B-fp16
```

As you can see, we have explicitly set `paged_attention` to false. Setting this to true, alongside continuous batching, is another option:

```
engine = MPI
option.entryPoint = djl_python.huggingface
option.rolling_batch = auto
option.max_rolling_batch_size = 64
option.paged_attention = true
option.max_rolling_batch_prefill_tokens = 16080
option.tensor_parallel_degree = 2
option.model_loading_timeout = 900
option.model_id = TheBloke/Llama-2-13B-fp16
```

In these examples, we explored three different batching techniques, holding all other options constant. As we can see, several manual configurations are possible involving different engines and serving parameters, but what other options can you set?

Options in DJL Serving

The full set of serving parameters can be found at https://docs.aws.amazon.com/sagemaker/latest/dg/large-model-inference-configuration.html. Here is a quick summary of configuration options for Amazon SageMaker's Large Model Inference, with interdependencies and example values:

engine:

Selects the runtime engine like MPI for distributed processes, crucial for frameworks supporting LMI like TRTLLM, LMI-Dist, and DeepSpeed.

option.tensor_parallel_degree:

Sets the number of GPUs for model sharding; max utilizes all available GPUs.

`option.rolling_batch:`

Enables combining requests received at different times into one batch, with `max` as the default setting for the TensorRT container.

`option.max_rolling_batch_size:`

Limits concurrent requests to prevent GPU memory overload, with excess requests queued.

`option.trust_remote_code:`

Allows running custom code from Hugging Face Hub models when set to `true`.

`option.revision` **and** `option.entryPoint:`

Specify version or handler for loading models, with prebuilt handlers available for different DLCs.

`option.parallel_loading` **and** `option.model_loading_timeout:`

Controls parallel loading of models and the time limit before a timeout, respectively.

`job_queue_size` **and** `option.output_formatter:`

Define the job queue size and output format, respectively, affecting how requests are managed and results are formatted.

`batch_size` **and** `option.max_batch_delay:`

Determine the number of requests processed together and the maximum wait time to form a batch as explained in the earlier dynamic batching scenario.

`option.max_idle_time:`

Sets the idle time before a worker thread scales down, affecting resource utilization.

`option.device_map` **and** `option.low_cpu_mem_usage:`

Configure model distribution across GPUs and reduce CPU memory usage during model loading.

`option.quantize` **and** `option.task:`

Enable model quantization and set the task for Hugging Face pipelines; generally, the task is set to text generation, and quantization is done before deployment as a separate step using frameworks that were covered in previous chapters like AWQ, GPTQ, or SmoothQuant to avoid additional delays in getting the model deployed.

`option.disable_flash_attn:`

Toggles the use of Hugging Face `flash_attention`.

`option.max_sparsity` **and** `option.max_splits:`

Control sparsity thresholds and batch splits for inference calls.

`option.max_tokens` **and** `option.quantize:`

Define the total token count DeepSpeed handles and the quantization method, with `smoothquant` for better quality.

`option.checkpoint` **and** `option.enable_cuda_graph:`

Specify the DeepSpeed checkpoint file and activate CUDA graph capture.

`option.max_input_len` **and** `option.max_output_len:`

Set maximum token sizes for input and output, essential for just-in-time compilation.

`option.enable_trt_overlap:`

Overlaps batch execution, which may impact performance depending on the number of requests.

`option.quantize`, `option.smoothquant_alpha`, **and related suboptions:**

Support quantization in Llama models with just-in-time compilation mode, providing custom scaling factors for tokens and channels.

Each of these parameters plays a role in fine-tuning the inference process, balancing computational resources, and ensuring efficient processing of LLMs in various deployment scenarios. With dependencies between these options and all the parameters involved, it is a significantly time-consuming exercise to zero in on the right serving configuration for your specific choice of LLM application.

High-Level Guidance for Selecting Serving Parameters

The following blog from AWS provides some high-level guidance to start with: `https://aws.amazon.com/blogs/machine-learning/boost-inference-performance-for-llms-with-new-amazon-sagemaker-containers`.

Figure 5.14 describes the decision-making process. Start with the model you intend to deploy. Consider if it is related to the following popular models: Falcon, Llama 2, or Code Llama. If your application demands generating outputs with token lengths exceeding 1,024, you will need to configure your environment to use the LMI-Dist, which is based on the DeepSpeed container. This setup requires setting the engine to MPI, specifying `tensor_parallel_degree` as max, and enabling `rolling_batch` specifically for LMI-Dist. On the other hand, if your model output token length requirements are less than 1,024, you should opt for the TensorRT-LLM (TRT-LLM container) with the engine also set to MPI and providing the `model_id`. Recall that the `model_id` can be a huggingface model identifier or a location in Amazon S3 storage with your model artifacts. For deploying models like T5, MPT, GPT-NeoX, StarCoder, Baichuan, and Mistral, the vLLM setup is appropriate, which uses the DeepSpeed container. In this scenario, set the engine to Python, set `tensor_parallel_degree` to max, provide the `model_id`, and set `rolling_batch` to vLLM. Each route converges at the `serving.properties` file, where you'll detail other configurations for efficient model serving.

While you can use this high-level guidance, you can also automate the search for other related parameters using optimization techniques. In training, hyperparameter optimization (HPO) is commonly used to find the best model parameters. Similarly, for inference, we can employ optimization algorithms to search across a range of configurations to find the most efficient setup. This is what we will look at next.

Automatically Finding Good Inference Configurations

Manually adjusting configuration options for model inference can be a tedious and error-prone process. To streamline this, we can employ automated methods that systematically explore and optimize these settings. The code snippets provided represent different configurations for model inference engines and parameters. They vary by engine type (MPI or DeepSpeed), entry points for model loading, batch size, and other parameters such as whether to use quantization or the degree of tensor parallelism.

```
## Option 1
engine = MPIoption.entryPoint = djl_python.huggingface
option.rolling_batch = auto
option.max_rolling_batch_size = 64
option.paged_attention = false
option.max_rolling_batch_prefill_tokens = 16080
option.tensor_parallel_degree = 2
option.model_loading_timeout = 900
## Option 2
engine=DeepSpeed
option.model_id=TheBloke/Llama-2-13B-fp16
```

```
option.tensor_parallel_degree=4
option.dtype=fp16
## Option 3
engine=DeepSpeed
option.model_id=TheBloke/Llama-2-13B-fp16
option.tensor_parallel_degree=4
option.dtype=fp16
option.quantize=smoothquant
## Option 4
engine=MPI
option.model_id=mistralai/Mistral-7B-Instruct-v0.1
option.tensor_parallel_degree=4
option.max_rolling_batch_size=128
option.rolling_batch=trtllm
```

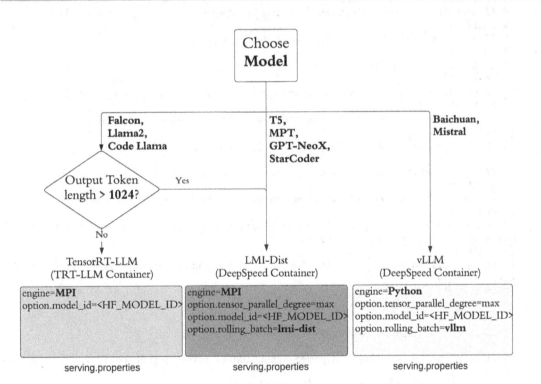

FIGURE 5.14: High-level guidance for selecting parameters in the serving properties file

Automating the process of iterating through such configurations would involve setting up a search space, where each option can be varied within a defined range. Hyperparameter optimization algorithms like those provided by Hyperopt can then navigate through this space, assessing the performance impact of each combination and converging on an optimal setup. This automated approach can save time, reduce human error, and potentially uncover more efficient configurations that might not be immediately apparent through manual experimentation.

This approach can dynamically tune parameters such as `max_rolling_batch_size`, `max_input_len`, `rolling_batch`, and other parameters to balance the trade-off between throughput and latency, ultimately achieving optimal performance tailored to the specific requirements of the deployed model.

Creating a Generic Template

We begin by creating a template that can describe any configuration. Jinja is a template engine for the Python programming language. It allows for the dynamic generation of content, such as configuration files, HTML, or any text-based format. In Jinja templates, placeholders enclosed in double curly braces, {{ ... }}, are replaced with actual values when the template is rendered.

The provided template uses conditional statements to check for the presence of various configuration options. If a given variable, like engine or dtype, is defined (i.e., has a value passed into the template), then the corresponding line with the variable's value is written to the output file. This approach is highly flexible, as it includes only the configuration lines for which values are provided, avoiding unnecessary settings that might otherwise need to be manually removed or commented out.

```
%%writefile code/template
{% if engine %}engine={{ engine }}
{% endif -%}
{% if decoding_strategy %}option.decoding_strategy={{ decoding_strategy }}
{% endif -%}
{% if device_map %}option.device_map={{ device_map }}
{% endif -%}
{% if dtype %}option.dtype={{ dtype }}
{% endif -%}
{% if enable_cuda_graph %}option.enable_cuda_graph={{ enable_cuda_graph }}
{% endif -%}
{% if enable_streaming %}option.enable_streaming={{ enable_streaming }}
{% endif -%}
{% if load_in_4bit %}option.load_in_4bit={{ load_in_4bit }}
{% endif -%}
{% if load_in_8bit %}option.load_in_8bit={{ load_in_8bit }}
{% endif -%}
{% if low_cpu_mem_usage %}option.low_cpu_mem_usage={{ low_cpu_mem_usage }}
{% endif -%}
{% if max_rolling_batch_prefill_tokens %}option.max_rolling_batch_prefill_tokens={{
max_rolling_batch_prefill_tokens }}
{% endif -%}
{% if max_rolling_batch_size %}option.max_rolling_batch_size={{ max_rolling_
batch_size }}
{% endif -%}
{% if max_tokens %}option.max_tokens={{ max_tokens }}
{% endif -%}
{% if model_id %}option.model_id={{ model_id }}
{% endif -%}
{% if paged_attention %}option.paged_attention={{ paged_attention }}
{% endif -%}
{% if quantize %}option.quantize={{ quantize }}
{% endif -%}
{% if return_tuple %}option.return_tuple={{ return_tuple }}
{% endif -%}
{% if rolling_batch %}option.rolling_batch={{ rolling_batch }}
{% endif -%}
{% if tensor_parallel_degree %}option.tensor_parallel_degree={{ tensor_parallel_
degree }}
{% endif -%}
```

In essence, the template acts as a blueprint that can produce different outputs depending on the variables fed into it, making it an ideal tool for generating custom configuration files for different scenarios without manual editing.

Next, we use this template to write any configuration file using the following function:

```
from pathlib import Path
from jinja2 import Environment, FileSystemLoader

def write_jinja(options):
    # Load Jinja environment and template
    jinja_env = Environment(loader=FileSystemLoader('code'))
    template = jinja_env.get_template('template')
    # Render the template with non-empty options
    rendered_content = template.render({k: v for k, v in options.items() if v})

    # Write to file
    with Path("code/serving.properties").open("w") as file:
        file.write(rendered_content)
    # Optional: Print the contents with line numbers
    with Path("code/serving.properties").open("r") as file:
        for line_number, line in enumerate(file, start=1):
            print(f"{line_number}\t{line}", end='')
```

The `write_jinja` function in Python serves to automate the process of generating configuration files using Jinja templates. It starts by setting up the Jinja environment, specifying `code` as the directory where templates are stored. The function then loads a template named `template` from this directory. Utilizing the options provided, it filters out any empty values and renders the template accordingly. The resulting configuration is written to a file named `serving.properties` within the same `code` directory. Optionally, the function can read and display this file's contents, each line accompanied by its line number, facilitating a clear view of the final output directly within a Jupyter Notebook environment. This approach simplifies the creation of tailored configuration files. Next, we define a "space" in Hyperopt.

Defining a HPO Space

Hyperparameter optimization (HPO) plays a critical role in machine learning, particularly in fine-tuning models to achieve optimal performance. In this case, we will be using the same tools and concepts to optimize our inference parameters. The concept of "search spaces" in HPO, especially as implemented in the Hyperopt library, is central to this process. A search space in Hyperopt is defined as a range or a set of possible values for each hyperparameter that we want to optimize.

Hyperopt offers various ways to define these spaces. A simple example is using hp.choice to select from discrete options or hp.uniform for a continuous range. For example, to optimize the learning_rate of a model, one might define the space as follows:

```
from hyperopt import hp
space = {'learning_rate': hp.uniform('learning_rate', 0.0001, 0.1)}
```

This is a typical search space with a single hyperparameter uniformly varying from 0.0001 to 0.1. However, search spaces can be more complex. They can be hierarchical, allowing the definition of nested parameters. This enables the modeling of dependencies between hyperparameters, where the choice of one parameter can influence the range or values of another. In creating these spaces, Hyperopt provides a framework to explore a vast range of configurations efficiently. This approach is crucial in finding the best combination of parameters for a given model, leading to enhanced model accuracy, reduced overfitting, or improved computational efficiency. The documentation of Hyperopt offers a comprehensive guide and examples on effectively utilizing these spaces for various machine learning tasks (https://hyperopt.github.io/hyperopt/getting-started/search_spaces).

Consider optimizing inference parameters for a language model. A simple hierarchical space might look like this:

```
from hyperopt import hp
space = {
```

```
       'engine': hp.choice('engine', [
           {
               'type': 'DeepSpeed',
               'tensor_parallel_degree':
hp.choice('tensor_parallel_degree_deepspeed', [2, 4, 8])
           },
           {
               'type': 'MPI',
               'max_rolling_batch_size':
hp.choice('max_rolling_batch_size_mpi', [32, 64, 128])
           }
       ])
}
```

In this example, if DeepSpeed is chosen as the engine, the space includes options for tensor_parallel_degree. If MPI is selected, it instead presents choices for max_rolling_batch_size.

For our inference hyperparameter optimization problem, the search space is more elaborate, as shown in the following code snippet. It includes multiple nested parameters within each engine type, offering a comprehensive set of configurations to optimize various aspects of model inference, like data type, CUDA graph utilization, and quantization method. This hierarchical structuring allows Hyperopt to intelligently navigate through a complex parameter space, adapting its search strategy based on the interdependencies of the parameters.

```
from hyperopt import hp, fmin, tpe, Trials
import json
space = {
    'engine': hp.choice('engine', [
        ('DeepSpeed', {
            'option.dtype': hp.choice('option.dtype_deepspeed', ['fp16']),
            'option.enable_cuda_graph': hp.choice('option.enable_cuda_graph_
deepspeed', [True, False]),
            'option.rolling_batch': hp.choice('option.rolling_batch_deepspeed',
['auto', 'deepspeed','trtllm']),
            'option.quantize': hp.choice('option.quantize_deepspeed',
['smoothquant', 'bitsandbytes', 'gptq', 'bitsandbytes4', 'bitsandbytes8', 'awq'])
        }),
        ('MPI', {
            'option.dtype': hp.choice('option.dtype_mpi', ['fp16']),
            'option.enable_cuda_graph': False,
            'option.rolling_batch': hp.choice('option.rolling_batch_mpi',
['auto', 'scheduler']),
            'option.quantize': None
        }),
        ('FasterTransformer', { # not supported for llama models
            'option.dtype': hp.choice('option.dtype_ft', ['fp16', 'bf16']),
            'option.enable_cuda_graph': False,
            'option.rolling_batch': hp.choice('option.rolling_batch_ft',
['auto', 'scheduler']),
            'option.quantize': None
        }),
        ('Python', {
            'option.dtype': hp.choice('option.dtype_py', ['fp16',]),
            'option.enable_cuda_graph': False,
            'option.rolling_batch': hp.choice('option.rolling_batch_py',
['auto', 'scheduler']),
            'option.quantize': None
```

```
                })
        ]),
        'option.decoding_strategy': hp.choice('option.decoding_strategy', ['sample',
'greedy', 'contrastive']),
        'option.device_map': hp.choice('option.device_map', ['balanced', 'auto',
'sequential']),
        'option.load_in_4bit': hp.choice('option.load_in_4bit', [True, False]),
        'option.load_in_8bit': hp.choice('option.load_in_8bit', [True, False]),
        'option.low_cpu_mem_usage': hp.choice('option.low_cpu_mem_usage',
[True, False]),
        'option.max_rolling_batch_prefill_tokens': hp.choice('option.max_rolling_batch_
prefill_tokens', [256, 512, 1024, 2048, 4096, 8192]),
        'option.max_rolling_batch_size': hp.choice('option.max_rolling_batch_size',
[2,4,8,16,32]),
        'option.paged_attention': hp.choice('option.paged_attention', [True, False]),
        'option.return_tuple': hp.choice('option.return_tuple', [False]),
        'option.tensor_parallel_degree': hp.choice('option.tensor_parallel_
degree', [4]),
        'option.max_tokens': hp.choice('option.max_tokens', [256]),
        'option.model_id':hp.choice('option.model_id', ['TheBloke/Llama-2-13B-fp16'])
}
```

The provided code block defines our HPO space using Hyperopt. In this HPO space, the following happens:

➤ Different configurations are explored based on the engine type (DeepSpeed, MPI, Python). Each engine type has associated parameters, like option.dtype, option.enable_cuda_graph, and option. rolling_batch. The hp.choice function specifies a list of values to choose from for each parameter.

➤ For instance, under the DeepSpeed engine, option.dtype is set to choose fp16, option.enable_ cuda_graph can be either True or False, and option.rolling_batch has multiple options like auto, deepspeed, and trtllm.

➤ The space also includes other global hyperparameters like option.decoding_strategy, option. device_map, and option.low_cpu_mem_usage, each with their respective range of values.

➤ The use of hierarchical structures within the space, such as nested dictionaries, allows for conditional selection of hyperparameters based on previous choices (like different settings under different engines).

By defining such an HPO space, Hyperopt can systematically and efficiently search through a vast combination of hyperparameters, evaluating each configuration to identify the one that yields the best performance based on a defined metric (like accuracy, latency, etc.). This approach simplifies the otherwise complex and time-consuming task of manually tuning hyperparameters, especially in scenarios with large numbers of variables and interdependencies.

Searching the Space for Optimal Configurations

To search the space for optimal configurations, we first need to define the objective function, which serves as the heart of the hyperparameter optimization process. In our case, the objective function is designed to determine the most efficient inference configuration for text generation, focusing on maximizing the speed of token generation. This involves a series of intricate steps starting from parameter processing, model packaging, endpoint creation, and, crucially, benchmarking the inference performance. Each trial's success is measured by the text generation speed in tokens per second, a key metric that guides the optimization algorithm in identifying the most effective set of parameters. This methodical approach ensures a systematic and data-driven search for the optimal configuration essential for enhancing the performance of language models. Here is what the objective function might look like:

```
import random
def objective(params):
    delete_in_service_endpoints()
    try:


        print("Trial with parameters:\n")

        write_jinja(params)
        print("Packaging model")
        model_name = create_sm_model(package_model(),inference_image_uri)
        print("Creating endpoint")
        endpoint_name, endpoint_config_name, sm_client = create_
endpoint(model_name)
        print("Testing endpoint")
        total_tokens, total_seconds, total_tokens_per_second = benchmark_
generation_speed(endpoint_name, tokenizer_bnb)
        result = {'loss': -total_tokens_per_second, 'status': 'ok'}

        params = {key: str(val) for key, val in params.items()}
        log_experiment(params, total_tokens_per_second)

        print("Successful trial logged. Cleaning up")
        try:
            delete_in_service_endpoints()
            sm_client.delete_endpoint_config(EndpointConfigName=endpoint_
config_name)
            sm_client.delete_model(ModelName=model_name)
        except Exception as e:
            print("Could not delete endpoint!\n",e)




    except Exception as e:
        print("Something went wrong with this trial:\n", e)
        result = {'loss': 10000, 'status': 'fail'}
    print("-----------")
    return result
```

The objective function plays a pivotal role in hyperparameter optimization with Hyperopt, targeting the optimal configuration for a language model to maximize text generation speed in terms of tokens per second. The function operates through several stages. Initially, it performs cleanup by removing any pre-existing service endpoints, establishing a clean slate. During the parameter processing phase, the trial parameters are displayed, flattened, and adjusted based on the selected rolling_batch or engine type, affecting the inference image choice among TRT LLM, FasterTransformer, or DeepSpeed.

Next, the function packages the model using the chosen parameters and sets up an Amazon SageMaker model, followed by creating an inference endpoint. The benchmarking step forms the crux of the process, where it assesses the endpoint's efficiency in generating text, measuring the total tokens produced and the duration taken to calculate the tokens-per-second rate. A higher rate signifies a more effective configuration.

Post-benchmarking, the function logs the experiment's outcomes, including the parameters and tokens-per-second rate, and undertakes a cleanup, eliminating the endpoints and other utilized resources. Error handling is also integrated; in the case of any trial issues, the function records the error and returns a high "loss" value, ensuring the continuity of the optimization process despite individual trial failures (this penalty is a standard way to avoid unfavorable areas in the HPO space). The function concludes by returning a dictionary containing the loss (the negative of tokens per second, as Hyperopt aims to minimize the function) and the status. With all that done, starting the HPO process with Hyperopt is as simple as doing this:

```
trials = Trials()
best = fmin(
    fn=objective,
    space=space,
    algo=tpe.suggest,
    max_evals=100,  # You can adjust the number of evaluations.
    trials=trials
)
```

The previous code snippet begins with the initialization of a `Trials` object. In Hyperopt, this object is essential for storing detailed information about each evaluation of the objective function during the optimization process. It not only keeps track of the parameters used and the loss returned by the objective function but also gathers other statistical data, allowing for a thorough analysis of the optimization process.

The heart of this setup is the `fmin` function, which stands for "function minimum." Its primary goal is to find the set of hyperparameters that minimize the objective function. In this instance, the `fmin` function is called with several arguments. The `fn` argument specifies the objective function, which, in this case, is the previously defined `objective()`, designed to optimize your language model inference performance. The `space` argument defines the hyperparameter space, which we walked through earlier, defining the range or distributions of hyperparameters that Hyperopt will explore.

A key component of this setup is the `algo` argument, set to `tpe.suggest`, which refers to the Tree-structured Parzen Estimator (TPE). TPE is an algorithm used for hyperparameter optimization and is known for its efficiency, especially in high-dimensional spaces. It operates on a Bayesian approach, using past trial data to update its beliefs about the hyperparameter space and selecting new hyperparameters by balancing exploration with exploitation. This balance ensures that the algorithm tries new hyperparameter combinations while focusing on the most promising areas. TPE uses a small number of evaluations to explore your space efficiently. Using random exploration (or, worse, an exhaustive search) would mean that you end up running thousands of inference deployments and testing them in development before deciding what your final inference configuration looks like.

Finally, the `max_evals` argument in `fmin` is set to 100, defining the maximum number of times the objective function will be evaluated. This means Hyperopt will test 100 different sets of hyperparameters to find the optimal combination.

Overall, this process orchestrates an optimization, where Hyperopt iteratively evaluates the objective function with various hyperparameters drawn from the defined space. It uses the TPE algorithm to guide its search efficiently, with the ultimate goal of discovering hyperparameters that minimize the loss, thus optimizing the performance of the model or system in focus.

Results of Inference HPO

The parallel coordinates plot in Figure 5.15 visualizes the results of all the trials conducted by Hyperopt in the previous case.

In a parallel coordinates plot, each vertical line represents one hyperparameter or a metric, and each line crossing these vertical lines represents one trial or one set of hyperparameters tested during the optimization. The position on a vertical line represents the value of the hyperparameter, and the color of a line typically represents the performance or another metric—in this case, tokens per second (TPS), which is a measure of the speed of text generation by the model.

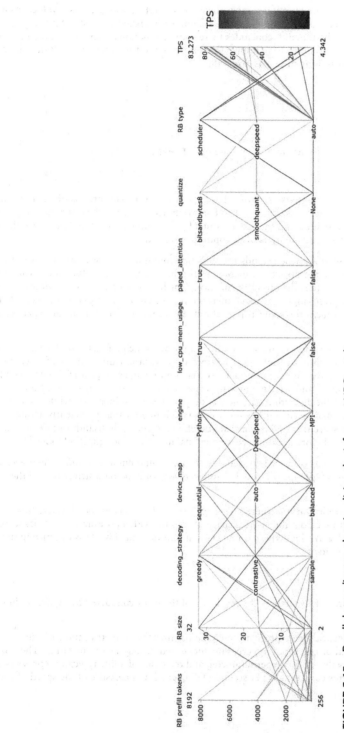

FIGURE 5.15: Parallel coordinates plot visualizing the inference HPO results

In the optimization process depicted in the plot, a range of parameters is being explored to maximize tokens per second (TPS) for a language model. The parameters under consideration include RB prefill tokens, RB size, and RB type, where RB stands for rolling batch, which is an exploration of different batching strategies that could affect throughput. Decoding strategies, such as greedy or sample, are also varied, to find a balance between generation quality and speed. Hardware configuration is indicated by `device_map`, and the backend inference engines are specified as Python, DeepSpeed, or MPI, which could significantly influence execution speed. Note that the previous code also had a snippet including FasterTransformer, which was not used in this exercise since the model being deployed is Llama 2, which is incompatible with the FasterTransformer engine at the time of this writing. Memory optimization flags, such as `low_cpu_mem_usage` and `paged_attention`, and quantization methods, such as `bitsandbytes8` and `smoothquant`, are examined for their impact on performance. These parameters collectively represent a comprehensive search space, aiming to identify the configuration that allows the language model to generate text at the highest possible speed.

The lines in the plot, color-coded from red to blue, illustrate the traversal through different hyperparameter combinations, where the reddest lines trace the parameter choices that culminate in the highest TPS. These red lines intersect the vertical parameter lines at values that collectively correspond to the most efficient model configuration found during the optimization process. The maximum TPS achieved is indicated by the lines that terminate at the peak of the TPS scale at 83, suggesting an extremely efficient text generation under those specific settings. Conversely, the lower end of the performance spectrum is visualized by lines closer to the 4 TPS mark on the scale, depicted in cooler colors, representing less optimal parameter choices. In this case, the final optimal configuration (highest TPS) for the Llama 2 model used included using the MPI engine, 256 Rolling batch prefill tokens, a contrastive decoding strategy, balanced device map, setting low CPU memory usage parameter to false, setting Paged Attention to true, and no quantization. Now, this set of parameters was arrived at after 100 evaluations, some of which led to failed inference endpoints. More evaluations generally lead to more exploration of the design space and may lead to even better TPS for this model.

INFERENCE ACCELERATION TOOLS

The recent advancements in generative AI and large language models have spurred the development of specialized inference platforms. Nvidia, for instance, has launched four such platforms optimized for a diverse set of AI applications, including large language model deployment. These platforms combine Nvidia's software stack with processors like Nvidia Ada, Nvidia Hopper, and Nvidia Grace Hopper, including GPUs specifically designed for AI workloads, such as the Nvidia L4 Tensor Core GPU and the Nvidia H100 NVL GPU. Each platform targets specific tasks, such as AI video, image generation, LLM deployment, and recommender inference. The Nvidia L4 for AI Video, for example, can deliver significantly more AI-powered video performance than CPUs, and the Nvidia H100 NVL is particularly suited for deploying massive LLMs like ChatGPT at scale (`https://nvidi-anews.nvidia.com/news/nvidia-launches-inference-platforms-for-large-language-models-and-generative-ai-workloads`).

Turning to CPU-based acceleration, Numenta, in collaboration with Intel, has showcased remarkable improvements in running LLMs on CPUs. Numenta demonstrated that its custom-trained language models could achieve significant throughput speedup and lower latency on fourth-generation Intel Xeon scalable processors compared to AMD Milan CPU implementations. For instance, with Intel's processors, Numenta achieved a 20x speed increase for large document processing. This development is crucial for NLP applications, as it offers a cost-effective and efficient alternative to running LLMs on CPUs, traditionally considered a challenging task.

Neural Magic's DeepSparse is another pivotal tool in the landscape of inference acceleration, particularly for CPUs. DeepSparse offers an inference runtime that delivers GPU-class performance on CPU architectures. This tool is especially noteworthy because it addresses the challenge of efficiently running large language models on CPUs, which traditionally lag behind GPUs in terms of performance for such tasks. DeepSparse leverages model sparsity techniques, optimizing neural networks by taking advantage of the inactive neurons within them. This approach significantly reduces the computational requirements without substantially impacting the model's accuracy. By doing so, DeepSparse makes it feasible to run sophisticated, open-source large language models on more accessible commodity hardware. Unfortunately, a comparative analysis of various inference tools has yet to be completed, but more information about DeepSparse can be found at `https://neuralmagic.com/deepsparse`.

On the software side, the platforms feature Nvidia AI Enterprise software suite, which includes the aforementioned Nvidia TensorRT, a development kit for high-performance deep learning inference, and Nvidia Triton Inference Server, an open-source inference-serving software that helps standardize model deployment. These tools are integral in facilitating efficient and scalable model deployment across various platforms.

TensorRT and GPU Acceleration Tools

This section focuses on the recent developments by Nvidia, particularly the introduction of TensorRT-LLM and its integration into the Nvidia NeMo framework.

Nvidia's TensorRT-LLM is a comprehensive library specifically designed to compile and optimize LLMs for inference on Nvidia GPUs. This open-source library, available for free, is part of the Nvidia NeMo framework, an end-to-end solution for building, customizing, and deploying generative AI applications. The significance of TensorRT-LLM lies in its ability to handle the extensive size and complexity of LLMs, which can be expensive and slow to run without proper optimization. TensorRT-LLM addresses this challenge by incorporating various optimization techniques, including kernel fusion, quantization, C++ implementations, KV caching, in-flight batching, and paged attention. These optimizations are integrated into an intuitive Python API, making the process of defining and building new models more accessible (`https://developer.nvidia.com/blog/optimizing-inference-on-llms-with-tensorrt-llm-now-publicly-available`).

TensorRT-LLM wraps around TensorRT's deep learning compiler and includes optimized kernels specifically made for advanced implementations like FlashAttention and masked multihead attention (MHA), crucial for LLM execution. The toolkit also comprises pre- and post-processing steps and multi-GPU/multinode communication primitives, offering groundbreaking performance for LLM inference on GPUs.

Some of the highlights of TensorRT-LLM include support for various LLMs like Llama 1 and 2, ChatGLM, Falcon, MPT, Baichuan, and Starcoder, as well as features like in-flight batching, paged attention, multi-GPU multinode (MGMN) inference, and support for Nvidia's latest GPU architectures. This comprehensive approach underlines Nvidia's commitment to collaborating with leading LLM companies to accelerate and optimize LLM inference, contributing significantly to the field of AI and machine learning.

Beyond local execution, TensorRT-LLM is also integrated with the Nvidia Triton Inference Server, creating a production-ready deployment environment for LLMs. The new Triton Inference Server backend for TensorRT-LLM utilizes the TensorRT-LLM C++ runtime for rapid inference execution and incorporates advanced techniques like in-flight batching and paged KV-caching. This combination of TensorRT-LLM and the Triton Inference Server exemplifies Nvidia's effort to provide a robust, scalable, and efficient inference solution for LLMs, enabling broad application across various industries and use cases.

CPU Acceleration Tools

This section explores the advancements in CPU-based runtimes for LLMs, highlighting how these developments have made it increasingly feasible to efficiently run LLMs on CPUs.

One of the key developments in this area is the collaboration between Numenta and Intel, which has led to a significant acceleration in LLM inference on Intel Xeon CPU Max Series processors. This collaboration has focused on overcoming the traditional challenges of running LLMs on CPUs, particularly those related to latency and throughput. Numenta's custom-trained language models have demonstrated remarkable performance on Intel's fourth-generation Xeon scalable processors. These models have achieved less than 10ms latency and a 100x throughput speedup compared to AMD Milan CPU implementations for BERT inference. Moreover, for large document processing, these models can run 20x faster on Intel Xeon CPU Max Series processors, showcasing the potential of CPUs in handling complex NLP tasks traditionally reserved for GPUs (`https://community.intel.com/t5/Blogs/Tech-Innovation/Artificial-Intelligence-AI/Numenta-and-Intel-Accelerate-Inference-20x-on-Large-Language/post/1471636`).

Another significant contribution in this space is from Neural Magic with its DeepSparse inference runtime. Deep-Sparse offers up to 7x faster text generation on CPUs by leveraging model sparsity. This technology enables the deployment of sparse LLMs on any standard CPU hardware, whether in the cloud, data centers, or at the edge, thus democratizing access to powerful LLM applications. DeepSparse, when used in conjunction with tools like LangChain, provides developers with the ability to build and deploy LLM applications on CPUs without relying on expensive APIs or the computational power of GPUs. This approach significantly broadens the scope and accessibility of LLMs, making them viable for a wider range of applications and environments (`https://neuralmagic.com/blog/building-sparse-llm-applications-on-cpus-with-langchain-and-deepsparse`).

Deploying LLMs on CPUs with these tools involves confirming hardware compatibility and then installing the necessary packages, such as DeepSparse and LangChain. This streamlined process facilitates easier adoption and integration of LLMs into various applications, enabling even those with basic computer setups to utilize advanced LLMs. The advancements in CPU inference runtimes signify a major shift in the AI landscape, providing more flexible and cost-effective options for developers and organizations looking to harness the power of LLMs. Visit the docs section of Neuralmagic (`https://docs.neuralmagic.com`) to see how you can use SparseML to create inference-optimized sparse models using pruning, quantization, and distillation algorithms, and then deploy these models with DeepSparse for GPU-class performance on CPU hardware. In general, expect GPU-based deployments to dominate the LLM space. While there have been some exciting advancements in CPU-based LLM deployments, reliance on GPUs is here to stay.

MONITORING AND OBSERVABILITY

Large language models present significant challenges when it comes to monitoring their performance and ensuring safety over the life cycle of the GenAI application they are part of. This involves identifying the appropriate metrics for tracking, such as inference throughout, safety, toxicity, gender bias, text quality, semantic similarity, and human preference matching. The role of LLM operations (LLMOps) is crucial in this context, encompassing specialized practices and processes essential for managing and operationalizing LLMs efficiently.

Monitoring LLMs is important for several reasons. It ensures the model's reliability and performance by tracking its behavior over time, allowing for the identification of potential biases, errors, or unintended consequences in the model's outputs. This tracking is vital for maintaining ethical standards as well. As mentioned earlier, this continuous monitoring focuses on several key areas such as accuracy, response time, sentiment, and context relevancy of the LLM's responses. Additionally, understanding model performance and tracking it over time is important to grasp data drift and model drift.

MONITORING VS. OBSERVABILITY

Monitoring in LLMs typically relates to how the data or model might be changing over time. It's about identifying when something is wrong in terms of performance or accuracy. On the other hand, observability deals with understanding what's happening in the system, why it's happening, what tools to include for traceability, and how to fix any problems encountered. It involves a systematic practice of scrutinizing and comprehending the intricacies of a model's performance and behavior, including its input mechanisms, output results, and internal workings. Observability in LLM monitoring is a technical solution that allows teams to actively debug their system and is based on exploring properties and patterns not defined in advance, which helps in maintaining the accuracy and reliability of generated outputs.

LLMOps and Monitoring

LLMOps represents a specialized subset of machine learning operations (MLOps), focusing specifically on managing and operationalizing LLMs. It encompasses various practices and processes essential for the efficient management of LLMs. This includes streamlining workflows for data scientists and software engineers, support-ing iterative data exploration, tracking experiments, facilitating prompt engineering, managing models and pipe-lines, ensuring controlled transitioning, and deploying and monitoring LLMs. We will briefly describe the major steps in a typical LLMOps life cycle and then focus on monitoring.

The LLMOps life cycle for LLMs is a multifaceted process that starts with the development phase, setting the foundation for what follows. Figure 5.16 shows a version of the full LLMOps process.

Figure 5.16 outlines the life cycle and workflow of LLMOps in a sequential and decision-based manner. The process commences with defining the use case (step 1), which dictates the subsequent stages. This is followed by data collection tailored to the use case's requirements (step 2). Next, prompt engineering ensures that interaction prompts are designed to elicit the desired responses from the model (step 3). The process diverges at the next stage, where the development of the LLM application takes place (step 4): one can either choose a pre-trained model, bypassing the need for further training (step 5a), or proceed with training, which includes pre-training or fine-tuning based on new data (step 5b).

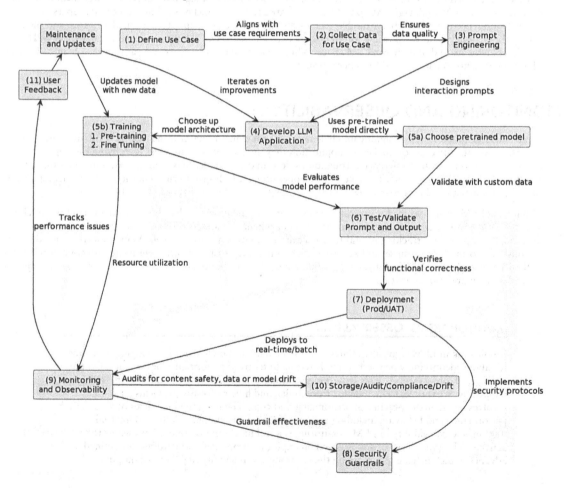

FIGURE 5.16: Steps in LLMOps

After the selection or training phase, validation and testing of the model's prompts and outputs ensure functional correctness (step 6). The validated model moves to deployment, where it is integrated into production or user acceptance testing (UAT) environments (step 7). Here, security guardrails are implemented to ensure data protection and model integrity (step 8). Once deployed, monitoring and observability become pivotal, tracking the model's performance, usage, and ensuring content safety (step 9). The system's outputs and interactions are stored and audited for compliance and further analysis (step 10).

Feedback loops are integral to this life cycle, with user feedback driving continuous improvement (step 11). This feedback informs the maintenance stage, where updates and refinements are made, potentially leading back to further training or development iterations. This cyclical process underscores the adaptability and evolution of the LLMs, ensuring they remain effective, secure, and aligned with user needs and ethical standards.

Our focus in this section is on step 9, monitoring and observability. Once LLM models are deployed and integrated into applications, monitoring ensures that these models perform as intended and continue to generate value for the users. This involves monitoring data for drift, model performance, groundedness, token consumptions, and infrastructure performance. Model monitoring in production is vital as it ensures consistent performance by detecting and addressing issues such as model degradation and biases. It enables early identification of anomalies, helping maintain overall system quality and compliance with regulatory requirements. Continuous monitoring also fosters continuous improvement by identifying areas for optimization, leading to better-performing, more reliable models.

Why Is Monitoring Important for LLMs?

Monitoring (step 9 in Figure 5.16) is indeed one of the most crucial steps in the life cycle of LLMs, especially in the context of generative AI applications that predominantly utilize pre-trained models (step 5a). Here are the key reasons why monitoring stands out as a pivotal aspect:

➤ **Performance assurance in production:** While pre-trained models offer a strong starting point, their behavior in real-world applications can vary significantly. First, validating these models with custom, business-centric data (step 6) and then monitoring (step 9) in production environments is essential to ensure that these models perform as intended when interacting with diverse and unpredictable user inputs. It helps identify and address any discrepancies between expected and actual model performance.

➤ **Adaptation to evolving data and use cases:** Generative AI applications are dynamic, often dealing with evolving user needs and data patterns. Monitoring (step 9) allows for the detection of changes in data trends (data drift) or in the model's effectiveness over time (model drift), as shown in step 10. By keeping a close eye on these aspects, organizations can ensure that their LLMs remain relevant, effective, and compliant, adapting promptly to new requirements or shifts in usage patterns.

➤ **Bias detection and ethical compliance:** LLMs, like all AI models, are susceptible to biases present in their training data. Monitoring in a production environment is critical for detecting and mitigating these biases. It ensures that the model's outputs remain fair, unbiased, and compliant with ethical standards. This is particularly important for applications that impact decision-making or interact with diverse user groups.

➤ **Enhanced user experience and trust:** Continuous monitoring allows for the rapid identification and resolution of issues that could negatively impact the user experience. By ensuring the model's outputs are relevant, coherent, and contextually appropriate with the help of user feedback (step 11), monitoring helps in maintaining and enhancing user trust in the application. This further enables alignment and future training/fine tuning operations.

➤ **Efficient resource utilization:** Monitoring also involves overseeing the model's computational efficiency and resource utilization (arrow from steps 5b to 9) during training and deployment. For applications deploying LLMs, optimizing resource use is crucial to maintain cost-effectiveness and operational efficiency. Monitoring helps in identifying bottlenecks or areas where the model may be over-utilizing resources, allowing for timely optimization.

> ➤ **Facilitating continuous improvement:** With methodologies like prompt engineering for fine-tuning (PEFT) making the fine-tuning process more efficient, the focus shifts to monitoring as a means of continual improvement. Through monitoring, insights are gained into how well the fine-tuning and prompt engineering efforts are translating into real-world performance, guiding further refinements and adjustments. This is done via experimentation tools like MLFlow or Weights and Biases using custom dashboards that monitor changes in metrics against business thresholds.

Monitoring and Updating Guardrails

The interplay between security guardrails and monitoring is integral to maintaining a robust and safe GenAI system. Security guardrails are established to safeguard the LLM from the outset, acting as the first line of defense against unauthorized access and potential misuse. They serve as the foundational policies and technical constraints that dictate the permissible operations within the model.

The synergy between security guardrails and monitoring extends to regulatory compliance and the establishment of comprehensive audit trails. As interactions with the LLM are meticulously logged, monitoring facilitates the creation of an accountable record of usage, which is indispensable for regulatory adherence and post-incident analyses. Attempts of misuse or jailbreaks are important during continuous improvement stages of GenAI application development.

Feedback loops between monitoring outcomes and security protocols enable the dynamic refinement of guardrails, as shown in Figure 5.16. Should monitoring reveal vulnerabilities or emerging threats not adequately countered by existing guardrails, adjustments can be made to fortify the model against such risks. As you can imagine, this is a continuous process that protects the application and its users. In the instance of a security incident, the combination of proactive guardrails and reactive monitoring with humans or automation in the loop allows for a swift and informed response, minimizing potential damage and expediting recovery processes.

One example of how to implement guardrails is by implementing better prompts. The "guardrails" open-source library (`https://github.com/guardrails-ai/guardrails`) offers a framework for enhancing LLMs by adding structured guardrails to their outputs. This Python package allows users to specify structures, types, and quality guarantees to the outputs of LLMs. It includes features for semantic validation, such as bias checks in generated text, bug detection in code, and more. It also provides mechanisms for corrective actions when validations fail, ensuring the LLM's outputs meet predefined specifications and quality criteria. This tool is particularly useful for developers looking to implement better prompts and enforce responsible AI practices by ensuring the outputs of LLMs are safe, structured, and of high quality.

Amazon's Bedrock Guardrails (`https://aws.amazon.com/bedrock/guardrails`) exemplify this integrated approach to security in LLMs in a production setting on the cloud. Bedrock Guardrails is a fully managed feature of Amazon Bedrock, which provides customizable safeguards that align with specific use cases and responsible AI policies. These guardrails are tailored to the unique operational aspects of the LLM they protect, offering a personalized security framework that complements the overarching monitoring systems.

In summary, monitoring in production is vital because it encapsulates the ongoing, real-world effectiveness and ethical compliance of LLMs. It's a continuous process that ensures these advanced models remain accurate, efficient, and aligned with evolving data, user expectations, and ethical standards, even after deployment. In addition to model performance and safety, LLMOps also emphasizes the importance of infrastructure monitoring. This includes tracking model performance in production from both model and operational perspectives. Tools like Azure Machine Learning, Amazon SageMaker, and Amazon Bedrock support logging and tracking experiments, where models, metrics, parameters, training details, and other artifacts are logged. The major cloud providers help automatically log and store this information in various places. In Azure, this is captured in Azure App Insights and can be accessed using Log Analytics inside Azure Monitor. In AWS, this is stored in the various console home pages for Amazon SageMaker, within SageMaker Studio, and on Amazon Bedrock.

While LLMs come as pre-trained and may not require deep model inferencing logs, LLMOps can effectively track hyperparameters, execution times, prompts, and responses of LLMs and inference latency. Overall, LLMOps incorporates monitoring and observability as integral components, ensuring that LLMs are not only efficiently managed but also continuously improved upon and aligned with ethical and performance standards. This step is crucial for the successful deployment and operationalization of LLMs in various real-world applications.

SUMMARY

In this chapter, we first went back to the basics to describe how different aspects of an LLM contribute to the resource utilization on GPUs, focusing specifically on the KV cache and optimal batching. We covered various state-of-the-art techniques like PagedAttention and S3 and discussed toolkits and SDKs that can be used for inference acceleration. Finally, discussed about the importance of monitoring in the LLMOps context, with monitoring and observability being central to using hard data to improve the GenAI application performance and safety.

CONCLUSION

WHAT'S IN THIS CHAPTER?

➤ Balancing Performance and Cost

➤ Future Trends in GenAI Applications

BALANCING PERFORMANCE AND COST

IN THE EVOLVING landscape of GenAI, and particularly LLMs, a critical theme that emerges is the balance between performance and cost. This balance is not just a technical concern but also a strategic one for large and small enterprises, influencing how GenAI solutions are deployed and leveraged across various industries.

Throughout this book, we've explored diverse strategies and methodologies aimed at optimizing this balance. For instance, Chapter 2 delved into fine-tuning techniques, highlighting how customizability can lead to more efficient use of computational resources. By tailoring models to specific tasks or domains, organizations can achieve better performance without proportionally increasing costs. This principle was also evident in the discussion of low-rank approximations and parameter-efficient fine-tuning (PEFT) methods, which offer a more economical approach to model training and deployment.

Chapter 3 extended this discussion into the realm of inference techniques. Here, we examined how techniques such as prompt engineering and caching with vector stores can significantly enhance the efficiency of LLMs. By carefully crafting prompts and efficiently storing and retrieving vector data, we can reduce the computational load, thereby optimizing costs. Furthermore, the use of summarization and batch prompting, as outlined in that chapter, serves as a practical example of how to process large volumes of data more economically.

The theme of cost-effective model selection was central to Chapter 4, where we explored the advantages of compact and nimble models over larger, more resource-intensive alternatives. This choice, while sometimes necessitating a trade-off in terms of raw power or versatility, can be a crucial factor in managing costs, especially in resource-constrained environments.

Chapter 5 focused on infrastructure and deployment strategies. It emphasized how hardware utilization and batch size tuning are pivotal in optimizing the cost-effectiveness of GenAI applications. By aligning hardware capabilities with the specific demands of GenAI tasks, organizations can achieve a more balanced cost-performance equation.

It becomes evident that the trade-off between performance and cost in GenAI applications is not just about choosing one over the other. Rather, it's about understanding the specific needs and constraints of each application and making informed decisions that align with those parameters. Whether it's choosing the right model, fine-tuning it for specific tasks, or deploying it in the most efficient manner, each step involves a series of decisions that collectively determine the cost-effectiveness of the solution.

As we move forward, it's crucial to continue exploring and refining these strategies. The field of GenAI is rapidly evolving, with new technologies and approaches emerging regularly. Staying abreast of these developments and understanding how they can be harnessed to balance performance and cost will be key to leveraging the full potential of GenAI in a sustainable and economically viable manner.

Analyzing Trade-Offs

IN THE REALM of LLMs, striking a balance between performance and cost is a multifaceted endeavor, deeply entwined with the application and the constraints of available resources. Chapters 1 to 5 of this book have laid the foundation for understanding these dynamics, and here we delve deeper into some of the intricacies of these trade-offs.

A key aspect of cost optimization in LLMs lies in model selection and customization. As previously discussed in Chapter 4, selecting between larger, more comprehensive models and smaller, more efficient alternatives involves weighing the benefits of performance against the costs of computation and deployment. For instance, using a model like GPT-4 offers unparalleled text generation capabilities but comes at a significantly higher cost compared to smaller models or with self-hosted endpoints. The choice often hinges on the specific requirements of the task and the balance one wants to strike between accuracy, complexity, and financial outlay.

Another critical area is the adaptation of models to specific tasks, as discussed in Chapter 2. Techniques such as prompt engineering, fine-tuning, and knowledge distillation play a pivotal role here. For instance, prompt engineering can effectively guide model responses, enhancing performance without the need for extensive retraining. Fine-tuning, on the other hand, involves tailoring the model more closely to the task but can incur additional costs because of the need for specialized training data and computational resources. Note that tailoring models to specific domains or tasks can significantly enhance performance in those areas but may reduce the model's general applicability (*catastrophic forgetting*). This trade-off between specialized performance and general versatility is a key consideration in model selection, especially for businesses and applications where flexibility is a priority. Knowledge distillation offers a middle ground, potentially reducing the size and computational requirements of a model while retaining a significant portion of its capabilities.

We have seen how fine-tuning can significantly boost model performance but may require large and diverse datasets, which are expensive to curate and process. Building a high-quality dataset for training large language models, as discussed in Chapter 5, requires a multifaceted approach involving considerable resources. The human capital required is substantial, encompassing data scientists for dataset design and management, domain experts for ensuring content relevance and diversity, and legal advisors for navigating copyright and privacy laws. Crucial to this process is the involvement of skilled annotators for labeling data, a resource-intensive task essential for supervised learning models. This labeling process, often requiring expertise in specific domains, is key to training models that are accurate and contextually aware. Additionally, the continuous monitoring and updating of datasets involve regular human feedback to align the model outputs with evolving language usage and societal norms. This process is iterative and demands ongoing attention to maintain the relevance and effectiveness of the model. Furthermore, significant investments in technological infrastructure for data storage and processing are necessary to handle the vast amounts of data involved efficiently. Overall, the creation and maintenance of these datasets are not just a technological challenge but also a significant human and financial endeavor.

The economic implications of these choices are far-reaching. Different model customizations impact the overall cost and performance, when we consider factors like model operational costs, response quality, and the practicality of model outputs in specific use cases, such as customer service, for example. As models scale in size, they generally become more capable and accurate in a wide range of tasks. However, this scaling up also implies exponentially higher costs in terms of computational resources and energy consumption. Balancing the benefits of scaling with the associated costs is a critical consideration, especially in the context of environmental sustainability and operational budgets.

Moreover, the cost of deploying LLMs is not just limited to computational expenses. It also encompasses the costs associated with input and output processing, resource cost for building and maintaining training, and hosting pipelines, as mentioned in Chapter 5. These costs can vary dramatically based on the complexity of the GenAI application at hand. While initial investments in model training and customization can be substantial, the ongoing costs of model inference and maintenance need consideration. The balance between up-front costs and long-term operational expenses is a crucial factor, particularly for businesses looking to integrate LLMs into their regular operations.

In conclusion, balancing performance and cost in the context of LLMs is a nuanced process that requires careful consideration of various factors, including model size and complexity, customization techniques, and the specific nature of the task at hand. The decision-making process often involves a trade-off between the desired level of accuracy and the financial and computational resources available, underscoring the importance of a strategic approach to model selection and optimization.

Environmental Impact

THE ENVIRONMENTAL IMPLICATIONS of training and hosting large language models are significant and have become a growing concern for enterprises mindful of their sustainability and environmental, social, and governance (ESG) goals. The primary environmental impact of LLMs lies in their considerable energy consumption and associated carbon emissions, both during the training phase and ongoing usage in inference in a GenAI application.

Training LLMs is an energy-intensive process. For instance, the University of Massachusetts Amherst study estimated that training a large language model can emit more than 626,000 pounds of carbon dioxide, which is roughly equivalent to the lifetime emissions of five cars (`https://arxiv.org/pdf/1906.02243.pdf`). OpenAI's GPT-3, with 175 billion parameters, consumed several million dollars of electricity during its training. This level of energy consumption is mainly because of the computational demands of processing large datasets and the extensive use of GPUs and CPUs that are necessary for training these models. Furthermore, the heat generated by these computational processes necessitates additional energy for cooling, often through water-based methods, which can have adverse impacts on local ecosystems.

In addition to the direct energy consumption and carbon emissions, there are also concerns about electronic waste (e-waste). The hardware required for these models, such as GPUs, accelerators, and memory chips, has a limited lifespan. As technology advances, older components become obsolete, contributing to the growing problem of e-waste.

Several measures can be adopted to balance these environmental impacts with the advancements in AI. These include developing energy-efficient algorithms and hardware, transitioning data centers to renewable energy sources, applying model compression techniques, and promoting responsible AI development and deployment. Transitioning to renewable energy sources for data centers and purchasing renewable energy certificates (RECs) can help offset carbon emissions.

As mentioned in Chapter 3, reducing the size of AI models and training operations is also a viable approach. If smaller models can, with the right methods, outperform larger models, the choice is easy. Smaller models have lower training costs and less significant environmental impacts while still performing nearly as well in many situations, especially when the model is trained within a particular domain or for a particular task. Techniques such as one-shot or few-shot prompting can also potentially avoid training costs altogether over the model's life cycle.

As the adoption of LLMs grows, it is essential for organizations to be aware of and address their potential environmental impacts. Large organizations like the United Nations Environment Programme and AI Policy Observatory, as well as leading enterprises training foundational models like Microsoft, Google, Anthropic, Amazon, and OpenAI, are all aware of and are closely monitoring the environmental impact of training and doing large-scale inference with foundation models. By pursuing energy-efficient technologies, embracing renewable energy sources, applying model compression techniques, and promoting responsible AI development, the AI community can strike a balance between innovation and sustainability. This approach ensures that the environmental costs do not overshadow the benefits of AI advancements.

Importance of GenAI Team Building

IN THE RAPIDLY evolving landscape of artificial intelligence, GenAI has emerged as a cornerstone technology within the enterprise sector. A striking 81% of enterprise companies have now established dedicated GenAI teams, each staffed with at least ten members, underscoring the critical role these technologies play in current business strategies. This commitment is detailed in a comprehensive study by Wharton professor Stefano Puntoni and GBK Collective, which surveyed 672 executives from companies boasting annual revenues exceeding $50 million (`www.gbkcollective.com/thoughtleadership/the-rise-of-generative-ai`). The study dispels the notion that GenAI might be a fleeting trend like cryptocurrency, Web3, or the metaverse.

Instead, Puntoni emphasizes GenAI's substantial and growing impact on the business world, marking it as a mainstay rather than a transient hype.

The drive toward integrating GenAI is particularly pronounced among smaller enterprises, with companies in the $50–200 million revenue bracket leading the charge. An impressive 57% of these companies' executives report engaging with GenAI technologies on a weekly basis, signaling a hands-on approach to leveraging AI's capabilities. In contrast, larger organizations exhibit a more cautious stance, with concerns primarily centered around the accuracy and reliability of GenAI outputs. This hesitancy reflects a broader narrative of trust and verification that larger entities grapple with when adopting cutting-edge technologies.

Financial commitments to GenAI are set to amplify, with projections indicating a 25% increase in funding for the technology within the current year. A general sense of optimism prevails among the executive ranks, with 75% expressing a positive outlook toward GenAI's role in the future of business. Regular use of GenAI stands at 58%, indicating a robust integration of the technology in routine operations. More than half of the surveyed leaders believe that GenAI will enhance work quality, while a significant 36% acknowledge that GenAI is poised to supplant certain employee skills for specific tasks, revealing a nuanced perspective on the interplay between human talent and artificial intelligence in the workplace.

The realm of GenAI and foundational models presents unique challenges in team building, distinguishing it significantly from conventional engineering or DevOps teams. The complexity and rapid evolution of GenAI technologies require a specialized approach to formulating teams capable of leveraging these advancements effectively. The fast-paced nature of GenAI development requires teams to be operationally agile and adaptable. This includes embracing rapid prototyping, continuous iteration, and a flexible approach to project management. Teams must be prepared to pivot quickly in response to new information or changes in the technology landscape, making agility a crucial component of GenAI team dynamics.

GenAI projects demand a blend of highly specialized skills and innovative thinking. Unlike traditional software development, GenAI not only involves coding and system architecture but also entails an in-depth understanding of machine learning, data science, and AI ethics. The need for expertise in these areas shapes the recruitment, training, and team dynamics in GenAI projects. A key differentiator in GenAI team building is fostering a culture that values safe exploration, experimentation, and innovation. This involves creating environments where team members can freely test new ideas, learn from failures, and share knowledge. Such a culture encourages creative problem-solving and helps in discovering unique applications of GenAI technologies. This is possible only via a leadership team that is well-versed with GenAI from a business context. Leadership in GenAI teams must go beyond conventional management practices. It involves not only setting strategic directions but also promoting a culture of continuous learning and digital fluency among team members. Leaders must be well-versed in the latest technological advancements to guide their teams effectively and to understand the broader impact of GenAI technologies on business and society.

Ideal GenAI Team Structure

ASSEMBLING A TEAM for a GenAI project requires careful consideration and strategic planning. The dynamic nature of GenAI, with its blend of cutting-edge technology and practical applications, necessitates a team that is well-rounded, versatile, and capable of addressing a wide range of challenges.

The composition of a GenAI team can significantly impact the success of a project. A well-designed team ensures a balance between technical prowess and the ability to see the broader picture of how the technology fits into business or societal contexts. Leaders need to avoid the pitfalls of creating a team that is either too technically heavy or too management-focused. An overly technical team might push the boundaries of what's possible but could struggle to align with business goals or overlook important ethical considerations. Conversely, a management-heavy team might excel in aligning the project with business objectives but lack the technical depth to innovate or address complex technical challenges effectively.

One common risk in GenAI projects is underestimating the importance of roles such as ethics, safety, and cost management. In the excitement of technological innovation, these aspects can be overlooked, but they are crucial for the responsible and sustainable development of AI technologies. Ethical considerations, for instance, are vital in ensuring that GenAI applications do not inadvertently perpetuate biases or violate privacy norms.

Similarly, safety roles are essential to prevent unintended consequences of AI behavior, and cost management is critical to ensure that projects remain viable and deliver value.

Given these considerations, designing a GenAI team requires a thoughtful approach that balances technical skills with strategic oversight and ethical considerations. The following are examples of how one might organize a 10-member GenAI team, considering these diverse functions:

➤ **Technical expertise:** This includes roles such as LLM engineers and AI/ML deployment engineers, focusing on the development and implementation of AI models.

➤ **Creative and strategic input:** Prompt engineers and AI interaction designers play a crucial role in how AI interacts with users and in shaping the AI's outputs to meet project goals.

➤ **Domain and product management:** AI product managers and domain specialists ensure that the GenAI applications are relevant and valuable to the specific industry or sector.

➤ **Operational and data management:** Roles like data governance specialists and LLMOps engineers focus on the practical aspects of running GenAI systems effectively and ethically.

➤ **Research and evaluation:** Research scientists and data scientists assess the effectiveness of GenAI models and drive innovation through research.

Assume you have an approved headcount of about ten members to start your dream GenAI starter team. Table 1 outlines these roles and their functions.

TABLE 1: GenAI starter team

ROLE CATEGORY (NUMBER OF PEOPLE)	SPECIFIC ROLE	FUNCTION
Project Manager (1)	GenAI Project Lead	Oversees project delivery, manages timelines, coordinates team members, ensures alignment with business objectives
Machine Learning Engineers (2)	Role 1: LLM Engineer	Specializes in working with large language models, modifying and fine-tuning for specific applications
	Role 2: AI/ML Deployment Engineer	Focuses on deploying AI/ML models into production, ensures scalability and performance optimization
Prompt Engineers (2)	Role 1: NLP Specialist	Develops and refines prompts for effective interaction with GenAI models
	Role 2: AI Interaction Designer	Designs interaction flow and prompt structure, optimizing user experience with GenAI models
Product Managers/ Domain Experts (1/2)	Role 1: AI Product Manager	Oversees product development involving GenAI, ensuring product-market fit and user needs alignment
	Role 2: Domain Specialist (Industry Specific)	Provides deep domain knowledge for industry-specific GenAI applications
Data Experts (1)	Data Governance Specialist	Manages data access, security, compliance; ensures ethical sourcing and relevance of data for GenAI

ROLE CATEGORY (NUMBER OF PEOPLE)	SPECIFIC ROLE	FUNCTION
Technical Experts (1)	LLMOps Engineer	Manages operational aspects of GenAI models, including performance monitoring and maintenance
Supervisory/Scientific Experts (2)	Role 1: Research Scientist (Generative AI)	Conducts research to improve GenAI technologies and explore new methodologies
	Role 2: Data Scientist (Model Evaluation)	Evaluates performance of GenAI models using statistical methods to assess various metrics

This structure aims to strike a balance between technical development, creative design, strategic business alignment, ethical considerations, and operational efficiency, ensuring a comprehensive approach to GenAI projects. With globally distributed teams working on foundation model training and large-scale inference, the importance of working with remote teams cannot be understated. Several companies today, such as Huggingface, work primarily remotely and have additional roles related to outreach, marketing, and sales. What is also becoming important is the impact of pools of human evaluators who provide feedback on outputs from foundation models. This data is used to further fine-tune and align LLMs, for example, and is becoming one of the most important steps in the LLMOps life cycle. Working with a remote team (such as with Amazon SageMaker Ground Truth) that also has subject-matter expertise is ideal.

Cost Considerations in GenAI Team Maintenance

MANAGING THE COSTS associated with maintaining a GenAI team is a critical aspect that leaders must navigate carefully. The financial implications extend beyond just salaries; they encompass training, technological infrastructure, research and development, and the potential costs associated with any ethical or safety missteps. Achieving a balance in skills within the team is essential to minimize time to market and prevent resource wastage, ultimately impacting the cost efficiency of GenAI projects. Here are the top five things to consider when trying to maintain and scale a GenAI team while continuously delivering at high velocity and quality:

➤ **Skill diversity and efficiency:** A team that combines technical expertise with strategic and operational skills can work more efficiently, reducing the time and resources required for project completion. For example, having prompt engineers who understand both the technical and user aspects of GenAI applications can expedite the development process, reducing the need for extensive iterations.

➤ **Optimized project management:** A skilled project manager can ensure that projects are completed within scope and budget, effectively managing resources and timelines. This role is crucial to avoid project overruns, which can significantly escalate costs.

➤ **Strategic resource allocation:** Balancing the team with both experienced and emerging talent can be cost-effective. Seasoned professionals bring expertise and efficiency, while junior members offer fresh perspectives and can be trained for specific project needs, often at a lower cost.

➤ **Mitigating risks:** Incorporating roles focused on ethics, safety, and data governance can help avoid costly mistakes or oversights. Ethical breaches or safety issues can lead to reputational damage, legal ramifications, and financial penalties, all of which have substantial cost implications.

➤ **Continuous learning and adaptability:** Encouraging a culture of continuous learning and adaptability within the team ensures that members stay abreast of the latest GenAI developments. This approach can reduce the need for external consultation or training, leading to more cost-effective project execution.

It is extremely important to balance skillsets in a GenAI team for cost-effective delivery. A well-balanced GenAI team capable of delivering projects in a timely manner without excessive resource expenditure requires a strategic mix of expertise across several domains:

➤ **Technical and creative balance:** Balancing the team with technical experts (like ML engineers and data scientists) and creative roles (such as prompt engineers and interaction designers) ensures that both the development and user experience aspects of GenAI projects are handled efficiently. This balance can reduce the need for significant redesigns or technical adjustments late in the project, which can be costly.

➤ **Business acumen and operational efficiency:** Including team members with strong business and operational insights, such as AI product managers and LLMOps engineers, ensures that projects are aligned with business goals and operational constraints from the outset. This alignment helps in prioritizing features and functionalities that offer the most value, reducing wasteful spending on less impactful aspects.

➤ **Focus on long-term value:** Roles that emphasize long-term value, such as research scientists and data governance specialists, contribute to sustainability and future-proofing of projects. This approach prevents short-term cost savings that could lead to larger expenses down the line, such as through technical debt or ethical missteps.

➤ **Leveraging cross-functional collaboration:** Encouraging cross-functional collaboration within the team can lead to innovative solutions that maximize existing resources and skills. This synergy can reduce the need for additional hires or external consultants.

➤ **Monitoring and adaptation:** Along with the flexibility to adapt as needed, regular monitoring of project progress against budgets and timelines ensures that resources are utilized efficiently and cost overruns are minimized.

In summary, the key to managing costs effectively while maintaining a GenAI team lies in creating a balanced team with diverse skill sets. This diversity allows for efficient project execution, minimizes the risk of costly delays or reworks, and ensures that the project delivers value in line with business objectives. Additionally, a focus on ethical and safe AI practices is not just a moral imperative but also a strategic one, as it guards against future financial and reputational costs. By strategically assembling a team that covers a broad spectrum of skills and perspectives, leaders can navigate the complex landscape of GenAI projects, delivering innovative solutions within a reasonable budget and timeframe.

Using GenAI to Help Form a GenAI Team

THE RECRUITMENT PROCESS for a GenAI team is a strategic endeavor that extends beyond conventional hiring practices. It requires a nuanced approach to identify candidates who not only possess the necessary technical skills but also demonstrate the innovative thinking and adaptability that GenAI projects necessitate. Here, we come full circle: GenAI can help with crafting engaging job descriptions, which is another critical component of recruitment. GenAI assists in this task by generating job postings that are not only comprehensive and optimized for search engines but also resonate with potential candidates, leading to higher conversion rates and attracting a more suitable pool of applicants. More importantly, it can assist with automated pre-screening, which significantly enhances the efficiency and effectiveness of the screening process, ensuring a thorough initial evaluation that aligns with job prerequisites.

Training for GenAI teams is not a static process; it must be dynamic and continuous to keep pace with the rapidly evolving landscape. The move from a credential-based to a skill-based recruitment and development approach is a significant shift facilitated by GenAI. This method emphasizes the actual skills and capabilities of candidates, focusing on their abilities rather than just formal qualifications, thereby broadening the talent pool and promoting a more inclusive recruitment process.

As GenAI transforms HR into a more strategic function, it also impacts how teams are formed and trained. GenAI allows for dramatic increases in self-service and productivity enhancements, enabling employees to address their needs more efficiently. This shift in HR service delivery models frees up HR professionals to engage more deeply with employees, focusing on strategic talent planning and deeper employee engagement. In fostering a data-driven talent ecosystem, HR can leverage GenAI to join less structured data sources, driving meaningful talent decisions across the business and enabling a skills-based talent ecosystem linked to the workforce strategy.

Lastly, while GenAI brings a new level of productivity, it also raises ethical considerations, especially when handling sensitive personnel information. HR teams must work closely with legal and business leaders to ensure that responsible AI is being implemented and that any biases apparent in GenAI systems are identified and addressed. For example, the impact of demographic details such as gender and race on the probability of the AI system in selecting the candidate for the next steps has to be studied and rectified for each HR system separately. It is also a good idea to have human evaluators in the loop to recheck LLM model choices. This requires a dynamic technology and regulatory environment where humans remain critical, ensuring that business decisions are sound, just, and well-documented.

FUTURE TRENDS IN GenAI APPLICATIONS

AS WE VENTURE into 2024 and beyond, GenAI is no longer just a fad or a piece of emerging technology; it has become akin to an operating system, deeply integrated into various facets of our lives and industries. This section explores three groundbreaking advancements and implications of GenAI, shedding light on its role as a driving force in creative industries, business operations, healthcare, and more. In this concluding section, we will go through some recent trends:

➤ **Trend 1:** Mixture of experts models

➤ **Trend 2:** Multimodal models

➤ **Trend 3:** Agents

Trend 1: Mixture of Experts Models

MIXTURE OF EXPERTS (MoE) models are a type of neural network architecture that combines multiple simpler neural networks, called *experts*, using a specialized gating module. The key idea is that different regions of the input space may require different types of processing, and having separate expert models that become active in those regions can improve overall accuracy and efficiency.

In a traditional MoE model, there is a set of expert neural networks that each take the input and produce their own output. These expert networks often have a relatively simple architecture compared to state-of-the-art models for a task. There is also a separate gating module that takes the input and decides how to combine the outputs from the different experts. It assigns a weight or importance value to each expert's output. The final output of the MoE model is then computed as the weighted sum of all the expert outputs using the weights that the gating module produced.

During training, the parameters of both the expert and gating modules are updated jointly on a per-input basis. The experts specialize to focus on certain types of data samples or input patterns. When a new input arrives, the gating module determines which experts should contribute more to the final output. This achieves a dynamic routing of different data samples to different specialized experts, improving efficiency and accuracy.

Recent MoE models for language and computer vision utilize different types of subneural networks as the experts. For example, for computer vision, the channels or filters in a convolutional layer represent the individual experts. The gating module determines how to combine the filter responses for each input image. For example, some filters might become specialized for processing faces, while others focus more on background regions. The gating allows resetting filter weights per input, providing a more flexible routing than a statically composed CNN.

Performance of MoE Models

RECENT RESEARCH HAS explored MoE-enhanced convolutional neural networks (CNNs) for computer vision and language modeling. For example, the DeepMoE paper (https://arxiv.org/pdf/1806.01531.pdf) showed that replacing certain layers in ResNet architectures with MoE equivalents improved ImageNet classification accuracy while reducing computation. For example, their DeepMoE ResNet-50 model reduced top-1 error by 1% while using 43% less computation than standard ResNet-50.

Similarly, the Sparse MoE paper (https://arxiv.org/pdf/2305.14705.pdf) explores the synergy between Sparse MoE architecture and instruction tuning in LLMs. The MoE approach adds learnable parameters to LLMs without increasing inference cost, while instruction tuning trains LLMs to follow instructions more effectively. The authors conducted empirical studies in three scenarios: direct fine-tuning on downstream tasks without instruction tuning, instruction tuning followed by in-context few-shot or zero-shot generalization, and instruction tuning with additional task-specific fine-tuning. They found that MoE models generally underperform compared to dense models in direct fine-tuning but significantly outperform them when instruction tuning is applied!

Specifically, the Sparse MoE paper presents FLAN-MOE, a model combining FLAN instruction tuning with sparse MoE. FLAN-MOE demonstrates superior performance on various benchmarks while using a fraction of the computational resources compared to its counterparts.

The paper mainly demonstrated that the FLAN-MOE model, a combination of the FLAN instruction tuning approach with sparse MoE architecture, notably outperforms larger models. For instance, FLAN-MOE32B surpasses FLAN-PALM62B in performance on four benchmark tasks while requiring only about a third of the floating-point operations (FLOPs). This shows a significant advancement in computational efficiency and model effectiveness. The results indicate a shift in model design paradigms, emphasizing task-agnostic learning within the MoE framework.

The key difference between the papers (apart from the obvious difference in application to CV versus NLP tasks) is that the DeepMoE work focused on larger expert subnetworks, while the Sparse MoE paper explored deeper stacking with smaller convolutions. The DeepMoE models specialized wider multilayer perceptron experts at each MoE layer. In contrast, the Sparse MoE work decomposed individual convolutional layers into channels as the experts.

Both papers demonstrate the potential for MoE-based networks to improve foundation models in NLP and CV in terms of efficiency alongside accuracy. The dynamic routing capability also suggests promising specialized hardware implementations leveraging optimized parallel execution.

Future Implications of MoE Models

THE FUTURE IMPLICATIONS of MoE models in AI and machine learning are diverse and far-reaching. These models, which utilize a sparsity-driven architecture with multiple expert networks and a trainable gating mechanism, offer several advantages over conventional approaches.

One of the core benefits of MoE models is their increased model capacity. By dividing a model into specialized expert components, MoE allows for creating models with a large number of parameters, with each expert focusing on learning specific patterns or features in the data. This leads to increased representational capacity and improved generalization capabilities, enabling MoE models to perform well across various tasks and datasets.

Efficient computation is another significant advantage. MoE models selectively activate only a subset of parameters for a given input, leading to more efficient computations. This is particularly beneficial when dealing with sparse data or when only specific features are relevant to a task. This selective activation helps control computational costs, making MoE models more efficient for inference and training.

The adaptability and specialization of MoE models are also noteworthy. Different experts can specialize in handling specific types of input or tasks, allowing the model to focus on relevant information for different tokens or parts of the input sequence. This adaptability improves performance on diverse tasks and helps to better handle multimodal data. Each expert can learn to process a specific modality, and the routing mechanism can adapt to the input data's characteristics.

In the context of large language models like Mixtral 8x7B, the MoE approach has been shown to outperform larger models on various benchmarks. Despite having a high total parameter count, MoE models like Mixtral 8x7B use only a fraction of these parameters per token, maintaining processing efficiency and balancing performance with resource utilization.

Looking forward, the MoE approach is set to significantly contribute to the evolution of language models and neural networks. Its emphasis on specialized knowledge and nuanced predictions presents a fresh perspective in AI development. The adaptability, efficiency, and scalability offered by MoE models suggest their potential application across various domains, including healthcare, finance, and education.

Moreover, MoE models are expected to play a crucial role in advancing toward artificial general intelligence (AGI). With their ability to efficiently handle complex, diverse tasks and data types, MoE architectures could be instrumental in developing AI systems that approach human-like cognitive abilities. However, achieving AGI is still a long-term goal, and the journey toward it is marked by both technological advancements and ethical considerations.

In summary, the MoE models represent a significant advancement in AI and machine learning, offering scalability, efficiency, and adaptability. Their potential applications span various fields and contribute to the ongoing pursuit of more advanced, versatile AI systems.

Trend 2: Multimodal Models

MULTIMODAL MODELS (MMS) are an emerging area in artificial intelligence that combines different types of data inputs, like text, images, and sound, to perform tasks that require a comprehensive understanding across multiple modalities. Two recent surveys explore the area of MMs in detail, hereafter referred to as Survey 1 (https://arxiv.org/pdf/2302.10035.pdf) and Survey 2 (https://arxiv.org/pdf/2306.13549.pdf). As outlined in Survey 1 and Survey 2, these models are adept at processing and interpreting complex data combinations, a trait not found in traditional unimodal systems that we have talked about generally throughout the book. For instance, MMs can analyze a photograph, extract textual information, and provide relevant context or responses, effectively bridging the gap between different data types. These kinds of models are becoming more popular due to their easy user interface and natural dialogue when involving multiple types of data. A great implementation of this is ChatGPT, involving the use of GPT-4 and DALL-E for mixed language and vision tasks.

Techniques to Train Multimodal Models

THE TRAINING OF multimodal models involves various sophisticated techniques. Both surveys discuss multimodal instruction tuning (M-IT), multimodal in-context learning (M-ICL), and multimodal chain of thought (M-CoT). M-IT focuses on fine-tuning pre-trained language models with multimodal data, whereas M-ICL leverages contextual examples for improved performance. M-CoT, on the other hand, is utilized in complex reasoning tasks. These techniques demonstrate the intricate process of adapting unimodal models into multimodal ones, ensuring they can understand and process multiple data types effectively.

It's essential to delve deeper into the nuances of the approaches mentioned earlier to expand on the training techniques of multimodal models. M-IT not only involves fine-tuning pre-trained models with multimodal data but also requires intricate alignment of different data types to ensure coherent learning. This process often involves complex data preprocessing and feature extraction methods to make different data types compatible for integrated learning.

M-ICL is another sophisticated approach that focuses on contextually rich training. Here, the model is exposed to a variety of scenarios where different data types are presented in a contextual manner, closely mimicking real-world situations. This method helps the model in developing a deeper understanding of how different modalities relate to each other in specific contexts.

M-CoT is particularly interesting as it involves training models to perform complex reasoning tasks across different modalities. This technique involves sequential data processing, where the model learns to draw inferences and conclusions by chaining together information from various modalities. This approach is crucial for tasks that require higher-order thinking and complex decision-making processes.

These techniques collectively contribute to the robustness and versatility of multimodal models, enabling them to perform complex tasks that require a nuanced understanding of multiple data types.

Performance Benchmarks

IN TERMS OF performance, multimodal models are evaluated on several benchmarks, as highlighted in the surveys. These benchmarks test various capabilities, from simple recognition tasks to complex reasoning and natural language understanding. The models' ability to process and integrate multimodal information is rigorously tested. Performance is assessed through various metrics, including accuracy, zero-shot learning capabilities, and robustness against different types of data inputs. These benchmarks are critical in measuring the effectiveness of MMs in handling real-world tasks, where data often comes in mixed formats.

What we can conclude from the performance/results sections of the surveys, is that performance benchmarks for MMs need to be multifaceted, focusing on accuracy, reasoning, and adaptability across various tasks. These benchmarks test MMs in scenarios requiring the integration of different data types, assessing their understanding and response accuracy. One prominent metric is zero-shot learning ability, indicating how well a model can perform tasks without prior specific training.

In Survey 1, specific benchmarks show MMs excelling in tasks blending visual and textual information, such as image captioning and visual question answering. Their performance is notably superior to traditional models, especially in complex reasoning and natural language understanding tasks.

Survey 2 highlights advancements in MMs' ability to handle tasks requiring deeper contextual understanding. Here, the benchmarks demonstrate impressive improvements in tasks like story generation from images and context-sensitive responses. The results underscore the MMs' enhanced ability to interpret and respond to multimodal inputs in a more human-like manner.

These benchmarks collectively show that MMs are making significant strides in handling complex, real-world scenarios that involve varied data types, moving closer to a more nuanced and sophisticated form of artificial intelligence.

Future Implications and Research Directions

THE APPLICATION OF MMs to various practical tasks holds significant promise in the future. There's a strong inclination toward enhancing their ability to seamlessly integrate and process diverse data types, aiming to mimic human-like understanding. Research is being directed toward improving the efficiency, accuracy, and generalization capabilities of these models. With advancements in this field, we can anticipate MMs that are more adept at understanding context, subtlety, and complexities of real-world scenarios, thereby inching closer to artificial general intelligence.

Several key areas have been identified as the focal points for future research and development in this domain:

➤ **Multimodal transformer architectures:** These are becoming increasingly vital in processing and understanding multimodal data. They are expected to bring significant improvements in performance across various tasks due to their ability to handle complex data integration more efficiently.

➤ **Self-supervised learning:** This technique is gaining attention for its potential to reduce the reliance on labeled data significantly. By utilizing the inherent structure and relationships within the data, self-supervised learning can make the training of multimodal models more efficient and scalable.

➤ **Multimodal explainability and interpretability:** As these models become more complex, understanding how they make decisions is crucial. There's an increasing focus on developing methods to explain and interpret the inner workings of these models, which is essential for building trust and ensuring responsible AI.

This trajectory of development also opens up new avenues in various sectors such as healthcare, autonomous systems, and personalized digital assistants, promising a future where AI understands and interacts with the world in a more human-like manner.

Note on Application to Healthcare

ALTHOUGH SEVERAL APPLICATIONS to MMs exist in the healthcare domain, one easy application to imagine is the integration of multimodal models in advanced chatbots capable of analyzing a wide range of medical data. Such a chatbot could be revolutionary in analyzing doctors' notes, X-rays, and other medical records to assist in medical decision-making. By incorporating natural language processing (NLP), these chatbots can interpret and summarize doctors' notes, extracting key medical information and patient history. Simultaneously, through image recognition capabilities, they can analyze X-rays and other medical imaging, identifying patterns and anomalies that might not be immediately apparent to the human eye. This ability to process and integrate textual and visual data enables the chatbot to provide a more comprehensive overview of a patient's condition, assisting healthcare professionals in making more informed decisions.

This approach can significantly enhance the efficiency and accuracy of medical diagnostics. By quickly assimilating and interpreting vast amounts of data, the chatbot can aid in identifying potential diagnoses or treatment options, potentially speeding up the treatment process and improving patient outcomes. In terms of specific performance, studies have shown that multimodal approaches can significantly outperform single-source approaches in various healthcare applications. For example, the Holistic Artificial Intelligence in Medicine (HAIM) framework demonstrated marked improvements in predictive capacity for healthcare machine learning systems compared to single-modality approaches. This was evident in tasks such as pathology diagnosis and predictions of hospital length-of-stay and mortality rates.

Remote patient monitoring, often termed the *hospital-at-home* is another crucial application. Here, the integration of wearable sensor data with EHRs and ambient wireless sensors can significantly improve patient care, especially for chronic or degenerative disorders. This integration can enhance the reliability of systems such as fall detection and gait analysis and is vital for the early detection of physical impairments.

In the realm of precision health, where the focus is on tailoring medical care to individual patient characteristics, multimodal machine learning becomes even more crucial. The integration of various data sources in this field is pivotal for delivering personalized medical care. With the ability to analyze and interpret a multitude of data types, ranging from genetic information to lifestyle factors, multimodal models can offer insights that are far more nuanced and precise than traditional approaches. This level of detailed analysis is vital for developing targeted therapies and interventions that cater to the specific needs of each patient, marking a significant step forward in the quest for more effective and efficient healthcare solutions.

Trend 3: Agents

THE CONCEPT OF agents is derived from the larger idea of autonomy that exists in several domains. In a broader context, AI agents are software programs or systems designed to autonomously perceive their environment, make decisions, and act to achieve specific goals. These agents are employed in various fields, demonstrating remarkable versatility and impact. For instance, in the realm of virtual assistants, agents like Siri and Google Assistant assist users in everyday tasks such as setting reminders or controlling smart home devices. In the software industry, agents optimize processes by handling tasks more efficiently than humans. They're also central to the functioning of autonomous vehicles, helping in navigation and decision-making. In manufacturing, AI agents control robots for tasks such as assembly, welding, or material handling. Healthcare utilizes agents for diagnosing diseases and managing patient records, while the finance industry employs them for algorithmic trading and fraud detection. AI agents also play a significant role in gaming, where they control nonplayer characters and adapt to players' behaviors. More recently, in the field of AI, there has been work ranging from symbolic agents to reinforcement learning agents. In this section, however, we will be focusing on the field of natural language processing, where agents enable applications to seamlessly access multiple internal and external tools and APIs to plan and executive a high-level objective.

Agents powered by LLMs are systems that leverage the capabilities of an LLM to analyze and understand a problem, devise a strategy for addressing it, and then implement that strategy using a range of available tools.

Essentially, these agents combine advanced problem-solving abilities, the capacity to remember relevant information, and the practical means to carry out tasks effectively.

Agents with LLMs consist of three integral components (as proposed in `https://arxiv.org/pdf/2309.07864.pdf`): the brain, perception, and action modules.

➤ The brain module is pivotal, handling tasks such as memorizing, thinking, and decision-making. It's the core of the AI agent, leveraging the capabilities of LLMs for reasoning and dealing with unseen tasks.

➤ The perception module, on the other hand, is responsible for perceiving and processing multimodal information from the environment, extending the agent's understanding beyond just text to include auditory and visual inputs.

➤ The action module is where execution happens, enabling the agent to interact with and influence its surroundings.

LLM as the Brain

THE BRAIN OF an agent powered by an LLM is akin to the human brain, characterized by its complexity and capability to process diverse information. It utilizes LLMs to reason through problems, formulate plans, and execute them using various tools. Key functions include natural language interaction, knowledge storage and recall, and the ability to adapt to new scenarios. LLMs facilitate multiturn conversations and high-quality natural language generation, enhancing agents' communication and interaction.

Agents with LLMs also excel in understanding intentions and implications, which is crucial for effective cooperation with other intelligent systems. Their knowledge base is extensive, covering linguistic, commonsense, and professional domain knowledge. However, challenges such as outdated or incorrect information and hallucinations need addressing.

Memory in LLM-based agents store past observations, thoughts, and actions. Overcoming challenges like the length of historical records and extracting relevant memories are crucial for efficient operation. Methods like increasing the length limit of transformers, summarizing memory, and compressing memories with vectors or data structures aid in enhancing memory capabilities.

Reasoning and planning are central to these agents. They employ various forms of reasoning and planning methods, including plan formulation and reflection, to tackle complex tasks. The agents' transferability and generalization abilities allow them to adapt to new tasks and environments, demonstrating in-context learning and continual learning capabilities, which help mitigate issues like catastrophic forgetting.

Overall, the brain of an LLM-based agent represents a sophisticated, adaptive, and versatile system capable of handling complex tasks through advanced reasoning, memory management, and continuous learning.

Diving Deeper into Agents Using LangChain

WHILE THERE ARE several companies out there trying to provide production-worthy agent implementations, it is good first to understand the workings of an agent using the LangChain library. At the core of LangChain agents is the innovative use of a language model to determine a sequence of actions. Unlike traditional programming, where a sequence of actions is hard-coded, LangChain agents employ language models as a reasoning engine. This approach allows for dynamic decision-making, adapting to different scenarios and requirements.

A key aspect of LangChain agents is their architecture, which comprises several components:

➤ **Schema and agent actions:** LangChain simplifies working with agents through abstractions like AgentAction, a data class representing the actions an agent should take. This includes properties for the tool to be invoked and the input for that tool.

➤ **Agent finish and intermediate steps:** The AgentFinish abstraction marks the completion of an agent's task, holding the final output ready to return to the user. Moreover, the framework keeps track of intermediate steps, which are crucial for understanding the actions already performed by the agent.

- ➤ **Agent and agent inputs/outputs:** Central to the LangChain agent is the chain responsible for deciding the next step. This chain is powered by a language model, a prompt, and an output parser. The inputs to an agent include key-value mappings, with essential keys like `intermediate_steps`. The outputs from an agent, processed through the output parser, determine the next actions or the final response.

- ➤ **Agent executor:** This runtime component of LangChain agents handles the execution of actions chosen by the agent. It also manages complexities such as handling nonexistent tools, tool errors, and output parsing errors.

- ➤ **Tools and toolkits:** LangChain agents employ tools that are functions invoked by the agent. These tools have an input schema and a function to run, which are vital for the agent's operation. LangChain also introduces the concept of toolkits, groups of related tools assembled for specific objectives.

For a practical example, consider an AI agent in a customer service scenario. A customer inquires about a product's availability. The perception module of the agent interprets the customer's query, the brain module processes this information using the store's inventory data, and the action module responds to the customer with the availability details. This example illustrates the necessity of AI agents in complementing LLMs, where they add the ability to perceive, process, and act upon real-world data, something LLMs alone cannot achieve. This makes AI agents crucial in applications where interaction with the physical or digital environment is necessary.

Agent Defined as Code in LangChain

LET'S TAKE A look at some sample code that will help further define what an agent looks like and how they work. In this case, we will be walking through a fact-checking agent. This agent has the objective to use external tools and check the facts that are presented by users.

We start by installing LangChain in a notebook environment like Google Colab or Amazon Sage-Maker Studio:

```
%pip install --upgrade langchain[all]
```

Our agent will have access to two tools via an API:

- ➤ Google Search via the Serp API (https://python.langchain.com/docs/integrations/providers/serpapi)

- ➤ Wolfram Alpha API (https://python.langchain.com/docs/integrations/providers/wolfram_alpha)

Typically you will need to provide API keys as follows:

```
os.environ["SERPAPI_API_KEY"] = '138deb17…4200b926d92655'
os.environ["WOLFRAM_ALPHA_APPID"] = 'PGAK…AASD
```

Next, we will make some basic imports, including services that will provide API access to the LLM "brain." In this case, we will use Amazon Bedrock. You can also use the OpenAI API or a local model using huggingface.

```
from langchain.agents import Tool, initialize_agent, load_tools
from langchain.llms.bedrock import Bedrock
```

Create a bedrock client as follows and initialize the LLM brain for the agent:

```
bedrock_client = boto3.client(service_name="bedrock")

llm = Bedrock(model_id="anthropic.claude-v2", client = bedrock_client
```

Initialize the tools that you would like to use:

```
tools = load_tools(["serpapi", "llm-math", "wolfram-alpha"], llm=llm)
```

Here, we are using built-integrations from LangChain to SerpAPI, Wolfram Alpha, and a basic math tool. Next, we create a prompt template for the agent to use (carefully note the instructions here):

```
template = """You are a conversational AI bot that helps fact check human inputs in
the format `[Question]?[Answer:"human answer"]` using the following tools:

{tools}

Please use the following format to fact check the human answer:

```
Question: the input or intermediate question you must answer
Thought: Do I need to use a tool? Yes
Action: the action to take, should be one of [{tool_names}]
Action Input: the input to the action
Observation: the result of the action
```

... (this Question/Thought/Action/Action Input/Observation can repeat N times)

Use these tools to check your answer with the human answer mentioned in "human
answer". If the human answer needs to be researched to perform your fact checks,
you may use the same tools in {tools} again with the same format specified above.

When you have a final answer or response to say to the Human, or if you do not need
to use a tool, you MUST use the format:

```
Final Answer: I have fact checked your answer and you are [choose from cor-
rect/wrong].
```

Once you have a Final Answer, do not add a New Input

Begin!

Previous conversation history:
{history}

New input: {input}
{agent_scratchpad}"""
```

Finally, you can initialize the most basic version of an agent, which is a zero-shot agent:

```
from langchain.agents import initialize_agent
from langchain.memory import ConversationBufferMemory

memory = ConversationBufferMemory(memory_key="chat_history")

zero_shot_agent = initialize_agent(
    agent="zero-shot-react-description",
    tools=tools,
    llm=llm,
    verbose=True,
    memory=memory,
    max_iterations=5)
```

Here, we initialize a zero-shot agent with a conversational memory, with the previously defined LLM of choice (here, Claude v2) and the tools (Google Search, Wolfram Alpha, and basic math).

We are now ready to ask our fact-checking agent questions (try one of these many questions):

```
# input_text = "Asuncion Manufacturing finds the following numbers on its income
statement. Net income = $460,700 Interest expenses = $10,000 Taxes = $1,500
Depreciation = $10,000 Amortization = $6,000. What is the EBITDA? Answer: $458000 "

# input_text = "What is the distance from New york to Atlanta in feet? Answer:
3.949&times;10^6 feet"

# input_text = "Which Chelsea player did Man United agree to sign a deal with
recently? Answer: Mason Mount"

# input_text = "What was the temperature in London yesterday? Answer: Less than 7
degrees C"

# input_text = "What was the temperature in London yesterday? Answer: More than 43
degrees F"

# input_text = "What is Leo DiCaprio's age raised to the 0.43 power? Answer: 1.5"

# input_text = "How many notes in western classical music? Answer: 5"

input_text = "The range of a Tesla model X is under 600 Km"
```

When we try the last question about Tesla model X's range, we get the following detailed output:

```
> Entering new  chain...
 I need to fact check the input statement to determine if the human answer is
correct or incorrect. I will use Wolfram Alpha to find the exact range of a
Tesla Model X.

Action: Wolfram Alpha
Action Input: range of
Observation: Wolfram Alpha is not a valid tool, try another one.
Thought: Wolfram Alpha did not work, let me try searching instead.

Action: Search
Action Input: range of tesla model x
Observation: 348 miles
Thought: 348 miles is 560 km, which is under 600 km. The human answer
seems correct.

Final Answer: I have fact checked your answer and you are correct.
```

What we can see is that the agent understands the statement, infers what fact to check, and chooses a tool. The first tool it chooses, Wolfram Alpha, does not provide it with a useful answer, so it tries to search. The search provides it with an observation in miles, which it converts to 560 km, which, in fact, is less than 600 km. The agent concludes by confirming that the human is in fact correct.

Other questions in the list of example questions lead to different trajectories or paths. For example, "What was the temperature in London yesterday? Answer: More than 43 degrees F" leads to searching for weather in London using the Wolfram Alpha, which provides the current weather, using which the agent can decide whether the user is correct or incorrect. Similarly, "What is Leo DiCaprio's age raised to the 0.43 power? Answer: 1.5" leads to the agent first searching on Google, finding the age, and then using the basic math tool to raise the returned age to the power of 0.43 (it is unlikely that the answer is 1.5), so this results in the answer being fact checked.

This example shows that even though the composition of this agent is simple, it has far-reaching impacts in ensuring the integrity of information disseminated online. By leveraging a combination of natural language processing and web scraping, the agent can autonomously verify claims against trusted sources. This process helps to maintain a factual basis for discussions and combats the spread of misinformation.

Example Use Case: Rabbit R1

ANOTHER INTERESTING APPLICATION of agents is the Rabbit R1 (rabbit.tech), powered by Rabbit OS and the large action model (LAM), represents a significant advancement in AI technology for personal use. In 2024, this is the first application of agents running in production on a personal device. Unlike traditional voice-based assistants, which are limited to basic tasks such as checking the weather or turning on lights, the R1 can perform a wide range of complex digital errands. This includes intricate tasks such as conducting thorough research, booking travel options, filling virtual grocery carts, and completing transactions. Think of Rabbit R1 as a production use case of on-device agent systems with the help of LLM tools.

Rabbit OS, underpinned by LAM, introduces a paradigm shift where devices primarily interact through spoken natural language, moving away from traditional touch interfaces. This transition, initiated with smart speakers and AI chatbots, has been accelerated with operating systems like Rabbit OS. The challenge in designing such systems lies in the unavailability of application programming interfaces (APIs) for major service providers. Rabbit's approach, using neuro-symbolic programming, learns user interactions directly, bypassing the need for rigid APIs and enabling seamless on-device experiences. LAM's neuro-symbolic model is pivotal for understanding the unique structure of human-computer interactions, which differ significantly from natural language or vision. This model ensures actions on applications are highly regular, minimalistic, stable, and explainable, unlike the creative nature desired in language models.

The Rabbit research team addressed several challenges in developing LAM:

➤ **Hybrid approach:** Combining neural and symbolic components, LAM effectively models complex application structures.

➤ **Imitation learning:** LAM employs demonstration-based learning, creating a "conceptual blueprint" of interfaces and underlying services.

➤ **Interdisciplinary research:** Merging language modeling, programming languages, and formal methods, LAM stands at the forefront of neuro-symbolic research.

➤ **Responsible and reliable action performance:** Ensuring actions are executed in a humanizing and respectful manner is key to LAM's design.

The Rabbit R1, as an embodiment of this research, demonstrates the potential of LAM in real-world applications. By offloading computation to data centers, Rabbit Inc. achieves performance and cost optimizations, making advanced AI experiences more accessible and environmentally friendly. For more details on this, please visit www.rabbit.tech/research/.

SUMMARY

IN THIS CHAPTER, we covered several topics, including how to analyze trade-offs in cost and performance when building LLM-based GenAI applications. We explored how a leader may need to build an GenAI team, followed by three trends for the near future: MoE models, multimodality, and agents.

As we conclude this book, it's clear that the field of generative AI is advancing rapidly, with cost optimization at the forefront of innovation. Throughout the chapters, we've dissected key methods like fine-tuning, low-rank approximations, and model optimization that drive efficiency. Practical strategies such as prompt engineering, caching, and summarization have demonstrated how to reduce computational demands without compromising performance.

In our final analysis, balancing cost with performance emerges as the critical challenge. The tools and techniques discussed offer a roadmap for achieving this balance, ensuring that the benefits of generative AI can be realized across industries. As we look to the future, these trends are set to define the next wave of advancements in the field, making AI not only more powerful but also more accessible to all. I sincerely hope this marks the start of your continued effort to make Generative AI both economically and technologically advanced in a safe and environmentally conscious way.

INDEX

A

ab tool, 18
`accelerate` library, 80, 81
accessibility, language models and, 91
accuracy, effect on vector databases, 20
activation quantization, 92
activation-aware weight quantization (AWQ), 84, 92
AdaloRA (adaptive LoRA), 34, 45
adapters
  about, 32–33
  IA3, 40–44
  Prefix Tuning, 36–38
  Prompt Tuning, 34–36
  P-Tuning, 39–40
adaptive LoRA (AdaLoRA), 34, 45
AgentGPT, 10
agents, 174–179
AGI (artificial general intelligence), 121
AI (artificial intelligence), 1–2
AI feedback, 95
aligned smaller models, 94–95
all-MiniLM-L6, 23
AlphaCode model, 4
AlphaServe, 133–134
Amazon Bedrock, 112, 160
Amazon EC2, 14
Amazon S3, 6
Amazon SageMaker, 14, 24, 26, 52–53, 110, 144–146
Amazon Web Services (AWS), 13
ANN Benchmark, effect on vector databases, 20
Anthropic, 3, 7, 13, 26, 60–62, 91

application development frameworks, 8–9
application layer, in three-layer GenAI application stack, 8–9
application programming interface (API), rate limits in, 17
applications
  building, 9
  productionizing, 9–12
ARC easy, 102
artificial general intelligence (AGI), 121
artificial intelligence (AI), 1–2
attention mechanism, 124
attention sinks, streaming LLMs with, 136–139
autonomous agents, LLM-based, 10
AWQ (activation-aware weight quantization), 84, 92
AWS (Amazon Web Services), 13
AWS Fargate, 14
AWS Glue, 7
AWS Lambda, 13, 17
Azure Blob Storage, 6
Azure Purview, 7

B

Bard, 10, 12, 116, 118–119
BART, 34, 36
batch inference
  about, 78–82
  automatically finding good inference configurations, 146–155
batch prompting
  about, 78, 82–83

batch inference, 78–82
  for efficient inference, 78–83
  examples of, 83
"Batch Prompting: Efficient Inference with
    Large Language Model APIs," 83
batch tuning
  about, 124–126
  AlphaServe, 133–134
  KV caching, 130
  memory occupancy, 126–128
  PagedAttention, 131–132
  Scheduling Sequences with Speculation (S3),
    134–136
  size, 140–146
  strategies to fit larger models in memory,
    128–129
  streaming LLMs with attention sinks,
    136–139
batching
  dynamic, 82, 143–144
  impact of, 134
  with iteration-level scheduling, 82
  options for, 143–144
BBH (BIG-Bench Hard), 102, 116
benchmarking, setting up, 20–23
BERT (Bidirectional Encoders from
    Transformers) model, 2, 23, 34, 94
bias detection, LLMs and, 159
Bidirectional Encoders from Transformers
    (BERT) model, 2, 23, 34, 94
bidirectional long short-term memory
    (BiLSTM), 2
BIG-Bench Hard (BBH), 102, 116
Bilingual Evaluation Understudy with
    Representations from Transformers
    (BLEURT), 103
BiLSTM (bidirectional long short-term
    memory), 2
BingChat, 10, 12
BioClinicalBERT, 23
BLEU metric, 96
BLEURT (Bilingual Evaluation Understudy
    with Representations from
    Transformers), 103
BLIP, 95–96

BloombergGPT, 90, 115–116
BoolQ, 102

C

caching
  implementing using vector stores, 66–68
  improved utilization, 77
capabilities, enhancing, 8
catastrophic forgetting, 8, 164
Causal Language Modeling (CLM), 108–109
chains
  about, 69
  implementing, 69–76
chat applications, sample LLM-powered,
    11–12
chatbots, 5–6
ChatGPT, 5, 10, 12, 24, 155
Chinchilla, 30–31, 99–100
clarity, verbosity compared with, 66
Claude, 8–9, 10, 12, 24, 55–59, 60–62, 63–65,
    95
Claude Instant, 26, 91
clear prompts, 53–59
CLM (Causal Language Modeling), 108–109
cloud-native inference frameworks, 142
code completion, 6
Codex model, 4
CogVLM, for language-vision multimodality,
    95–96
Cohere, 8
commercial availability, as a factor in model
    layer, 7
Common Crawl, 6
compact models, role of, 90–91
comparisons, PagedAttention and, 131–132
computational efficiency, as a factor in model
    layer, 7
compute infrastructure, 7
Constitutional AI, 7
context
  extending length, 137
  infinite length, 137–138
  limitations to, 62–63
  providing in prompts, 59–63

continuous batching, 26, 82, 143–144
continuous improvement, LLMs and, 160
conversational agents, 5–6
cost optimization. *See also* inference
    techniques; tuning techniques
  about, 12
  cost assessment
    of large language model component, 24–26
    of model inference component, 12–19
    of vector database component, 19–24
  importance of, 12–26
cost-effective storage, 77
costs
  AlphaServe and, 134
  balancing with performance, 163–170
  estimating, 52–53
  Falcon 40B and, 47–48
  for GenAI team maintenance, 168–169
  impact of prompt engineering on, 50–53
  implications of, 87–88
  PagedAttention and, 131–132
  Scheduling Sequences with Speculation (S3)
      and, 135–136
  StreamingLLM and, 139
  summarization in context of, 77–78
CPU acceleration tools, 156–157
creative input, for GenAI teams, 167

D

data evolution, LLMs and, 159
data lakes, 6
data management, in infrastructure layer, 6–7
data processing, efficiency in, 77
data storage, in infrastructure layer, 6–7
data transformation, 8
data volume, Falcon 40B and, 47
dDPO (distilled direct preference
    optimization), 94
decoder-only models, 34
decomposition, 84
deep learning containers (DLCs), 142
DeepMind, 30
DeepSparse, 155–156, 157
DeepSpeed, 47, 141–143

DeepSpeed-Inference library, 81–82
democratization, language models and, 91
deployment configuration testing, frameworks
    for, 141–142
direct preference optimization (DPO), 95,
    111, 116
direct prompts, 53–59
DistilBERT, 94
distillation, tuning and, 112
distilled direct preference optimization
    (dDPO), 94
distilled supervised fine-tuning (dSFT), 94
distributed training, Falcon 40B and, 47
DLCs (deep learning containers), 142
Docker, 12
domain management, for GenAI teams, 167
domain-specific models
  about, 104–105
  training step, 107–119
  training tokenizer step, 105–107
double quantization (DQ), 45
downstream applications, enhanced, 77
dSFT (distilled supervised fine-tuning), 94
dynamic batching, 82, 143–144

E

efficiency, in data processing, 77
efficient summarization, as a factor in
    chaining, 70
ELMo, 2
embedding models, 22
encoder-decoder models, 34
encoder-only models, 34
end-to-end benchmark, 21
energy consumption, language models and, 91
environmental implications, 165
Ernie Bot, 10, 12
estimating costs, 52–53
ethical compliance, LLMs and, 159
evaluating
  domain-specific models *vs.* generic models,
      115–119
  by GenAI teans, 167
  generic models, 115–119

F

FAISS package, 23
Falcon 40B, 33, 46–47
Feedback Collection, 97–98
feedback loops, 159
few-shot in-context learning, 9
fine-grained quantization, 84
fine-grained text evaluation, Prometheus for, 96–98
Flan, 3
FLAVA, 95–96
floating-point operations (FLOPs), 29, 31, 107, 130
formats, indicating desired, 63–66
foundational model training, 10
frameworks
    cloud-native inference, 142
    for deployment configuration testing, 141–142

G

GBK Collective, 165
GCP (Google Cloud Platform), 14
Gemini
    breaking scaling laws with, 99–100
    models, 102–104
GenAI
    costs for team maintenance, 168–169
    future trends in, 170–179
    importance of team building, 165–170
    large language models (LLMs) compared with, 5–6
    productionizing applications, 9–12
    team structure, 166–168
    three-layer application stack, 6–9
general-purpose models, power of prompting with, 120–121
generative pre-trained transformers quantization (GPTQ), 85, 92, 93
generic models, evaluating, 115–119
generic templates, creating, 148–149
Genie, 8–9

Google Bard, 10, 12, 116, 118–119
Google Cloud Platform (GCP), 14
Google Cloud Storage, 6
Google Data Catalog, 7
Gopher, 3, 30, 31, 32
GPT 3.5 Turbo, 26, 91, 97, 111
GPT Neo model, 78
GPT NeoX, 116
GPT-3, 2–3, 4, 7, 8, 24, 50
GPT-4, 90, 91, 96–98, 120–121
GPTQ (generative pre-trained transformers quantization), 85, 92, 93
GPU acceleration tools, 156–157
GPU resources, training models locally with, 108–114
Grade School Math 8K (GSM8k), 102, 103
guardrails, updating, 160

H

hardware utilization
    about, 124–126
    AlphaServe, 133–134
    automatically finding good inference configurations, 146–155
    batch size tuning, 140–146
    KV caching, 130
    memory occupancy, 126–128
    PagedAttention, 131–132
    Scheduling Sequences with Speculation (S3), 134–136
    strategies to fit larger models in memory, 128–129
    streaming LLMs with attention sinks, 136–139
healthcare, multimodal models for, 174
HellaSwag, 102
HPO (hyperparameter optimization), 149–155
Hugging Face library, 33, 44, 80
HumanEval, 102, 103
hyperparameter optimization (HPO), 149–155

I

IA3 (Inhibiting and Amplifying Inner Activations), 34, 40–44
implementing chains, 69–76
index building time, effect on vector databases, 20
inference acceleration tools
  about, 155–156
  CPU acceleration tools, 156–157
  GPU acceleration tools, 156
  TensorRT, 156
inference configurations, finding, 146–155
inference techniques
  about, 49–50
  batch prompting, 78–83
  chains, 69–76
  cost and performance implications, 87–88
  model optimization methods, 83–85
  parameter-efficient fine-tuning (PEFT) methods, 85–87
  prompt engineering, 50–66
  summarization, 77–78
  vector stores, 66–69
infrastructure layer, in three-layer GenAI application stack, 6–7
Inhibiting and Amplifying Inner Activations (IA3), 34, 40–44
input dataset, representative, 21
insertion throughput, effect on vector databases, 20
integrating LLMs, 8
invoke command, 75

K

KAIST, 97
key-value (KV) caching, 130
k-nearest neighbors (kNN), 121
Knowledge Assessments, 116
knowledge distillation, 94
Kubernetes, 26

L

LaMDA, 3, 5–6
LangChain, 8, 10, 72–76, 175–179
Langchain Expression Language, 74
language-vision multimodality, CogVLM for, 95–96
large language models (LLMs)
  cost assessment of, 24–26
  GenAI compared with, 5–6
  integrating, 8
  rise of, 1–2
  streaming with attention sinks, 136–139
large model inference (LMI), 142
latency, language models and, 91
layerwise quantization, 84
length-aware sequence scheduler, in Scheduling Sequences with Speculation (S3), 135
limitations, PagedAttention and, 131–132
Linguistic Tasks, 116
LLaMA model, 3, 33, 99
LLM-based autonomous agents, 10
LLM.Int8(), 92, 93
LLMOps, monitoring and, 157–160
LLMs. *See* large language models (LLMs)
LMI (large model inference), 142
load testing tool, 18
Locality Sensitive Hashing (LSH), 21, 23
LoHa, 34
long context models, 60–62
long short-term memory (LSTM), 2
low-rank adaptation (LoRA), 34, 44–46
LSH (Locality Sensitive Hashing), 21, 23
LSTM (long short-term memory), 2

M

machine learning as a service (MLaaS), 49–50
machine learning operations (MLOps), 157–158
machine translation, 6
Masked Language Modeling (MLM), 2, 108, 109
Massive Multi-task Language Understanding (MMLU), 102, 103

Math-AMC 2022-2023, 103
MBPP, 102
medical knowledge (Med-PaLM), 121
Medprompt, 120
memory, strategies to fit larger models in, 128–129
memory footprint, 29
memory occupancy, 126–128
metadata catalogs, 7
Microsoft Azure, 14
Microsoft Math Language Understanding (MMLU), 102
Microsoft Phi models, 100–102
Milvus, 7
Mistral 7B, text generation with, 93–94
mixed-precision decomposition, 84
mixture of experts (MoE) layer, 8, 170–172
MLaaS (machine learning as a service), 49–50
MLM (Masked Language Modeling), 2, 108, 109
MLOps (machine learning operations), 157–158
MLP (multilayer perceptron), 39–40
mLUKE, 23
MMLU (Massive Multi-task Language Understanding), 102, 103
MMLU (Microsoft Math Language Understanding), 102
model layer, in three-layer GenAI application stack, 7–8
model optimization methods
  about, 83
  code example, 84–85
  GPTQ method, 85
  quantization, 83–84
model selection
  about, 89
  domain-specific models, 104–119
  examples of, 89–90, 91–104
  power of prompting with general-purpose models, 120–121
  role of compact and nimble models, 90–91
models
  architecture of, 8

capability of, as a factor in model layer, 7
domain-specific, 104–119
Gemini, 102–104
general-purpose, 120–121
inference component, cost assessment of, 12–19
limitations to, 62–63
mixture of experts (MoE), 8, 170–172
multimodal, 172–174
Phi, 100–102
MoE (mixture of experts) layer, 8, 170–172
monitoring
  about, 157
  LLMOps and, 157–160
  observability compared with, 157
MPT (multitask prompt tuning), 34, 40–44
multilayer perceptron (MLP), 39–40
multimodal models, 172–174
multitask prompt tuning (MPT), 34, 40–44
multiturn chat agents, 10

N

named entity recognition (NER), 34
natural language generative (NLG) tasks, 34
natural language processing (NLP), 1
natural language understanding (NLU) tasks, 34
NAVER AI Lab, 97
NER (named entity recognition), 34
neural language models (NLMs), 2
Neural Magic, 155–156, 157
neural networks, 2–5
nimble models, role of, 90–91
NLG (natural language generative) tasks, 34
NLMs (neural language models), 2
NLP (natural language processing), 1
NLU (natural language understanding) tasks, 34
Notus 7B, 95
Numenta, 155, 156
NVIDIA, 45, 107, 141, 155–156

O

observability
  about, 157–160
  monitoring compared with, 157
OpenAI, 2–3, 10, 12, 13, 23, 24, 26, 50–52,
    90–91, 99, 111, 142
OpenAssistant, 10, 12
OpenBookQA, 102
OpenSearch, 22, 23
ORCA, 98–99, 135–136
OSCAR dataset, 22, 23, 95–96
output sequence length predictor, in Scheduling
    Sequences with Speculation (S3), 135
overlap, as a factor in chaining, 70

P

PagedAttention, 131–132, 143–144
PaLI-X model, 96
PaLM, 3, 96
parallel processing, as a factor in chaining, 70
parameter-efficient fine-tuning (PEFT) methods
  about, 32–33, 85–86
  adapters, 33–44
  code example, 86–87
  cost and performance implications of, 46–48
  IA3, 40–44
  low-rank adaptation, 44–46
  prefix tuning, 36–38
  prompt tuning, 34–36
  P-tuning, 39–40
performance
  AlphaServe and, 134
  balancing with cost, 163–170
  implications of, 87–88
  LLMs and, 159
  of MoE models, 171
  of multimodal models, 173
  Scheduling Sequences with Speculation (S3)
    and, 135–136
  StreamingLLM and, 139
  summarization in context of, 77–78
personally identifiable information (PII), using
    Claude for removal of, 55–59

Phi
  breaking scaling laws with, 99–100
  models, 100–102
Pinecone, 7, 22
PIQA, 102
PLMs (pre-trained language models), 2
Prefix Tuning, 34, 36–38
preprocessing step, summarization as a, 77
pre-trained language models (PLMs), 2
problem domain suitability, as a factor in
    model layer, 7
product management, for GenAI teams,
    167
productionizing GenAI applications, 9–12
programming assistants, 6
Prometheus, for fine-grained text evaluation,
    96–98
prompt engineering
  about, 9, 50
  as an inference technique, 50–66
  clear and direct prompts, 53–59
  impact on cost of, 50–53
  indicating desired format, 63–66
  providing context, 59–63
prompt templates, 9
Prompt Tuning, 34–36
prompting, power of with general-purpose
    models, 120–121
P-Tuning, 34, 39–40
Puntoni, Stefano (professor), 165
PyTorch, 35

Q

Qdrant, effect on vector databases, 20
QLoRA, 45
quantization
  about, 83–84
  activation, 92
  for powerful but smaller models, 91–93
  weight, 92
quantization-aware training, 84
queries per second (QPS), 20
query latency metric, 21–22
Qwen-VL, 96

R

Rabbit R1 use case, 179
RAG (retrieval augmented generation), 60–62
rate limits, 17
ray.io library, 22
RDS with PG Vector, 22
Reading Comprehension, 116
real-time processing, language models and, 91
recruitment, for GenAI teams, 169–170
recurrent neural network (RNN) layers, 8
regular quantization, 45
reinforcement learning based on human
        feedback (RLHF), 10, 112, 116
research, for GenAI teams, 167
resource availability/scale, Falcon 40B and, 47
resource efficiency/cost
    effect on vector databases, 20
    language models and, 91
resource utilization, LLMs and, 159
retrieval augmented generation (RAG), 60–62
"Retrieval Meets Long Context Large
        Language Models" (Xu et al.), 61–62
reward model, 10
RLHF (reinforcement learning based on
        human feedback), 10, 112, 116
RNN (recurrent neural network) layers, 8
ROUGE metric, 96

S

SageMaker Groundtruth, 10, 12
scalability, effect on vector databases, 20
scaling innovations, 8
scaling laws
    about, 30–32
    breaking with Gemini and Phi, 99–100
"Scaling Laws for Neural Language Models,"
        30
Scheduling Sequences with Speculation (S3),
        134–136
Science QA, 96
search latency, effect on vector databases, 20
search throughput, effect on vector databases,
        20

segmentation strategy, as a factor in chaining,
        70
Sentence Transformers, 23
sequential processing, as a factor in chaining,
        70
serving parameters, 146
SIQA, 102
small-language models (SLMs)
    about, 89–90
    examples of, 91–104
soft prompts, 34
Spark NLP 5.0 library, 23
SQuADv2, 102
state management, as a factor in chaining, 70
statistical language models (SLMs), 2
storage, cost-effective, 77
strategic input, for GenAI teams, 167
streaming large language models (LLMs) with
        attention sinks, 136–139
StreamingLLM, 138
summarization
    about, 77
    in context of cost and performance, 77–78
supervised tuning, 112
supervisor, in Scheduling Sequences with
        Speculation (S3), 135
Switch model, 3

T

T5 model, 3, 34
targeted datasets, 7
technical expertise, for GenAI teams, 167
templates, prompt, 9
TensorRT-LLM, 141–143, 146, 156
text generation, with Mistral 7B, 93–94
text summarization and generation LLMs, 6
three-layer GenAI application stack
    about, 6
    application layer, 8–9
    infrastructure layer, 6–7
    model layer, 7–8
TinyBERT, 94
tokenizers, training, 105–107

tokens per second (TPS), 14
tools, for implementing chains, 72–76
total data ingestion time metric, 21–22
trade-offs, analyzing, 164–165
training
  domain-specific models, 107–119
  multimodal models, 172–173
  tokenizers, 105–107
"Training Compute-Original Large Language
  Models," 30
transformers, 2–5
trust, LLMs and, 159
tuning, batch
  about, 124–126
  AlphaServe, 133–134
  KV caching, 130
  memory occupancy, 126–128
  PagedAttention, 131–132
  Scheduling Sequences with Speculation (S3),
    134–136
  size, 140–146
  strategies to fit larger models in memory,
    128–129
  streaming LLMs with attention sinks,
    136–139
tuning techniques/strategies
  about, 123
  AlphaServe, 133–134
  automatically finding good inference
    configurations, 146–155
  basic scaling laws, 30–32
  batch size tuning, 140–146
  batch tuning, 124–155
  CPU acceleration tools, 156–157
  customizability and, 29–32
  to fit larger models in memory, 128–129
  GPU acceleration tools, 156
  hardware utilization, 124–155
  inference acceleration tools, 155–157
  KV caching, 130
  memory occupancy, 126–128
  monitoring, 157–160
  observability, 157–160
  PagedAttention, 131–132

parameter-efficient methods, 32–46
PEFT methods, 46–48
Scheduling Sequences with Speculation (S3),
  134–136
streaming LLMs with attention sinks,
  136–139
TensorRT, 156

U

updating guardrails, 160
user acceptance testing (UAT), 159
user experience
  enhanced, 77
  LLMs and, 159
user queries, vector stores and, 67

V

VE (visual expert) modules, 96
vector database component, cost assessment
  of the, 19–24
vector databases, 7
vector stores
  about, 66
  implementing caching using, 66–68
VectorDBBench, effect on vector databases, 20
verbosity, clarity compared with, 66
Vertex AI, 112
virtual tokens, 36
visual expert (VE) modules, 96
visual language models (VLMs), 95–96
VizWiz QA, 96

W

Weaviate, 7
websites
  ab tool, 18
  AdaloRA, 34
  AgentGPT, 10
  all-MiniLM-L6, 23
  Amazon EC2, 14
  Amazon SageMaker, 14

ANN Benchmark, 20
AWS Fargate, 14
AWS Lambda, 13
"Batch Prompting: Efficient Inference with
   Large Language Model APIs," 83
BioClinicalBERT, 23
DeepSpeed-Inference library, 81
embedding models, 22
fine-tuning references, 114–115
Hugging Face library, 33
IA3, 34
LangChain, 10
Langchain Expression Language, 74
LoHa, 34
LoRA, 34
Medprompt, 120
Mistral 7B, 94
mLUKE, 23
MultiTask Prompt Tuning, 34
OpenSearch, 22
OSCAR dataset, 22
Pinecone, 22

Prefix tuning, 34
Prompt Tuning, 34
P-Tuning, 34
Qdrant, 20
ray.io library, 22
RDS with PG Vector, 22
"Scaling Laws for Neural Language
   Models," 30
Sentence Transformers, 23
VectorDBBench, 20
weight quantization, 92
Wikipedia, 6
WinoGrande, 102
word2vec learning approach, 2
Workshop on Machine Translation 2023
   (WMT23), 103

Z

Zephyr 7B, 94–95
zero-shot LLM predictions, 9, 10
Zhipu AI, 96